"Gupta, George, and Fewer have written a bold, exciting, and surprisingly optimistic book. Steering clear of the usual cliches about how business can either destroy or remake society, they show clearly and realistically that firms and entrepreneurs can work effectively, profitably, and purposefully with government. The book will rekindle for many a sense of progress, and even of hope."

—Deborah Spar, Senior Associate Dean,
Harvard Business School,
Business in Global Society (BiGS)

"*Venture Meets Mission* highlights one of the key superpowers of democracies: mission-driven entrepreneurship. The authors paint a compelling picture of the future, one in which ventures and government can work together for national security and economic prosperity. This book is a must-read for anyone looking to merge their patriotism and purpose with profit."

—Michael McFaul, former US Ambassador to Russia;
Director, Freeman Spogli Institute, Stanford

"The world is changing fast, and we need leaders who can adapt and innovate. *Venture Meets Mission* is an inspiring guide for the next generation of government officials and entrepreneurs. Rep. Mike Gallagher and I have worked across the aisle to bring the best ideas from Silicon Valley to Congress. This book is perfect for anyone who wants to make a difference and solve the most pressing problems of our time."

—Ro Khanna, United States Representative
from California's 17th District

"*Venture Meets Mission* brings to life two powerful ideas: how to infuse a business with an inspiring mission and how working with the government can help businesses profitably achieve their mission. It is a great read for anyone thinking about working with the government to build their business while contributing to the public good."

—Charles Rossotti, Senior Advisor at The Carlyle Group,
CEO, American Management Systems,
and former US Commissioner of IRS

"This book presents a simple but powerful message for anyone in my generation looking for meaning in their work: rather than thinking about your career decisions as a series of tradeoffs between profit and purpose, look for mission opportunities where you can have the most catalytic impact. As someone now inspired to build an agricultural venture in East Africa between the government and the private sector, this book is a valuable resource."

—Shiro Wachira, Student in the Freeman Spogli Institute,
Stanford, '23; Innovation Fellow at Unlock Aid

Venture Meets Mission

VENTURE

Aligning People, Purpose,

MEETS

and Profit to Innovate

MISSION

and Transform Society

ARUN GUPTA,
GERARD GEORGE,
and
THOMAS J. FEWER

STANFORD BUSINESS BOOKS
An Imprint of Stanford University Press
Stanford, California

Stanford University Press
Stanford, California

Special discounts for bulk quantities of Stanford Business Books are available to corporations, professional associations, and other organizations. For details and discount information, contact the special sales department of Stanford University Press by emailing sales@www.sup.org.

Printed in the United States of America on acid-free, archival-quality paper

Cataloging-in-Publication Data available upon request.
Library of Congress Control Number: 2023005165
ISBN: 9781503636286 (cloth), 9781503637276 (ebook)

Cover designer: Will Brown

CONTENTS

PROLOGUE

"What's the word?" Arun greeted cheerfully as we sat down for lunch at Georgetown's Peacock Cafe in Washington, DC, in the autumn of 2021. That summer, Gerry had joined Georgetown University's McDonough School of Business as professor of entrepreneurship and innovation after having served as dean of a business school in Singapore. Arun taught a popular entrepreneurship course for MBA students at Georgetown. While our nonlinear life experiences could not have been more different, we shared a common passion in entrepreneurship and a belief in its potential to address larger societal problems.

For over twenty years, Arun was a venture capital investor, with his most recent focus on investments at the intersection of mission, technology, and entrepreneurship. Arun had entered the venture capital industry during the emergence of internet startups, seeing entrepreneurship as the most powerful solution to societal problems and as a positive force of disruption. His first ten years as a venture capitalist were focused on high-growth tech companies outside the government sector. In 2009, Arun began exploring collaborative investment opportunities with the U.S. government with the belief that the government's bespoke procurement process was not able to keep up with the speed of innovations from commercial technology platforms and emerging cyber threats from global adversaries. Cloud, social, mobile, big data, open source, and space innovation required the government to transform how it served its mission. While investing in and scaling up the mission-focused tech companies, Arun appreciated firsthand the cultural and alignment challenges the government faced in collaborating with the entrepreneurial sector. Matching the "venture startup time" to "federal procurement time" was difficult, but the need was clear and the market opportunity was large. Building companies at the intersection of mission, tech, and entrepreneurship had greater meaning, but required collaboration with leaders and teams that were driven by purpose and not solely by equity and options. It challenged Arun's preconceived notion that entrepreneurs, by themselves, could solve societal problems; in fact, these larger problems could only be solved by bringing together the innovation capabilities of entrepreneurs with the scale and reach that uniquely resided with the government.

Gerry's journey was parallel to Arun's, but in the academic world. He had spent the past twenty-five years as a professor studying and teaching entrepreneurship in the top business schools across the United States, Europe, and Asia. About a decade earlier, he was elected as an editor of a flagship business management journal. In that role, he coaxed management scholars to address the grand challenges facing humanity. At London Business School and Imperial College London, Gerry's research and teaching shifted to how ventures can be driven by purpose and the need for innovation to solve problems in health care, energy, and climate change. As academic director of Elite UK, he worked with London Stock Exchange's exceptional private markets team to curate a community of exciting and ambitious firms with the objective of developing a talented pool of entrepreneurs in a vibrant ecosystem of capital and support services. As dean of the Lee Kong Chian School of Business, Gerry had the opportunity to work with Singapore's forward-thinking leaders, students, and businesses with a purpose-driven mindset. When considering a pandemic-induced return to the United States, Gerry looked at a handful of leading business schools, but none inspired him more than the "common good" ethos in Jesuit education and Georgetown University's locational advantage to influence global impact. Gerry joined Georgetown as part of his personal journey to purpose.

Our lunch conversation was enthusiastically animated. We found ourselves sharing anecdotes and experiences that were common even though our career pathways were completely different. We discussed how building companies at this tripartite intersection of mission, tech, and entrepreneurship was not easy. There was a systemic distrust and misunderstanding between each, and we found that polarization about government ("mission") and entrepreneurship ("capitalism") existed even among university students. Students often used a misinformed "purity test" lens to judge all of government and all of entrepreneurship. The current system of higher education channeled students to pursue careers that provided external recognition versus mission-driven careers that fulfilled internal passions. Government was demonized for being the cause of all problems with its numerous breakthroughs and successes overlooked, and entrepreneurship was misunderstood as being the root of "billionaire" income inequality, with no acknowledgment of the values and mindset it represented—integrity, perseverance, optimism, resilience, adaptability. To solve large societal problems, these ecosystems needed to be brought in sync, but the "catalyst for change at scale" was missing.

Arun's understanding of this shortcoming through his venture experience and academic pursuits led him to create the "Valley Meets Mission" class that he taught at Stanford in Washington. His course highlights how entrepreneurial talents can be applied to solve societal problems at scale by collaborating with the government. He quips at the start of class that students should not waste their entrepreneurial talents on building Candycrush 3.0, hoping instead to inspire them to focus those talents at mission-driven for-profit ventures. Interestingly, as senior leaders and entrepreneurs spoke to students, he witnessed how the stories of success changed students' perceptions and triggered discussions about bridging the existing gaps. Students with consulting and banking job offers were inspired to trade them to pursue opportunities at cyber, climate, and civic tech startups and inside of government. While the speakers' stories motivated the students, the class discussions energized the speakers—entrepreneurs and government, technology, policy, and finance leaders alike.

Gerry's opening session on growing entrepreneurial ventures focused on the need for clarity of purpose. Our classroom discussions in the context of lived experiences of entrepreneurial changemakers served as the inspiration for this book. With Gerry's research on purpose, public-private collaboration, and entrepreneurship, we knew we had something important to share. We felt that there was a bigger reason our paths have crossed at this stage of our respective careers. We needed to capture our experiences to bring together a community of entrepreneurs, policymakers, and talented students around mission, tech, and venturing.

A couple of weeks later, we brought Thomas Fewer into the team. Thomas had just finished his PhD in business and political science at Drexel University and was studying how businesses interface with political and regulatory institutions as a postdoctoral fellow at Georgetown. Building from his prior experience in the aerospace and defense industry, Thomas's research was already asking important questions on how the private sector could be leveraged to support the government's mission, and how the two can collaborate to develop technology-based solutions to major societal challenges, including issues of climate, healthcare, and food security. Finally, our team was complete.

We began with a simple objective: to understand how people can create mission-driven ventures. We got to work in earnest and started reaching out. We interviewed entrepreneurs, leaders in government, investors, students, and ecosystem partners. We created a small team of undergraduate and MBA students who developed detailed case studies on each of these initiatives. We collected secondary data to cross-check our conclusions and circled back to our interviews. The enthusiasm for this topic was overwhelming. Everyone whom we reached out to gave time generously and freely shared ideas on how a deep and lasting change can be made collectively. We realized that while there was a groundswell of idealism, it was difficult for everyone to see how we can make it come together. We were pushing on an open door.

Venture Meets Mission

One

IDEALISM AND IMPACT

Transforming Society with the Optimism of Entrepreneurship and the Scale of Government

"We have the power to make this the best generation of mankind in the history of the world or make it the last," President Kennedy proclaimed before the United Nations in 1963.[1] Throughout the course of contemporary history, every generation has faced crossroads. And many in each generation have summoned their collective resourcefulness and resilience to reinforce democratic ideals by fostering a culture of innovation and collaboration across academic, government, and private institutions. Today's generation faces a similar opportunity.

The COVID pandemic made us all reflect. For the younger generations, the pandemic provided a much-needed pathway to self-expression, along which they felt empowered to reflect upon and articulate their core beliefs, values, and ideals.[2] History has shown countless examples of brave and forward-thinking young adults such as Claudette Colvin, a civil rights activist, or more recently, Malala Yousafzai, a Pakistani female education activist and 2014 Nobel Peace Prize laureate, who have risen to the forefront of public discourse on social issues.[3] Over the years, they have captured our imagination through their idealism and dogged determination, and as heroic drivers of social progress. The pandemic, however, seemed to capture this youthful lightning in a bottle, triggering a much broader social contagion of meaning and purpose among the younger generation.

This "generational reset" was not confined to the weeks and months of quarantining and social distancing. Our now post-pandemic world continues to see us all move toward a deeper, *purposeful* contemplation of "What can *I* do?"—a shift from idealism to action that emphasizes the role of the individual in building a better world for us all. And this is clearly reflected in a number of social trends among the younger generations. For instance, in spite of all of the misinformation surrounding the pandemic and other political topics, young people have grown *more* trusting of critical institutions in their lives: family members, medical professionals, and academic institutions. And we also saw that Generation Xers and millennials were the most active responders to volunteer during the pandemic.[4]

The resolve toward purpose was further strengthened following Russia's invasion of Ukraine. We watched in horror as Russian troops rolled into the villages and cities in sovereign Ukraine and engaged in haphazard shelling of a democratic nation. The United States, a country deeply politically divided and only one year removed from the storming of the Capitol building on January 6, was reminded of the sanctity of democratic ideals that it had taken for granted, as videos circulated of everyday citizens fighting to protect their liberal democracy from Russia's invasion. For most young Americans, and certainly those without recollection of the 9/11 terrorist attacks, this was the first time that a sovereign democracy was truly under attack. Having been socialized into society through the decades of political assault on the need for and role of government, young Americans watched a community of people, who only thirty years ago were living in a socialist state, risk their lives to preserve *their* democratic principles. This geopolitical threat was more than just another harsh reminder of the fragility of liberal democracy, which inspired many to ask themselves, "How can I do my part?"

This self-calling into service is not new, but one that many have experienced for centuries. Born and raised in Philadelphia, former U.S. National Security Advisor and author of *Battlegrounds: The Fight to Defend the Free World* Lieutenant General H. R. McMaster has always felt a call to serve his country. He attended the prestigious United States Military Academy before pursuing advanced degrees at the University of North Carolina. "I always wanted to be in the army, ever since I was three years old," says McMaster. "Originally, I thought I wanted to serve for five years and then pursue a degree in law. But I had such a great time serving my country, being a part of something much bigger than myself. It was tremendously rewarding. I did not plan out my career in any way, but every assignment was an opportunity to make a real difference."[5] So, what does this call sound like? With the start of a second career at the Hoover Institution and Stanford University, McMaster explains the call as "a motivation, a desire, and a drive to serve the country by contributing to a fuller understanding of the most important challenges and opportunities we face internationally and as a way to bring Americans together to build a better future."

And the Ukraine war has shown a fundamental shift in how major geopolitical conflicts will now unfold, as this is truly the first digital, networked, and decentralized war. In an increasingly interconnected and globalized world, people are finding that there are many ways in which they can contribute their efforts. Everyday citizens began fundraising for relief efforts. Vigilante hacking groups came together to disrupt Russian intelligence. And the technological preeminence of American and British companies began to provide satellite data to the Ukrainian military, mitigate cyberattacks, track and seize Russian financial assets globally, and flag propaganda and disinformation on social media. Despite the dramatic effects of the pandemic and Russia's war on Ukraine, there remains a hopeful sense of optimism and an abundance of energized individuals searching for purpose. But it's become quite clear that this wasn't only about finding purpose.

Purpose, which can be understood as an individual's or group's selected and stated objective,[6] is inherently inward looking. Purpose does not rest upon any recognition of the wider role or responsibility of the individual or group in society, nor necessarily couple their objectives with those of the larger community.[7] People were surely looking to find meaning in their lives, but this meaning was not about their own needs.

No, this was an outward purpose—a *mission*. A desire to serve their communities, to protect their ideals, to drive change. Mission is markedly different from purpose in that it's oriented to be outward looking.[8] It's about seeking to create public value and achieving collective goals, one reason the term is often affiliated with the initiatives of government and public actors.

The time is now to mobilize this sense of mission to tackle the larger problems of society. *But how?* It appears that this question has become difficult to answer, as our current vernacular does not reflect the complexities that our young people desire. Amid a backdrop of polarization, a new form of bifurcation has stricken them—one of society's doing. We are led to believe that only two options exist to define our professional careers and personal lives: "do good" or "make money." Academic and political systems reinforce these silos, as does the language used in society: public sector ("do good") *versus* private sector ("make money"), nonprofit ("do good") *versus* for profit ("make money"). Society presents us with this artificial binary-choice construct, in which each path carries external judgment—"inefficiency and idealism" or "innovation and greed." To unlock this trapped generational energy and address the most pressing problems of society, we must create a new construct.

PROBLEMS ABOUND

So where can this renewed sense of mission begin to look for places to make an impact? Well, it doesn't take a policy expert to realize that governments have struggled to keep pace with the large societal challenges at hand such as climate change, cybersecurity, income inequality, or food insecurity, among others. Unfortunately, geopolitical conflicts and national self-interests have often been prioritized over the well-being of global communities. In many instances, we see that governments fail to address some of society's biggest problems.

In fairness, it is not that governments have turned a blind eye to social, ecological, and economic issues during the past century, or proliferated their thorniness. To the contrary, we find ample evidence that governments around the world are paying attention to, and making investments in, solving these problems. For example, the 2016 Paris Agreement on climate was negotiated and agreed upon by 196 parties with an ultimate goal of keeping the mean rise in global temperature below 3.6 degrees Fahrenheit (2 degrees Celsius).[9] In 2019, nine countries from the Middle East and North Africa chose to become early adopters of the World Bank's Human Capital Project, which aims to encourage governments to invest in people as the most valuable asset of every country.[10] And in 2021, the government of Norway and the Food and Agriculture Organization of the United Nations partnered with the International Maritime Organization and thirty countries for the Glo-Litter Partnerships Project, designed to tackle maritime litter and clean up the world's oceans.[11]

Clearly, these endeavors show a commitment by governments. However, it is also apparent that they are falling behind the private sector in innovative capacity. According to the federal workforce data from the U.S. Office of Personnel Management, in June 2018, the number of workers in government jobs over sixty years of age was almost double that of those under thirty years of age, with only 3 percent of the high-technology jobs staffed by workers under thirty.[12] This is in stark contrast to the technology businesses, where the average age of workers is between thirty and forty years. This age gap in government does not help expose agencies to emerging technologies, systems, methodologies, and approaches that are being instructed in our academic system.

Quite simply, the best minds choose careers that they find fast-paced and innovative. And while the United States is seen as a magnet for global innovation talent, its lead is concerningly shrinking.[13] Data from the World Intellectual Property Organization suggests that one in ten inventors with patents migrate, and more than half of them move to the United States.[14] However, historically, America used to capture over 50 percent of innovators from OECD countries;[15] this has now fallen to about 40 percent. Moreover, while the tech talent is flocking to the United States as venture capital investments have surged from $7 billion in 1995 to over $130 billion in 2020, it is geographically concentrated in areas farther away from centers of government, creating a slow-burn-ing crisis of tech innovation around mission.[16] Ninety-one percent of venture funds in the country are invested in San Francisco (69 percent), Boston (11 percent), and New York (11 percent).[17]

And this can be traced to the technological capability of the government as compared to the private sector. Toni Townes-Whitley, an accomplished businesswoman who served as Microsoft's president of U.S. Sales for Regulated Industries and is now the CEO of Science Applications International Corporation, describes how private-sector technology significantly outpaces government capability: "The government is far too often running at half-mast even in the procurement process. This prevents the adoption and implementation of state-of-the-art technology and innovations, raising significant national security concerns as well. Extant government regulations and procedures have further handicapped the ability of the government from adopting the much-needed innovations. And I think this really puts them at a disadvantage in how they are able to recruit young talent that is looking for work at the cutting edge of technological breakthroughs."

Governments also aren't facing the same geopolitical game as they did in the past. The rules and players have changed, and this has added to the difficulty of the task at hand. Not only are the players on the board reshuffled as the great power competition between democracies and autocracies intensifies, but also the board itself is changing as the topology of national security threats has become more complex. In a connected world where digital information is paramount, new threats are emerging that did not exist two decades ago. As data becomes the "new oil," adversaries take new forms and organizational structures. As seen in Ukraine, battlefields are now extended to digital networks—landline, wireless, and satellite—and financial networks—the Society for Worldwide Interbank Financial Telecommunication. Data has become a key driver of strategic partnerships; for instance, Western allies openly shared Russian invasion plans and provided satellite data to Ukraine,[18] and China's "belt and road" initiative provides critical communications infrastructure to countries in exchange for an ability to collect global data.[19] Adversaries are not limited to nation-state actors and include decentralized crime organizations and terror groups that operate with minimal traceability. In this digitized world, where the methods and identity of wrongdoers are opaque, safeguarding critical infrastructure has become an even higher priority.

The pandemic also evidenced how emerging and unforeseen existential threats can constrain the ability of governments to work toward society's most pressing challenges. We saw the vast economic and physical losses that countries face when unprepared for an outbreak. But it led to advances in CRISPR (RNA-based gene-editing technology) for creation of the COVID-19 vaccine,[20] at the cost of a fall in the barriers to develop biotechnology that can be weaponized. In addition to the digital-based threats to national security, governments are now acutely aware of biosecurity threats.

The pandemic exposed a "postcode effect" of success or failure in life, and it's quite concerning.[21] Social inequalities increasingly point to a future that sees where a person is born as having a more significant effect on their lifetime opportunities, earnings, and overall health and well-being than their drive, passions, and efforts.[22] This is not limited to domestic inequalities. Looking at national debt levels, we can observe the emergence of an ever-increasing gap between rich and poor countries. And it appears to only be getting worse as global actors engage in predatory lending. For example, as China's "belt and road" initiative increases its influence in the eastern hemisphere, developing nations are held hostage by their high-interest infrastructure loans, veiled behind an unfounded philanthropic guise.[23] As a result, the national debt levels in Sri Lanka and Pakistan have ballooned, halting development, progress, and stability.[24]

So where do we stand? The U.S. government is outpaced by the private sector in technological breakthroughs by the day. The threats the nation confronts grow complex and unidentifiable. And the pandemic has brought to the fore the inequalities in society. While governments possess the ability to help scale innovations and solutions through financial and regulatory levers, the social, technological, ecological, and economic indicators show that governments are unable to solve these problems alone. Without a better approach to problem solving than relying on the government alone, we will continue to see the proliferation and urgency of "demand side" problems waiting to be solved become weightier and seemingly intractable.

But the government is no longer positioned as a producer of breakthrough innovation as it was in the past. The previous model of a vertically integrated style of government innovation has been replaced with a network-ecosystem approach. Going back only sixty years, we saw a completely different strategy for how the government pursued innovation. "Moonshot" programs related to the space race (Mercury, Gemini, and Apollo) saw a model of government-led innovation. The government brought together the best technological minds, funded research and development, and provided the national vision for innovation and advancement. But today, it is becoming apparent that there remains a need for the government to provide that same vision with directed capital—while using its unique scale and influence to align and incentivize a more developed private capital and human talent ecosystem to solve current "moonshots" or "grand challenges." Even looking at the evolution of the space industry, we can observe this trend. What was once an industry dominated by NASA has now seen the growth of a number of commercial partners (SpaceX, Blue Origin, Axiom, and so on), all orchestrated by the government. In the face of today's challenges, the government becomes an initiator and organizer of impact and scale, but the private sector becomes the driver of innovation.

INTERSECTIONAL ENTREPRENEURS

In 1965, American businessman, engineer, and cofounder and chairman emeritus of Intel Corporation Gordon Moore observed that the number of transistors in a dense integrated circuit doubles in about every two years—an observation that most will recognize as "Moore's Law."[25] While this observation is inherently technical in nature and has been heavily linked to the development of the semiconductor industry, we recognize it as a reflection of a broader empirical relationship, one in which the gains in production experience and technology development yield an accelerating rate of technological innovation.

Recent innovations in processing power and artificial intelligence, for example, point to a simple truth: we live in an increasingly uncertain future. The technology advancements have accelerated the under-going social, economic, and environmental changes in and around our lives—the way we interact with each other, the way we exchange with each other, and the way we shape our planet. This moving backdrop not only complicates the uncertainty surrounding the grand challenges of contemporary society, it also calls into question who would be the most suitable agents for addressing and tackling these problems.

This fast pace of change also brings with it potentially complex solutions that carry unintended consequences. While it would be a noble pursuit to strive for a permanent and lasting solution to these problems, it is entirely unrealistic. We cannot simply develop a long-term plan for the future. As effective as it may be in implementation at the time, a lasting solution may grow ineffective as society continues to innovate and advance. Thus, when considering the larger societal issues, we must first grow comfortable with uncertainty and change. We must test, learn, and reiterate solutions, because we are likely to find the very assumptions of our long-term plans to be incorrect but we will not know until we test. We must accept that failing itself is not failure, but that settling is. We need to become comfortable with a mindset in which we are testing hypotheses—hoping to fail quickly on those showing limited promise and doubling down swiftly on those that may lead to innovations that will power us forward.

Who *should* we call to arms to tackle an uncertain future characterized by pressing social issues? While government bodies are certainly the most powerful agents with a robust resource base, history has proven their bureaucratic features to be quite rigid and inflexible—not exactly the ideal traits of an agent meant to bend and shift in response to a changing environment. And we already acknowledged that the government is seeing itself less as an innovator, and relying more heavily on the private sector. Nonprofits surely provide a unique approach to promoting the public good, but their capacities for scale and ability to mobilize resources are limited relative to traditional for-profit ventures. We should remove the preconceptions that working toward a higher purpose is decoupled from the ability to make money.

Wouldn't those with an entrepreneurial mindset be most suited to address such challenges? Think about it: there is truly nothing more entrepreneurial than building a solution to a problem, especially a problem that in most cases is a moving target. While entrepreneurs possess the drive and flexibility to tackle these challenges, it is becoming apparent that those best suited to thrive in the face of uncertainty and tackle large systemic problems are teams and groups with intersectional perspectives. Intersectionality reflects nonlinear career paths in which people follow their passions and broaden their skills and knowledge through various roles in different industries and sectors. To find a powerful driver of flexibility and innovativeness in the problem-solving process, we need to embrace the view that those who thrive are those who draw from a breadth of experience and perspective to think outside the box. So how can you build intersectionality? Toni Townes-Whitley is a perfect example of someone who has built career intersectionality. Townes-Whitley says, "You need to find the diagonal path where you can extend your curiosity while pursuing your passions. Look for the vertical opportunities to learn something new, and complement this with horizontal opportunities to apply what you've learned. All the while, keep an open mind to new experiences that you may not have considered before." When reflecting upon the value of intersectionality in careers, Townes-Whitley offers a final piece of advice: "Be a triple-threat athlete. They are always the most valuable players on the court."

General McMaster affirms, "The best way to tackle these challenges is through interdisciplinary perspectives and effective collaboration around these complex problems and opportunities." Recalling his time on the National Security Council, he adds, "Design thinking is key to solving these complex problems…framing these challenges with an eye towards strategic empathy [that is, viewing complex challenges from the perspective of others] helps you take an inventory of the vital interests at stake so you can understand why this is important." According to McMaster, "history is the organizing mechanism around which we can build strategic competence."

The discourse points us to a conclusion about our collective future: the world belongs to those with diverse perspectives and who embrace the values of entrepreneurship. It's quite simple. People, communities, and institutions embracing these principles will thrive, while those who do not may lag behind.

MISSION: HARNESSING THE POWER OF COLLECTIVE PURPOSE

The role of business in society is being questioned by academic, business, and political leaders alike. While this topic has a storied history in philosophy, economics, and political philosophy literature, recent dialogues have come forth to challenge the long-standing assumptions of these fields. Turning to the scholarly progress on grand societal challenges[26] and how business can contribute to the United Nations's Sustainable Development Goals, we observe an emerging theme that delineates a central and important role for a firm—one in which it is *a part* of society rather than *apart* from society.[27] No longer do the thought leaders and classroom instructors consider "generating economic returns for its owners" as the guiding principle objective of a firm. Instead, they advocate that businesses should embrace a model in which broader groups of stakeholders—and society as a whole—matter for the effective governance and performance of the firm, and the fulfillment of its mission. In this view, businesses should be embedded in society and responsible for all of our interests and well-being.[28]

Business leaders have embraced this principle. This is perhaps best evidenced in the 2019 Business Roundtable declaration, in which prominent leaders of the business community endorse the concept that the purpose of a corporation extends beyond its shareholders to include stakeholders and the communities in which they operate.[29] This was not a superficial corporate declaration—it was a concerted step in a continued journey toward progress, a step which started back in 2011 when the group put into action their initiative "Taking Action for America" by prioritizing job creation and national economic growth.[30] And as put by Salesforce founder and CEO Marc Benioff, "It's time for a new capitalism, a more fair, equal, and sustainable capitalism that actually works for everyone....A system in which corporate purpose is based on a fundamental commitment to all stakeholders—customers, employees, partners, communities, the planet, and society—rather than just shareholders."[31] No longer are the major societal issues of our time in the rear-view mirror of corporate executives—they sit right on the top of their "to do" lists.

This "mission"-oriented business strategy is much more than a strategy, it reflects the people of the business. Toni Townes-Whitley suggests that the adoption of a social mission is all but a requirement for businesses these days; to retain employees, they have to find something socially interesting or they will lose their people. "It's quite simple. Everything is pushing towards either the harm of what you're doing to society, or the benefit," says Townes-Whitley.

While academics present the legitimacy of this movement, and executives mobilize attention and resources, it is the startups and growth ventures that lead this charge.[32] As small enterprises, they have the flexibility to quickly mobilize resources and adapt their capabilities to deal with uncertainty. As consumers and end-users increasingly pressure businesses to consider a broader range of stakeholders, morals, and missions in the pursuit of financial returns, growth ventures are often the "first responders" to the call for purposeful business. This is perhaps most evident by the recent growth in the number of certified B Corp companies[33] that has tripled in the last five years to thirty-five hundred (across seventy countries)—highlighting how mission has spread through them like wildfire.[34]

Even with this renewed sense of mission, just as governments alone cannot solve these problems, neither can the private sector. "Look at the budgets that the government works with," says Townes-Whitley. "It doesn't matter how large a business's revenues and profits are, they're never even going to get close to what's being managed at the National Institute of Health." Take the COVID-19 vaccine, for example. While the private sector mobilized human and financial capital, the federal government, at around $20 billion, committed the most resources under Operation Warp Speed.[35] The response to the pandemic, in the form of public-private collaborations around vaccine development and supply of protective equipment, highlights the importance of businesses working with the government to solve the big problems.

Niloofar Razi Howe, who serves on the boards of large financial services institutions and government advisory boards, recognized the importance of these partnerships. Razi Howe sees these arrangements as the most practical way to tackle big problems, saying, "If you want to scale solutions that make the world a better place, you can't do it without the government. Governments possess unmatched resources, logistics, and distribution capabilities which make the solutions of business meet the problems in society far better, far faster." So, what characterizes the optimal government-venture relationship? According to Razi Howe, "In these partnerships, the government isn't actually doing the innovation, the innovation is happening in the private sector. And to me, that's the perfect partnership." But these relationships have to be founded upon meaning; as she says, "Creating solutions for your country and for society are the most meaningful and joyous things you can do—finding purpose in tackling problems you know nothing about while preserving the ideals of a liberal democracy."

The convergence of these themes—the generational reset and focus on mission, the proliferation of societal problems and the limitations of government, and the acceleration of uncertainty and importance of entrepreneurial values—brings us to a pivotal moment. We need to build mission-driven solutions to society's most pressing problems. It is time to power up entrepreneurship, but with a key difference. Mission-driven entrepreneurship means constructing businesses around the goals of the government. While these goals may, and often do, overlap with those of the social entrepreneur, the goals of mission-driven entrepreneurship can best be summarized in the preamble of the United States Constitution: those that help the government "establish justice, insure domestic tranquility, provide for the common defense, promote the general welfare, and secure the blessings of liberty to ourselves and our posterity."[36]

We need to embrace the idea that in order to truly make impact at scale possible, entrepreneurs need to see the government as a partner and not an obstacle. While this reads as an easy transition—a cognitive rewiring from foe to friend—there are a number of growing frictions. Among academic circles and discussions on interorganizational relationships, trust has been seen as the key driver of any partnership—public or private. Trust reduces the chance of opportunism. Trust reduces the costs to contract agreements or structure monitoring processes. You can probably see where we are going here. Do you trust your government? Do you believe that your leaders have your best interests in mind? Chances are that you don't.

In fact, government leaders are the most distrusted leadership group of any institution surveyed by the Edelman Trust barometer, with 66 percent of survey respondents worrying that they're being actively lied to by those in power.[37] The approval rating for the U.S. Congress has gone so low that lice, root canals, and the lines at the Department of Motor Vehicles have higher approval ratings.[38] It doesn't appear to be a partisan issue, either. On both sides of the political spectrum, the loudest voices against trust in our institutions appear to be coming from the extremes. Pundits and the political elite speak about their immense distrust in government, while the other disenfranchised members voice distrust in capitalism. This paints a grim picture of our future.

Francis Fukuyama, a renowned political scientist, says that classical liberalism is in a state of crisis.[39] Though current colloquial use of "liberalism" in the United States is a label for left-of-center politics, Fukuyama refers to liberalism as a doctrine that first emerged in the second half of the seventeenth century that argued for the limitation of the powers of governments through law and constitutions, and allowing and creating institutions that protect the rights of individuals and peacefully manage diversity in pluralistic societies. He writes that liberalism is a "big tent" that covers a range of political views but converges on the foundational importance of equal individual rights, law, and freedom. Fukuyama goes on to say that in democracy there are "elections to guarantee that the state represents the interest of as much of the population as possible and not just the elites that are running the state."[40] For proof of liberal democracy's positive impact, he points to the transformation of Asian countries in a matter of decades. Hong Kong, Japan, Singapore, South Korea, and Taiwan adopted key liberal institutions such as protection of private property rights and openness to international trade, which helped position themselves for global trade and market-based capitalism. But now, he sees that these liberal ideas face a crisis because the fundamental principle enshrined in liberalism—one of tolerance—is being fast eroded through political action, distrust, greed, and violence.

For the first time in recent memory, society's trust in business has exceeded the trust placed in its government. In fact, both business and academic institutions are significantly more trusted than the government among the American public, with Edelman Trust Barometer finding trust in business is 11 percent higher than trust in government,[41] and Morning Consult finding that trust in colleges and universities is 20 percent higher than trust in government.[42] And this is problematic for a government increasingly seeking innovation and collaboration with the private sector and academia. It is even more worrying for students and entrepreneurs seeking to start mission-driven ventures that will rely on the government for scaling their impact. Fukuyama sees social trust as the key to unlocking social and economic prosperity.[43] Fukuyama argues that only those societies with a high degree of trust will be able to create flexible organizations that are able to compete in the global economy. Trust means that people have faith that business and government have their best interests in mind. It means that entrepreneurs have faith in their governing institutions and are willing to take risks to push the boundaries of innovation and change. And for the government, it means that business is a partner in the pursuit of mission, and not a barrier. But we clearly face a trust deficit—and are looking upon a generational opportunity to repair this triangle of trust between civil society, business, and government with a model in which venture meets mission.

PIVOTAL MOMENT

A natural question demarcating the importance of our proposed compact is, *Why now?* We observe five fundamental shifts that make this a pivotal moment.

First, technology and business model innovations have enabled societal progress by easing the burdens of our daily lives and producing opportunities for ventures to strengthen the social fabric of society. As put by Jason Matheny, CEO of RAND Corporation and former coordinator for technology and national security at the White House National Security Council, "a large part of our population has been left behind—economically, in education, in measures of health and opportunity. At the same time, we face challenges from climate change, from aging, from the costs of chronic health problems, and we need to figure out solutions."[44] Where do these solutions lie, according to Matheny? Technological progress. "Among the things that will end up mattering the most are the competition between democracy and autocracy, and proving that the democratic system can still function in a much more complicated world than the one in which it was originally designed."

Many emerging technologies that were not present a decade ago will be a valuable source of solutions to our most pressing problems. Technological opportunities that allow us to reconsider our current processes and routines are arising in unforeseeable places. For example, extended reality (virtual and augmented) in education is estimated to receive $12.5 billion in funding from the federal government in 2025.[45] A digital water market is emerging that uses sensors, internet-of-things devices, and artificial intelligence to collect, communicate, and monitor water data. This market is expected to reach $20 billion by 2030,[46] and is focused on improving water quality and management in many developing countries and regions. Only by embracing technological innovations will we be able to create impactful solutions.

Second, targeted social-outcome resource deployment has become a characteristic of contemporary business environments. A tsunami of capital has flowed into social and sustainable business as investors and shareholders flock to businesses that are making meaningful investments in society. Most prominently, multibillion-dollar success stories of such mission-focused companies as Tesla, SpaceX, Palantir, Anduril, Gingkoworks, National Resilience, and the list goes on. These examples have served to break down the perceived dichotomy between profit and purpose, while making meaningful impact to national security and societal challenges. In addition, the government is now a viable market for private-sector innovations with more spending getting allocated for tackling large problems. With limited availability of top talent, we see a virtuous cycle of opportunity for profit to attract top talent for solving purposeful problems. Finally, no longer are financial metrics the defining characteristic of company performance. Science-based social performance targets yield more accurate measurements of companies' social impact. And businesses' transparency of this effectiveness is making social investing more and more feasible.

Third, we observe an emerging narrative of purposeful venture successes that highlights the role of government. It's easy to think about the most successful entrepreneurs of our time as self-made forward-thinkers, but this isn't entirely true. Most ventures behind the most impactful innovations were heavily subsidized by the U.S. government. Take SpaceX and Tesla, for example, companies that revolutionized space exploration and the automotive industry. Both of these companies received billions of dollars in government funding in research and development, and most of the technologies they employ were, in one way or another, funded and created by the U.S. government. The successes in problem solving with the government's support are giving momentum for action, with this narrative reverberating around not only the proven purpose-led ventures, but also the early stage ones.

Fourth, we cannot overlook the implications of the Russian invasion of Ukraine on the global business environment—and more important, on the ideals of a democratic society. As countries continue to restrict individual expressions and freedoms, the West is threatened by ideologies that contrast its open and inclusive democratic ideals. There have been calls for successful Western businesses to respond to Russia's aggression by withdrawing their operations from the Russian market, and many of those have. Digital and economic networks have transformed the topology of the battlefield. As General McMaster explains, "Businesses are becoming more a part of geostrategic competitions and [are] sitting at the intersection of critical infrastructure." In the face of the Russian invasion of Ukraine, we saw these businesses display the same sense of mission that we all felt when Russian troops invaded a sovereign, democratic nation: we must protect freedom.

Finally, as geopolitical rivalries accelerate, so too does "techno-economic" competition among nations for technological and economic superiority. As put by Jordan Blashek, cofounder and president of America's Frontier Fund, a mission-driven investment firm seeking to reinvigorate the nation's innovation and manufacturing prowess, "We are at the dawn of a new great-power technology race waged between democracies and autocracies. If we do not act now, by 2030 the United States could lose its edge in microelectronics, AI, quantum, and synthetic biology to our adversaries. At a time when technology is the 'high ground' for economic and national security, that is not a risk we can take. We need new companies that can reinvent supply chains, help governments solve the hardest social problems, and promote inclusive prosperity across the country. We face a generational responsibility to unleash American ingenuity once again for the benefit of free people around the world."

Increasingly, we see that democratic nations are in an innovation race with autocracies. Autocratic regimes can quickly mobilize financial and human capital around strategic priorities by suppressing any opposing perspectives and creating a unifying message. An October 2022 intelligence report by the Special Competitive Studies Project observed an increase in hostile global actors exploiting opportunities in technical surveillance and building up their digital infrastructure.[47] And while this may be a cause for concern, history and research have shown that democracies consistently outperform autocracies in innovation.[48] This is because innovation challenges the status quo, relies on free and open exchange of ideas, and thrives when people are willing to take risks, three features that fundamentally conflict with the interests of autocratic regimes. In fact, most innovations in autocracies largely occur through the tightly controlled military, and thus these innovations often fail to yield any sort of wider social benefit to the population. Compare, for example, how U.S. investments in NASA in the 1950s, 1960s, and 1970s produced significant "trickle down" innovation in the commercial markets, whereas similar Soviet investments yielded research and technology that never left secret government facilities.[49]

In response to these autocratic investments in digital infrastructure, the United States is making a number of investments in critical technologies that demonstrate a serious concern over the complex and deeply intertwined future of international relations and technology. The

CHIPS and Science Act and the Inflation Reduction Act both demonstrate the commitment of the U.S. government to cultivating domestic innovation in technology-critical areas, such as climate, semiconductor, space, energy, and cyber, all of which have implications for national security, economic policy, and America's standing on the global stage.

The CHIPS and Science Act, which started under the Trump administration and passed in a historically bipartisan vote in the Biden administration, will transform America's domestic manufacturing base. Specifically, the legislation has been applauded for its approach "to enable a much wider array of communities across America to participate in, and reap the benefits of, the changing economy." Gina Raimondo, the fortieth U. S. Secretary of Commerce, remarked that "with these transformational investments, [the United States is] reimagining [the] national innovation ecosystem well beyond Silicon Valley and Silicon Alley to create new technology innovation and manufacturing hubs throughout the country."[50] The bill authorizes twenty new regional technology and innovation hubs throughout the United States, to more evenly distribute the economic benefits of innovation beyond the existing innovation centers of Silicon Valley, Seattle, and Boston. The legislation mandates that at least one-third of these hubs must be small or rural communities (fewer than two-hundred-and-fifty thousand people).[51] At the same time, coming off of the heels of the COVID-19 supply chain crisis, CHIPS will transform America's supply chains from "just in time" (efficiency) to "just in case" (resiliency).[52] Much as the space race served as the proxy competition during the Cold War, the techno-economic race will serve as the new battlefield for liberal democracy.

When talking about U.S. global competitiveness and the growing geopolitical and economic challenge in China, Secretary Raimondo says, "The return on our investment [in CHIPS] is the achievement of our national security goal." Secretary Raimondo goes on to say, "My job isn't to displace the private sector: it's to lay the foundation to allow American businesses to do what they do best, innovate, scale, and compete....We need the private sector, including business, labor, and universities, to work with us to ensure America's long-term prosperity and security. We are pushing on all fronts, all at once. And we need to do it all together."[53]

Manish Bapna, the CEO of the Natural Resources Defense Council, expects that "the Inflation Reduction Act will unlock unprecedented public and private investment to produce solar panels, advanced batteries, electric cars, and other building blocks of the clean energy economy. It's helping to strengthen and diversify supply chains for clean energy investment that globally topped $800 billion in 2022 and is on track to reach $2 trillion a year by 2030." Bapna goes on to emphasize that "there's more at stake here than market share. The clean energy economy will reshape everything about our world—how we generate and distribute energy, how we commute and travel, how we build and live in cities, how we produce and consume food, and even how we earn a living. It will alter the wealth of nations, shift the balance of power and remake the geopolitical map of the world. Climate technology is fast becoming one of the commanding heights of the global security landscape, no less than the production and acquisition of fossil fuels has been for more than a hundred years."

Bapna also adds that recent geopolitical events will have an impact on how to construct supply chains for the new economy, saying, "Russia's invasion of Ukraine has reminded us, once again, that energy security requires energy independence. We won't achieve that by replacing fossil fuel dependence with corresponding dependencies around the materials and technology that support renewable energy. What's needed are more durable, diverse, and inclusive supply chains for the new clean energy economy. That's the way to achieve energy independence—and energy security—in the twenty-first century."

VENTURE MEETS MISSION

In this book, we follow stories of individuals, entrepreneurial ventures, and public servants who answered a call to mission. Through their expert perspectives and experiences, we propose an action plan to construct this meaningful model for impact. With the generational opportunity to create mission-driven impact, we must first rebuild trust among society, business, and government. In other words, we need a collectivity that builds on the power of partnership between private and public enterprise, fosters the sense of purpose and meaning, and shuns the polarizing labels of shareholder capitalism or government. This calls for a new vernacular in which "Venture Meets Mission" is a broader social perspective for innovation and shared prosperity. We need to dispel any notion of profit versus purpose, which forces an artificial choice between the two, and instead frame it as a discussion between business and society. The reframing of Venture Meets Mission helps bridge our sense of idealism and willingness to action with the convergence of people, purpose, and profit, and, importantly, through partnership.

And we would be remiss to overlook the fact that the viability of a Venture Meets Mission ecosystem is only possible in a liberal democracy. Not all governments are benign, and this is a fact that truly matters. Not only do the assumptions of efficient markets rely on the freedom for producers to select their product offerings and consumers their consumption choices, but the very premise of entrepreneurship relies on the freedom to think independently and freely in the pursuit of innovation. In nations without such democratic ideals, the inertia of the status quo as promoted by the autocratic regimes hinders the pursuit of meaningful innovation and economic growth. And of even more concerning, when such innovations occur, corruption in the governing institutions can lead to the expropriation of private-sector breakthroughs, which can disincentivize entrepreneurship altogether.[54] Quite simply, the ideals of a liberal democracy provide the best foundation for the Venture Meets Mission ecosystem to thrive.

With this in mind, we open Chapter 2 with a review of the barriers to action, tracing these largely to perceptions of incompatibility between entrepreneurship and the government. We note the importance of "humanizing government" and "personalizing entrepreneurship" in rebuilding trust between these groups. In Chapter 3, we discuss the design challenges that government-venture arrangements are likely to face. Through expert opinions of government officials, entrepreneurs, and investors, we identify five key uncertainties that deteriorate trust between ventures and the government. For entrepreneurs seeking to construct mission-driven ventures, in Chapter 4 we present actionable organizing principles by which they can build their ventures to rebuild trust with the government and work toward scaling their impact. Through cases of successful ventures, we highlight the strategies of entrepreneurs in bridging the trust gap between their businesses and the government. In Chapter 5, we dive deeper into the government's trust deficit problem, and discuss the ways that the government can rebuild trust with entrepreneurial ventures. We note the importance of the government's ability to dictate national strategy and mobilize a venture ecosystem around societal issues. Then, in Chapter 6, we highlight a number of individuals who are building their careers in the Venture Meets Mission ecosystem. These individuals, in one way or another, are all working toward bridging the gap between ventures and the government. Finally, in Chapter 7, we conclude with a look into the future of government-venture arrangements and observe fast-paced and growing areas for impact. This future is best summarized by Jason Matheny of RAND Corporation: "We should be aiming to improve the world as much as we can with whatever resources we have. The future could be really brilliant if we dedicate ourselves to solving the world's most important problems."[55]

Two

SHARED VALUES

*Rediscovering the Common Ground Between
Entrepreneurs, Government, and Society*

In the days leading up to January 20, 2017, Mathew Lira, at the time
a senior advisor to House Majority Leader Kevin McCarthy, was
scrambling with his colleagues to find a way to get the Tested Ability
to Leverage Exceptional Talent (TALENT) Act to the White House
before President Barack Obama left office. The bill, which had received
bipartisan support in the House and Senate, would make law a program
enabling technologists to serve in temporary tours of government duty.
Just three days before the Inauguration, the bill had passed unanimously
in the Senate, meaning that President Obama's signature was the only
thing remaining for the bill to become a law. A central motivation behind
the legislation was to provide the program with a bipartisan imprimatur;
a united act, despite their otherwise contentious relationship, between
Congressional Republicans and the Obama administration. The clock
was close to hitting zero. The night before the Inauguration, as the outgoing administration was shutting down, it was no longer possible to
deliver the legislation to the White House. It seemed that all hope for
that bipartisan moment had been lost. Then, the staffers realized, while

the process for delivering legislation to the outgoing White House had ended, the outgoing president travels to the Capitol on Inauguration Day and remains in office until noon. Through a bipartisan backchannel network, the question was asked, If presented with the legislation at the Capitol, would the president sign it? And so, on the morning of January 20, 2017, after President Barack Obama arrived at his holding room in the Capitol, the Clerk of the House presented the legislation for signature. As President Obama's last official act, at 11:07 a.m., the TALENT Act became law.[1] This lesser-known story about bipartisanship and public service is exactly what a well-functioning democracy looks like.

Yet it's likely you've never heard this story. Instead, in every media outlet, we are reminded of the political, economic, and social issues that divide us. For decades, political polarization has been a defining element, with partisan animosity increasingly breaching nonpolitical social relationships, such as those held among members of civic associations, workplace groups, and even personal groups and families.[2] The United States has prospered over the past decades, with total wealth held by Americans increasing from $43 trillion in 2001 to $141 trillion in 2021.[3] But this distribution of wealth has become skewed, with the bottom 50 percent of the population growing their wealth from $1.29 trillion to $3.76 trillion (191 percent) in contrast to the top 10 percent that has increased from $26.85 to $98.75 trillion (267 percent). If you compare absolute wealth differences, the top 10 percent hold 2,626 percent more wealth than the bottom 50 percent. These numbers are even more stark if we consider only the top 1 percent.[4] The widening wealth gap between the rich and the poor has made income inequality a major threat. Social inequalities too have gripped the modern American society, as reflected in the recent #MeToo and Black Lives Matter movements.[5]

And as the media remind us of our political, economic, and social divisions, it appears that we all hold different values, different beliefs, and different ideals. And this is concerning for societal trust, which in a liberal democracy promotes social cohesion and facilitates collective action. Social divisions, such as those related to the polarized political state, have a direct effect of undermining trust.[6] The philosophical disagreements among Americans, even among the polarized partisan groups, are quite small when it comes to underlying values differences.[7] It's the perceived or even felt differences that are deteriorating trust.

But we can look to research in social psychology to derive a more optimistic picture of our collective future. When confronting a common threat (in either a physical or existential form), individuals feel a greater sense of shared responsibility and tend to break away from self-focus and competitive isolationism. When people are driven to create social bonds with fellow community members on the basis of reciprocal inter-dependence, they redefine themselves as part of a larger system with a larger mission. They provide support when they have excess resources, skills, and abilities, and receive help from others when they are in need. As the philosopher Jean-Paul Sartre so elegantly writes, "The peculiar character of human-reality is that it is without excuse. Therefore, it re-mains for me only to lay claim to this war."[8] Nothing brings a sense of community and responsibility like a shared threat. Sartre's depiction of the mission mindset in the face of threats underscores the perceived responsibility an individual feels toward the community to aid in the fight against threats.

This was evidenced, too, in the selflessness by which we stepped up to help fellow citizens in the face of the pandemic. Individuals upended their daily routines to engage in quarantining to protect others from po-tential exposure, created and wore makeshift masks to decrease the like-lihood of contagion, and reduced their mobility to avoid public spaces that could act as "super spreader" events.[9] In addition, businesses and individuals donated heavily to causes that supported the containment of the virus.[10] Similar behavior was seen in the aftermath of the Russian in-vasion of Ukraine. As volunteers signed up to house Ukrainian refugees, foreign nationals signed up to fight for a country to which they had no ethnic or religious ties—solely to defend the ideals of democracy.[11] World Central Kitchen is a perfect example of a venture acting with purpose and shared responsibility. By innovating food systems and incorporating locally led solutions to build resilience, World Central Kitchen was able to provide nearly three hundred thousand daily meals to refugees in Ukraine, Poland, Romania, Moldova, and Hungary following the in-vasion. But this wasn't an outlier event. The Afghan refugees following the U.S. troop withdrawal, the migrants on the U.S.-Mexico border, Hondurans and Puerto Ricans hit by hurricanes Eta and Maria—all were fed by World Central Kitchen–led initiatives.

We have a renewed sense of mission. And this only happens by elevating our common objectives and harmonizing our values.

BARRIERS TO ACTION

Good intentions are not enough to yield tangible impact. Moving from intent to action is an entirely different ballgame. It requires *agency*. Agency is the capacity of individuals to act on their own will and consistent with their value system; it is social engagement informed by the past but oriented toward the present and the future.[12] We see how this social engagement can make us question what values are important, as the world is presented and perceived through divisive and polarized lenses. Agency is our own ability to act on those values. Perhaps it is the millennials' reprise of the movie *Mr. Smith Goes to Washington*, but the underlying question that confronts us is, *How do I turn good intentions into effective actions?*

It is no surprise that self-serving behaviors contribute to an array of negative externalities and societal problems. When you act with a complete focus on yourself, you can forget or disregard how you may be hurting others. Many disciplinary and professional groups place a heavy emphasis on identifying techniques to change potentially harmful behaviors. While it seems straightforward, a deep dive on the topic has proven it anything but. We can turn to examples from academic research, where a team in the United Kingdom created a taxonomy of *93*(!) distinct behavioral-change techniques as methods to initiate interventions.[13] Some interventions were based on expected consequences and rewards, which served to motivate or present action. Conversely, we can turn to how people adopt fitness goals and follow through with self-improvement via physical exercise. Three factors that serve to bridge the intention-action gap: planning processes, maintaining self-efficacy, and control and feedback.[14] Planning processes, for example, precede the

initiation of behavior as we develop mental representations of future situations and appropriate courses of actions. This, in turn, helps us overcome an intention gap. Corporate leaders grapple with this challenge,
with 93 percent of Fortune 500 CEOs and 82 percent of employees be-
lieving that their companies should encompass prosocial goals, but only
42 percent confident about how to actually achieve these.[15] However,
business researchers suggest that turning intention into action can be as
simple as clearly defining purposeful goals.[16]

The complexity of the intention-action problem can be traced to a
series of deeply intertwined individual, social, and contextual barriers
that make it hard for us to act upon our intentions. The individual factors—those related to us as people—shape our ability to act. For example, individuals are more likely to act when they have direct and more
information about the problems they face because there is an inherent
tendency to fear undertaking any action toward an unknown objective or
outcome. Social factors—those related to our interpersonal relationships
and social surroundings—shape our orientation to act. Having a high
social status and a strong and powerful social network, for instance, influences willingness to (not) act due to the potential reputational impact
of (in)action. Contextual factors—those related to the circumstances of
the situation—suggest that attributes about the problem itself may influence the likelihood of action. For example, when we perceive our path
to a potential outcome or solution to be cumbersome, costly, or long, we
are less likely to take action.[17] Or, a graduating college student might
have an option to enter public service to proactively further her goals
in helping build a better world, but the lack of financial support or role
models might stop her from even considering it. We list some of these
intention-action barriers in Table 2.1.

With so many barriers to action, it can appear intimidating to mobilize around good intentions. Fortunately, an increasing number of
success stories are emerging—a growing number of entrepreneurs have
been able to channel their mission into their businesses and work alongside public agencies to deliver social value.

Factor	Barrier
Individual	Lack of financial support
	Not enough time
	Incomplete knowledge
	High risk aversion
	Distanced moral responsibility
	Short-term thinking
	Low intrinsic motivation
	Low self-efficacy
Social	Sense of isolation
	Lack of role models
	Low social status
	Lack of political power
	Low community awareness and concern
	Social biases and discrimination
Contextual	Complexity of problem
	Poor infrastructure support
	Competing political interests
	Low societal trust

TABLE 2.1. Intention-Action Barriers. Source: Think Insights.

A FOCUS ON MISSION

We are searching for and finding meaning in our careers.[18] And this is an important, and often overlooked, consideration of the future of society. As we find meaning in our work, we are able to explore a renewed sense of mission in for-profit ventures that address the issues of the community. Not only do these ventures fulfill individual purpose by addressing some national or societal needs, they also create economic value. This lowers the intention-action barriers by providing intrinsic meaning, promoting a sense of collectiveness, and fostering societal trust. By combining the potential of free enterprise (that is, innovation and growth) with principles that promote societal progress and mutually beneficial outcomes, we have seen how entrepreneurs can harness the power of capitalism for social good. These enterprises are operationally no different from those that are entirely profit-driven, except in their functionality, which is built upon the vision to improve the lives of the nation and others.

Need *more* evidence that the dichotomy between profit and purpose is disintegrating? A 2016 Global Entrepreneurship Monitor study found that nearly half of all new ventures had social underpinnings, its highest percentage in the past century.[19] Moreover, the sheer number of ventures has exploded since COVID-19, highlighting people's concerted shift to entrepreneurial endeavors. In 2020, the United States saw a 23 percent increase in new business applications over 2019, reaching a new all-time high.[20] Together, the proliferation of entrepreneurial undertakings and the rise of social agenda suggest that their sense of purpose is not constrained to philanthropic pursuits and nonprofits, but includes purpose-driven for-profit endeavors. We need a new vernacular to highlight that capitalism and mission must not be mutually exclusive.

Take Nathaniel "Nate" Fick, U.S. State Department Ambassador at Large for Cyberspace and Digital Policy, author, entrepreneur, and former CEO of Endgame, an information security company that specializes in defensive digital security intelligence and big data analysis software. Nate, a former Infantry and Reconnaissance officer in the U.S. Marine Corps, knows what it means to pursue a career with mission focus, having done so despite pivoting from a military career into the nonprofit world and then into the business world. So, how does one merge their purpose into a for-profit enterprise? Nate says, "You need to create a business that means something for society. You are wrapping the soft qualitative elements of what you are about, what's important to you and what's important to society, around the hard quantitative core of generating economic value and returns."

When Nate left the military, he was trying to figure out the next steps in his journey. He says, "I thought about my military experience. What I liked was building and leading teams. I wanted to find a way to keep doing that. So, I enrolled in business school because, if nothing else, it seemed like a socially acceptable path. I eventually met some folks who were running a public policy research organization in Washington, and I was asked to lead a nonprofit organization. The organization had a mission that was very important to me. Classmates looked down at me for running a nonprofit, but as a leader it was a terrific training ground for what would come next. I took this experience and continued to follow a mission I believed in." Nate goes on to discuss how his mission remained even through his pivot from nonprofit to for-profit, "After four years of running a nonprofit, I got back on the track I envisioned myself on. I found a company with a great mission around cybersecurity. I was not interested in the next ride-sharing or dating app, I was interested in technology with a mission. I realized there were important problems that needed to be solved, problems that meant something to me, and problems that I could actually help solve."

ELEVATING COMMON OBJECTIVES
AND HARMONIZING VALUES

Large societal problems cannot be addressed by entrepreneurs alone. These challenges need to be addressed in partnership with governments to find actionable, scalable, and legal solutions. The 2020 World Economic Forum (WEF) Action Agenda explicitly states that entrepreneurs will be *the* driving force behind addressing the major societal challenges, and that government actors need to recognize them as "important allies" in this fight.[21] It displays actions recommended by the WEF for the entrepreneurs and governments to help make their collaborative relationships more effective. But both camps have deeply ingrained biases about the functionality and values of the other. And this is deterring the much-needed trust.

So wherein lie these biases? Most prominently, government and entrepreneurial functioning are evaluated differently in regard to outcomes and processes. When the government is judged on the outcomes it produces, its failures are often highlighted and its successes overlooked. A Brookings report that analyzed the largest government failures from 2001 through 2014 lists the 9/11 terrorist attacks at the top as a failure of oversight and Hurricane Katrina as a failure in operational effectiveness.[22] In sharp relief is the public interest in and recognition of the

Defense Advanced Research Projects Agency (DARPA) for producing world-leading technologies such as stealth fighter jets and the internet. However, this is more of an exception than the rule. In contrast, when entrepreneurs and venture capitalists are judged on outcome, the successes are often highlighted and not the failures. This can be seen in public awareness of success stories (such as Microsoft, Google, Amazon, Tesla), and forgotten monumental failures (for example, Quibi's $1 billion "fumble" in 2020[23]). As Arun quips in his class, "If venture capital funds were judged like government funds, no one would invest in a venture fund. We are measured on our winners in the portfolio and the government is measured on the losers in its portfolio. This has a radical impact on behavior—VC plays to win and government plays not to lose." Interestingly, venture funds are judged by their best outlier deals and the aggregate portfolio returns, with the losses seen as an investment in innovation. "The biggest secret in venture capital is that the best investment in a successful fund equals or outperforms the entire rest of the fund combined," says Peter Thiel.[24] Ironically, for government funds, the losses are magnified because they are easier to quantify than the successes, and the negative political repercussions are considered more newsworthy.

When the government is judged on the process, it is often perceived as slow and inefficient. For example, according to a 2019 survey of Americans, 55 percent believe that the government should do more to solve societal problems.[25] Yet there remains a perception that the government is "wasteful and inefficient," with 56 percent of respondents having this position. Moreover, 42 percent of the population believe that government regulations on business do more harm than good, highlighting the antagonistic position that many hold toward the government's role. This is underpinned by studies that find Americans to have a negative view of the federal government and a more positive view of business. For example, in the late 1960s, around 77 percent of U.S. adults trusted the government most of the time, while in 2015, only 19 percent of U.S. adults expressed this same sentiment, and over 50 percent strongly believed that many things that the government is doing are better left to businesses and individuals.[26] Clearly, there remains a trust deficit in the government's ability to efficiently operate and perform functions that businesses may do better.

Similarly, stereotypes of the processes of entrepreneurship and those that undertake new ventures remain profound among society. In 2017, *Harvard Business Review*, in its assessment of perceptions of entrepreneurs, found that people are most likely to describe male entrepreneurs as "arrogant" and "aggressive" and female entrepreneurs as "careless" and "inexperienced."[27] A 2020 survey by Kings College in London found that 50 percent of adults perceive money as being one of the biggest motivators for entrepreneurs, while only 27 percent see entrepreneurs as problem solvers.[28] Furthermore, 20 percent believe that entrepreneurs are self-interested, 15 percent believe them to be ruthless, and 13 percent see them as egocentric. And let's not be mistaken, the stereotypes of the entrepreneurial process are not limited to motivations but extend to demographics as well. When Mark Zuckerberg proclaimed that "young people are just smarter," he unintentionally perpetuated a long-standing stereotype that entrepreneurs are typically young, male, and white.[29]

Not only are there biases in the perceptions of what the government and entrepreneurs do and produce, there is also an inherent tension between the perceived values of government and entrepreneurship, such as in regard to risk tolerance. Not surprisingly, the nature of government agencies as tax collectors and public service providers means that transparency and accountability are paramount—which is not necessarily true in private enterprise, as the Theranos fraud saga and 2022 collapse of the FTX cryptocurrency exchange can attest. The purpose of government as a social control agent responsible for maintaining the integrity of public safety suggests that any risk-taking may jeopardize its ability to uphold complete public safety. In contrast, entrepreneurship rewards innovation and risk-taking, despite the high probability of failure. This produces risk-averse government actors, who are tasked with avoiding failure, as compared to private firms that are judged on their ability to produce economic gains and overcome failure. A cultural dichotomy therefore exists between the government and private actors in regard to the amount of risk each is comfortable assuming.

The Partnership for Public Service realizes this. This nonprofit, nonpartisan organization holds a mission to inspire a new generation of civil servants and transform the way government works. Max Stier, the founding president and CEO, describes the mission of the organization: "Our proposition is that no organization gets better if all you do is kick it. If you want to solve problems with such a risk-averse workforce, you've got to be able to create some real upside. Right now, there's typically downside for them if something wrong happens, and if something good happens and you make a positive impact, it often doesn't matter." So how do we make it matter? Stier's group has created the Samuel J. Heyman Service to America Medals (Sammy awards), recognizing the work of outstanding public servants. Stier explains the motivation for creating these awards. "The Sammy awards give federal employees the recognition and the lift they deserve for their outstanding and impactful work. We often hear that they feel like Cinderella and the carriage has come. Not only does it inspire the workforce to continue to serve, but it provides powerful examples to others, both inside and outside our government, of the amazing work of our public service employees."

Here again, the agency problem is at play. Our discussion highlights the problems of perceived functionality and incompatible value systems. Perceptions of entrepreneurs as extractive and self-serving contrast with those of the government as a protective and inclusive body for societal functioning. The perceived inefficiencies and slow-moving nature of government bodies contrast with the perceived highly efficient and innovative nature of small businesses, along with varying degrees of risk tolerance between them. These differences don't just suggest an incompatibility between public and entrepreneurial actors to partner, but also compel professionals seeking to promote positive social change to make an "either or" choice between them. In addition, they prevent the reconciling of trust between these groups, as these deeply ingrained biases and misconceptions prevent a real understanding of common objectives and mutual values.

So how do we bridge this gap and enable partnership between a mission-oriented enterprise and the government? We need to shift the "either or" trade-off of these groups to "both and," and this can be done through personalizing entrepreneurship and humanizing government.

PERSONALIZE ENTREPRENEURSHIP

Perceptions of entrepreneurship across various geopolitical borders and national cultures affect people's attitudes toward it. This influences the likelihood that individuals will choose entrepreneurship as a career choice, receive support from family, friends, and institutions as potential business founders, and be ambitious to undertake new ventures after previous failures or exits. Therefore, besides the individual, social, and contextual factors that influence the intention-action link, the cultural factors, which relate to perceived opportunities, capabilities, and willingness to fail, also have an effect on entrepreneurial undertakings.[30]

Who are entrepreneurs? Changing perceptions of "what entrepreneurship is" and "who is an entrepreneur" are critical to transforming intention into action. This requires a deep engagement with the characteristics of who entrepreneurs *actually* are: all of us. Entrepreneurship is not exclusively a business-oriented pursuit. In fact, entrepreneurship is applicable to—and practiced in—all facets of our daily life—as an individual, in our families, at work, and as a mindset. Most of us are already entrepreneurs. We just don't know it yet.

Let's take a look into the values and abilities of being entrepreneurial, as listed in Table 2.2.

Entrepreneurial integrity means embodying honesty and transparency in the business, following through with promises and commitments to stakeholders, acting and constructing routines and operations without bias or prejudice, and showing respect for everyone. These are not only virtuous pursuits in any facet of life, but also yield strong reputations for entrepreneurs and businesses, great employee and customer satisfaction, and high-quality products and services.[31] Integrity will help ventures win the trust of their customers, build better relationships and partnerships, and recruit and retain the best employees.

For entrepreneurs, humility means reducing one's own sense of entitlement, expressing gratitude and appreciation to others, and practicing mindfulness. These processes have been found to help strengthen the entrepreneurs' social bonds; form a basis for overall self-improvement, learning, and growth; and increase the competitiveness of the venture

Integrity is the quality of being honest and having strong moral principles. It refers to the content of a person's character, and is seen in instances when people do what they say they're going to do, and remain accountable for their previous actions and intentions.

Humility is the quality of being humble, when people set aside their ego and understand their own imperfections and limitations.

Courage is the choice and willingness to confront uncertainty. Courage means having the conviction to venture into uncharted territory and assume risks without any guarantee of success or knowledge of the outcomes.

Optimism is the hopefulness and confidence that one has about the future or about a specific endeavor or outcome.

Adaptiveness is akin to flexibility, which is the quality of being able to change one's actions and frameworks to meet different conditions. Adaptiveness is seen through non-linear behaviors that cannot be prescribed in sequences of steps, but are changed to meet current conditions.

Resilience is the ability to cope with and recover from crisis or difficulty—being able to accept uncertainty but also face a high degree of failure.

Empathy is a capacity to understand and share the feelings of others' experiences from their frame of reference and is the capacity to place oneself in another's position.

TABLE 2.2. Being Entrepreneurial. Source: David Bozward; Ewing Marion Kauffman Foundation; Kenan Institute of Private Enterprise, UNC Kenan-Flagler Business School.

in the marketplace.[32] In a venture, having humility can help an entrepreneur attract investors and build a more positive and effective team culture.[33] Humility empowers entrepreneurs to surround themselves with executives smarter than they are and be comfortable with "not needing to be right" but rather "always doing what's right."

In an entrepreneurial pursuit, courage is seen in the practicing of self-awareness and self-discipline.[34] Courageous entrepreneurs are notably more confident in their ability to face adversities and setbacks, which promotes a sense of hope and optimism while reducing the impact of stress. More important, courage is a personal attribute that is positively related to overall life satisfaction.[35] For ventures, courage helps in the pursuit of innovation, as doing things differently requires a commitment to a larger vision.

Optimism is a central attribute of the entrepreneurial process, as entrepreneurs tend to be far more optimistic than the general public. For example, in a survey in the late 1990s, researchers found that in spite of 96 percent of all businesses failing within ten years, one-third of venture founders were "absolutely convinced" that their venture had a zero percent chance to fail, and 81 percent believed their venture had more than a 70 percent probability of survival.[36] When entrepreneurs embody optimism, they tend to display more creative ways of thinking and are more likely to generate new ideas, they're more likely to be decisive and undertake pursuits, and they are more likely to bounce back after a setback.[37] Moreover, researchers at the University of Michigan have found that ventures undertaken by optimistic entrepreneurs tend to have higher overall levels of performance.[38] For ventures, the importance of optimism is perhaps best summed up by seventeenth-century French prime minister Francois Guizot: "The world belongs to optimists. Pessimists are only spectators."[39]

Adaptiveness is a defining characteristic of a successful entrepreneur, who is able to meet industry and market volatility and operational hardships head-on, without panic or pessimism. By making them able to change to meet existing opportunities, or bend to adjust to existing threats, adaptiveness enables businesses to build sustainable competitive advantages.[40] For ventures, adaptability is a key feature of being able to grow amidst uncertain market conditions.

Undertaking a new venture is a risky decision, which makes the ability to act in the face of uncertainty and overcome adversity quite difficult. Entrepreneurial resilience is seen in the ability to reflect upon one's choices and decisions, the practice of being present, maintaining a larger vision, and accepting failure as an inherent part of the process.[41] Research has observed that, besides lowering overall stress and anxiety and enabling entrepreneurs to overcome failure, resilience allows people in general to experience positive emotions more frequently.[42] Resilience helps stabilize ventures amidst the market and financial turbulence that may not be experienced by corporations.

As entrepreneurs are surrounded by their stakeholders—employees, customers, investors, and the local community—it is important that they understand the needs and concerns of these groups. Moreover, since entrepreneurship is about creating innovative solutions for communities, understanding these groups is a key requirement to running successful ventures. To show empathy, entrepreneurs need to engage with, take the perspectives of, and integrate the stakeholders into the purpose of the venture. Research has shown that empathy fosters ventures with social impact. Empathy can help a venture better attract customers and build trust with stakeholders.

These values are often overlooked by society once a venture is successful, but most successful entrepreneurs will confirm that that these values are what enabled them to get through the difficult stretches. Reggie Aggarwal, who cofounded Cvent, a software-as-a-service (SaaS) company, alongside Dave Quattrone and Chuck Ghoorah, recalls being a fourteen-year overnight success story. Having started his company in the peak of the dotcom rush in 1999, Reggie, as the CEO, had to reduce staff from 125 to 25 in 2001. He and his team, with only $400,000 left in the bank, scrapped and clawed for the next decade before they raised their next institutional round in 2011 prior to going public. "You learn a lot about yourself and your team's values and the importance of entrepreneurial values and culture to succeed. You make the sacrifices you need to make to succeed, but ironically when you do succeed very few remember the sacrifices you made except your team, family, and close friends."

"You don't need to start a company to be entrepreneurial," says Jonathan Silver, the former head of the federal government's multibillion-dollar clean energy investment fund and current chair of the Global Climate Council at Apollo Management. "It's a mindset, not a vocation. I think and act like an entrepreneur, even though I'm not launching a new venture. My current positions require the same creativity, flexibility, ability to overcome obstacles and understanding of how to build organizations that I needed when I was both an operating executive and a venture capitalist. I also realized somewhere along the way that it was possible to be 'entrepreneurial' in building a career. I didn't need to follow a specific path. I could carve my own. I went back and forth between the public and private sectors, between large organizations and small ones. I took jobs because they interested me, not because they would lead to something else. Mostly, I wanted to do work I found intellectually stimulating and emotionally resonant. And I became much better at executing what I wanted to do as I developed multiple frames of reference."

In addition to autonomy in career development, Silver goes on to say, "nearly everything we do in our daily lives can be linked to an entrepreneurial mindset. Entrepreneurship really is the way you engage in personal growth. You try, you fail, you try again. You work outside your comfort zone; you try new things. You see what works and what you like. You refine that. Nearly everything we do in our daily lives has elements of the entrepreneurial spirit embedded in it in some way, shape, or form."

A personal approach to entrepreneurship therefore means growing and thriving together. It means taking risks and being resilient. It means not being content with the status quo. Carol Dweck, a Stanford professor of psychology, writes about the importance of mindset. She notes that being entrepreneurial shares characteristics of a growth mindset. "In a growth mindset, people believe that their most basic abilities can be developed through dedication and hard work—brains and talent are just the starting point. This view creates a love of learning and a resilience that is essential for great accomplishment."[43]

Family can also be seen as an entrepreneurial endeavor. Entrepreneurship and family have long been associated due to the frequency and history of family-owned businesses in the United States, which resulted in the accumulation of intergenerational resources, skills, and knowledge at the household and family levels. Family firms constitute 90 percent of all business enterprises in the United States, totaling around 5.5 million businesses.[44] However, an entrepreneurial mindset in the family context transcends any type of business venture. Think about it: there is truly no more mission-driven entrepreneurial undertaking than building and raising a family. Here, two cofounders establish their own community, with its own purpose. And they join forces to achieve their common goal. They make important and continuous decisions of what values and goals will define their family and how these will be passed along to future generations of the family. An entrepreneurial mindset means fostering strong family relationships by enabling a willingness to see each other's values and ideas, encouraging others to find their passion and meaning, intergenerational mentoring and resource sharing, and developing a collective sense of mission and purpose. It means a willingness to test and learn and being comfortable with failure while developing a resilient mindset to make the next generation better prepared for an uncertain world than the previous one. This approach underscores that everyone, especially families, is inherently entrepreneurial.

Intrapreneurship, the deployment of an entrepreneurial mindset in an existing organization, has become a desirable framework for corporations to create new value, which is why we have seen a proliferation of these initiatives across corporate America in recent years. According to Bill Autlet, managing director of the Martin Trust Center for MIT Entrepreneurship, entrepreneurial values not only are associated with startups, but are "a way of creating value with new products, new ways of running businesses, and with a number of assets that you control. But also, assets that you don't control. So, entrepreneurs can exist in corporations, and corporations need them more and more."[45] Intrapreneurs embrace entrepreneurial values such as questioning the status quo and taking bold, inventive, and efficient approaches to address problems of stagnation that stymie large and established organizations.[46]

So where does intrapreneurship play out? Not only in for-profit organizations. Consider coaching a youth basketball team. This "organization" is a collective of many people doing different roles. As the coach, you are responsible for creatively and strategically developing a playbook. You coordinate practice schedules and equipment usage. The players independently and collectively practice and develop their skills. Each one of these members is critically important for the success of the team. And each one has the potential to be a leader and make a difference for the team. The most successful teams are those that harness their entrepreneurial values: trust your teammates; adapt to new situations; have resilience to overcome adversity; have the courage to take the last shot; employ empathy to help a teammate; use humility to improve your game; and be optimistic that you can win every game. The entrepreneurial mindset among sports teams in particular is so important that famed basketball coach Mike Krzyzewski encourages it not only on the court, but also in his classes in the Fuqua School of Business at Duke University. When talking to his incoming players, Krzyzewski says, "Don't go to school here, be a part of the school. Be an entrepreneur for creative thinking." We all have the opportunity to be entrepreneurs in our organizations. Even if those organizations don't necessarily appear entrepreneurial.[47]

Entrepreneurship is also a societal phenomenon. Noted author and educator Peter Drucker suggests that entrepreneurial values are a defining and central feature of society. In societies with high entrepreneurial values, change is accepted as a normal and healthy process, and doing something different is encouraged as opposed to doing something similar to what has already been done.[48] According to Efosa Ojomo at the Clayton Christensen Institute for Disruptive Innovation, an entrepreneurial society is driven by innovation and is one in which entrepreneurs are richly rewarded for breakthroughs and the government depends on the ingenuity of innovators to make the society more prosperous.[49] Economic cultures that promote a willingness to pursue opportunities and innovations, a tolerance for uncertainty and failure, and an efficiency to deploy human and financial capital have produced some of the greatest social innovations for the global economy.

So where do we see the value of personalizing entrepreneurship amidst an uncertain and turbulent world? Harvard Business School professor Bill Sahlman made an optimistic case for the future of the world we're in right now in a 2020 talk titled "Entrepreneurial Solutions to World Problems."[50] Sahlman claims the power of response lies in "the startup and venture capital—these are the two greatest inventions of the twentieth century." Quite a powerful assertion, which he then proceeds to defend: "The risk and uncertainty of the present moment make the entrepreneurial process particularly valuable." He argues, "Entrepreneurs acquire financial, human and other resources to run structured experiments, and then investors give only enough money to run a sensible experiment." The venture capital model exists to identify great people with outstanding ideas and give them money to run structured experiments that reveal information about the team, the competition, and the opportunity. The bottom line: "kill losing projects, accelerate winners."

One ambitious venture Sahlman describes is Moderna—a somewhat controversial company, with a clearly innovative, game-changing approach. It is an American biotech firm focused on drug discovery and development based exclusively on messenger RNA. Moderna is "attempting to insert synthetic mRNA into the living cells of patients that would reprogram their cells to create their own therapies and vaccines, rather than those therapies and vaccines being created externally and injected as with conventional medicines." The company has worked on treatments in the therapeutic areas of cardiovascular, metabolic, and renal diseases, as well as selected targets for cancer. In recent times, Moderna has been working on delivering the COVID-19 vaccine.

We are all entrepreneurs. The values of entrepreneurship extend far beyond the misconceptions of entrepreneurs as individualistic capitalists.

HUMANIZE GOVERNMENT

Why do governments exist? Historians suggest that governments originate from the need to protect people from conflict and provide law and order. Governments emerged as people realized that protection was easier if they stayed in groups, creating the basis for sovereignty, or the right of a group to be free outside of outside interference. As civilizations advanced, so too did government responsibilities, extending to the economy and social services. And although rules and responsibilities of the government vary across time and region, governments "provide the parameters for everyday behavior for citizens, protect them from outside interference, and often provide for their well-being and happiness."[51] As Roy Kapani, founder and CEO of ECS and serial government tech entrepreneur, says, "The private sector organizes resources efficiently, governments help to organize society."

And in the United States, the government has grown to substantial size. With a 2020 GDP of nearly $21 trillion, it can be difficult to truly comprehend how big the U.S. government actually is. Take, for example, just one part of it, California. With more than $3 trillion in economic output and a labor force of only 20 million, compare California's economy with that of India, which is $2.9 trillion and 519 million, respectively.[52] And the list goes on and on, with comparable numbers between Texas and Brazil, New York and Canada, and Pennsylvania and Saudi Arabia. With only 4.3 percent of the population, the United States produces nearly 25 percent of the world's GDP.[53] And the number of employees that exist to keep the wheels of the U.S. government turning is similarly substantial. For the past forty years, the total number of federal, contract, and grant employees hovered at around 10 million.[54]

Nonetheless, every day we hear an ongoing parade of media segments about government inefficiency and red tape. Since the mid-1980s, Americans have consistently—and increasingly—believed that the federal government is wasteful in how it spends money. In fact, Americans estimate that over half of every tax dollar that goes to Washington, DC, is wasted on bloated government programs and pork barrel spending.[55] While state and local governments are perceived by the public as slightly more efficient, perceptions of government as inefficient are still ubiquitous at all levels, and highly correlated to the low level of trust in the government.[56]

But this perception of a wasteful government is overstated, and it highlights a bigger problem—Americans' general lack of understanding about what the government *actually* does and what services it provides. For example, in a 2013 survey of the American public, people believed that around 28 percent of the federal budget was spent on foreign aid, when it was only around 1 percent.[57] The survey of government waste on the dollar discussed above? Experts estimate that real government waste is only pennies on the dollar.[58]

So, what's driving these misconceptions about government spending and efficiency? Journalists, academics, and politicians are quick to present this as public ignorance, but it's really a problem of language. The American public's lack of understanding of the functioning of government has been traced to the jargon surrounding policy terms that differs among the political elite (policymakers and scholars) and the mass public, which is further divided by socioeconomic status, ethnicity, and political affiliations.[59]

People understand government programs differently.[60] For example, many Americans with lower education levels believe "foreign aid" to be overseas military spending, while those with higher education levels perceive this to be humanitarian aid. Americans define government waste as different things, constructed largely through an ideological lens. In a survey of one thousand Americans in 2014, 40 percent defined waste as programs they disapprove of, 20 percent as government corruption and "pork" spending, and 10 percent as overpayments for services.

These results suggest limited understanding among the American public about what waste is and what government produces, rather than what the function of the government is. According to Roy Kapani, "Greater insight needs to be placed on the differences between mandatory government spending and discretionary spending. Most of what people see about the government is on the discretionary side. But that is an incomplete picture. Take the National Parks police for example. When the government shuts down and the National Parks are closed, you are still spending 70 percent of the government's budget."

This also highlights another challenge. Whereas testing and failing is viewed as an inherent and necessary part of the entrepreneurial pursuit of innovation and change, government testing and failing toward this aim is seen as wasteful and problematic to national interests. But many of the government's most impressive outcomes were produced through innovation-based processes that comprised the very same iterations of success and failure.

Much of the American public would be genuinely surprised to know not only that the U.S. government is behind many scientific breakthroughs which are interwoven into their daily lives, but also that the technological capability of the U.S. government is sometimes ahead of the commercial market. A few key inventions whose development was government funded include the Doppler radar (1945), MRI (1946), microchips (1958), barcodes (1974), wind energy (1980), the hepatitis B vaccine (1986), the Human Genome Project (1988), smartphone components

(1992), touch screens (1998), self-driving cars (2004), Siri (2011), and the coronavirus vaccine (2020).[61]

Surprised at these technologies or how quickly they were developed? You shouldn't be. U.S. government public research funding has had an impact on nearly every aspect of daily life around the world. Success stories of valiant and brave entrepreneurial undertakings such as Apple, Google, and Tesla all benefitted from government funding and research. Take the Apple iPhone, which accounts for around one-fifth of all new smartphone sales in the world.[62] Every single "smart" technological component of the iPhone was developed with government funding—the internet, GPS, touchscreen, voice recognition, battery, and hard drive.[63]

We often think of the government as only creating the preconditions for entrepreneurship and business: good education and skilled labor, conducive infrastructure and access to capital, and incentives for business creation. However, this narrow view of government doesn't reflect reality. The U.S. government is one of the biggest venture investors in the world, and responsible for nearly all radical innovations of the past century.[64]

Todd Stottlemyer, government and technology industry executive for thirty years and currently CEO of CNSI, a health care software company dedicated to improving the health of millions of Americans, has long observed the role of the federal government as a cultivator of innovation. "A lot of people think Silicon Valley just grew because you had all these entrepreneurs flocking to California. This couldn't be farther from the truth," says Stottlemyer. "Silicon Valley was created with deep investments by the federal government into university and commercial research, especially around national security. The biggest technological and societal challenges have always been tackled with government funding into public and private research. Always," he underlines.

In no area is this more evident than Operation Warp Speed, a federal effort that supported COVID-19 vaccine candidates to accelerate development. The partnership between the Department of Health and Human Services and Department of Defense (DoD), in tandem with pharmaceutical companies and manufacturers, served to accelerate vaccine development and mitigate infectious transmission risk. With the goal to develop, manufacture, and distribute hundreds of millions of vaccine doses within a year—a goal criticized by many as a pipedream—the federal government, in tandem with its private partners, was able to develop and scale up the COVID-19 vaccines.[65] This kind of cooperation is also evident in the appeal to startups to share recent and real-time optical and satellite radar imagery of Ukraine and Eastern Europe to assist with military and humanitarian efforts in the region. For example, an appeal to industry groups by Ukraine-based EOS Data Analytics has led to many small businesses in the space sector, such as Noosphere in Menlo Park, California, to answer this call and join forces with the U.S. Intelligence Community with the goal of preserving Ukraine's sovereignty.[66]

While these are great examples of government's initiatives, it must not be mistaken that the role of government is limited to supporting the advancement of rapid and innovative solutions. People interact with the fruits of government labor in every aspect of their daily lives. Driving to work? The road you are driving on was funded by government money and the safety standards of your car were created and enforced by the government. Having lunch in the park? The government ensures the safety of your meal by keeping the park safe and secure and the air you breathe clean. The list goes on and on of all the ways the government permeates daily life. Access to subsidized commodities, public transportation systems, critical infrastructure and national defense, and social programs are all the most recognizable and central examples of how the government has an impact on our daily lives and promotes economic stability and growth. According to economist John Keynes, "The important thing for Government is not to do things which individuals are doing already, and to do them a little better or a little worse; but to do those things which at present are not done at all."[67]

And the government itself has undergone significant transformation, which has improved its ability to form the bedrock of our daily lives while pushing the boundaries of technological innovation. This is due to the tireless work of public servants pushing to positively transform government while maintaining the larger mission. Look no farther than how the United States Postal Service (USPS) was able to adapt to respond to the pandemic. "COVID-19 brought an urgent shift in mission for the USPS, as the nation faced a shortage of test kits and surging infection rates," says Pritha Mehra, the chief information officer at USPS. "Postmaster General Louis DeJoy was approached by the White House to distribute test kits across the nation to every household, a monumental task which required a critical shift to modern scalable technologies. Bringing together this mission and an elegant technical solution, we were able to quickly create a platform which accepted 44 million orders daily."

Ann Dunwoody, a retired general of the United States Army and the first woman in United States military history to achieve a four-star officer rank, is a great case of a public servant who worked to positively transform government. At a time when many C-suite and board members were predominantly male, Dunwoody rose through the army ranks, working to challenge bureaucracy, bias, and parochialism.

Dunwoody recalls, "I fought the system my entire career. I couldn't stand the waste of the government that I witnessed, like seeing the use of manual spread sheets to manage a $400 billion enterprise. But it was an uphill climb to make these changes. It wasn't until I was a three-star general that I had the clout and ability to make the case to the army chief of staff for some important changes to property accountability. And then I looked to transform how we approached solving problems. First, I led an initiative to attract the best and brightest from all walks of life into my organization, seeing the value in diversity of thought versus seniority and old think. Second, I was successful in creating more partnerships with industry, to discuss best business practices to provide real-time logistics systems and end-to-end "factory to foxhole" visibility that provided transparency for everyone in the entire chain of command. Undoubtedly, diversity and transparency have helped strengthen operations."

Dunwoody's story also highlights the role of social innovations produced in the public sector. In the last twenty years, doors have continued to open for women in the military, with equal pay and opportunities for more women to serve in roles they were previously seen as unfit for. The entire federal government remains ahead of the private sector in ensuring equal pay for women. In 2020, it was found that the average woman working full time made only 83 cents for every dollar paid to their male counterparts.[68] In contrast, women in the federal government made 93 cents to the dollar.[69] While there certainly remains work to do in both the private and public sectors, such social progresses have been successful in humanizing the government.

Dunwoody recalls how humbling the public's response to her appointment was. "I had a lot of firsts in my career, and many of those were because women were just starting this journey of integration [with the men]. But I was never prepared for the promotion to four-star general, and what came with that. It was humbling to be recognized in letters from people I never met. And I mean duffel bags full of cards from people around the world. Veterans, men, women, daughters, mothers, fathers. Everyone was saying that they're glad this moment had arrived—for all of us. Because now, they can tell their young daughters that they could be anything they want to be, including a four-star general. It was humbling to represent that kind of change."

These discussions highlight the innovativeness and value of government. So, how do we recalibrate the perception of government from being inefficient, wasteful, and unconducive to that of an enabler of solutions to modern societal problems? We need to understand how the government agencies pursue *no-fail* missions to appreciate their low risk tolerance. Contrary to private ventures, which often pursue innovation through risk-taking and trial and error, government initiatives have really no room for error or failure. Ninety-six percent of new businesses fail within the first ten years of existence.[70] What would happen if the government had the same failure rate? Routine occurrences such as riding on interstate highways, sending your packages in the postal service, and even having lunch in the park could all become potentially hazardous and dangerous activities. Recent catastrophes such as the Norfolk Southern train derailment in Ohio in 2023 and the Boeing 737 MAX plane crashes in Indonesia and Ethiopia in 2018 and 2019 are examples of the disastrous consequences when the government does not meet its no-fail mission. It is important to understand the role and purpose of government in protecting the public, and why the government can be, at times, a risk-averse agent without an exclusive focus on efficiency in mind.

We need to see government through a humanistic lens—in which it is not a bloated enterprise of bureaucracy, but one of service workers and patriots. The misinformation surrounding the function of government highlights the lack of recognition and celebration of noteworthy and inspiring achievements of government and its employees. Humanizing the narrative of government is best carried out by the Partnership for Public Service, which honors excellence in the federal workforce and inspires others to go into public service. According to the company, these honorees "[w]hether they're defending the homeland, protecting the environment, ensuring public safety, making scientific and medical discoveries, or responding to natural and man-made disasters, put service before self and make a lasting difference."[71]

The breadth of opportunities across government for individuals to explore their personal social interest spans nearly every sector—energy, climate, economic development, food insecurity, national security, health care—and the list goes on. For example, Sonal Shah served as deputy assistant to the president and director of the Office of Social Innovation at the White House, leading the efforts across government agencies to introduce social innovation, including financial innovations, impact metrics, and the role of technology. The Humans of Public Service (HOPS) organization is another group working to break down the misconceptions of government. Using the same approach as the Humans of New York photography project, HOPS tells stories of government workers to remind people that "the government is filled with familiar faces like family members, neighbors and that person you bump into at your local store. Public servants care about their community and want to deliver impactful services, often under challenging circumstances."[72] And leading storytellers such as author Michael Lewis are beginning to tell more of these stories through various ongoing projects. Lewis's book *The Fifth Risk* talks about the brilliant work of federal workers and public servants, whose knowledge, dedication, and proactivity keep the wheels of government turning.

And one does not have to look far to see the pathbreaking and self-less work of government employees. Take Gregory Robinson, for example. Born the ninth of eleven children to tobacco sharecroppers in rural Danville, Virginia, Robinson attended a segregated elementary school before earning a bachelor's degree in math from Virginia Union University (where he had a football scholarship), and a bachelor's degree in electrical engineering from Howard University. In 1989, Robinson joined NASA as a manager at the Goddard Space Flight Center, rising up the ranks to eventually become the director of the Webb Space Telescope Program. From humble beginnings, Robinson became responsible for one of the most advanced scientific undertakings in human history and rightly was named to the *Time* 100 list of most influential people in 2022. Robinson's story shows that in the face of adversity, the American dream and a commitment to public service is still possible. While stories of corrupt and selfish politicians contaminate the perception of public servants, stories like that of Gregory Robinson are much more ubiquitous throughout the government—highlighting a true commitment to serve.

By humanizing the government, we can break down the damaging stereotype of the government as bloated, inefficient, and incompatible and replace it with the spirit of entrepreneurship.

A CAPACIOUS SENSE OF "WE"

Value systems underpin our beliefs, frame intentions, and guide actions. These value systems that are foundational for liberal democracies are slowly being tested and frayed. As a society, we have been subtly but profoundly reframing our value systems on what is ethical, what is good, and what is shared. And now, we seem to be in a place where we see more that divides us than what brings us together. Recent events are forcing us to "revalue" our shared values, and recalibrate what is needed to elevate our common objectives.

We need a more capacious sense of "We." The American constitution's three most powerful words are We the People—a collective belief that coming together despite our perceived differences will preserve the ideologies that underpin classic liberalism and democracy itself. One powerful mechanism is to harness mission—the collective sense of purpose—by bringing together the scale and goals of government with the power of free enterprise and the talent and passion in civil society.

Broad-brush characterizations of entrepreneurs as extractive and self-satisficing are inconsistent with the entrepreneurial values held by these individuals, who see themselves as optimistic and empathetic agents of social change, and who act with integrity and courage. The depiction of government as an inefficient institution that impedes progress and change is inconsistent with the innovative and inclusive solutions that government has introduced into everyday life. Not only are the misconceptions factually incorrect, the values of entrepreneurship and government are hardly orthogonal. Government and entrepreneurs can be two birds of a feather—change makers who pursue innovative solutions to address pressing societal problems.

The preconceptions of antagonistic and incompatible actors need to be dismantled and reforged with trust. There is simply no "purity test" between choosing the better of entrepreneurship and government agency. Both are interested in progress and change, both embody a sense of purpose and mission, and both are underpinned by values that stem from a concern for others. This may be difficult to achieve in an age of digital and physical echo chambers, which prohibit people from finding a "middle ground." However, it is only through acceptance of the real vision and mission of entrepreneurs and government that we can foster serious discourse and exchange between these groups and enable them to work together to solve societal problems.

INSEAD Business School studies innovation patterns across the world. Their Global Innovation Index provides a robust evaluation of the most innovative countries in the world by looking at a mix of science and innovation metrics. In 2021, the top ten most innovative countries in the world were Switzerland, Sweden, the United States, the United Kingdom, the Republic of Korea, the Netherlands, Finland, Singapore, Denmark, and Germany, all democracies.[73] Entrepreneurial culture is rooted not only in the climate of innovation, public infrastructure, labor skills, and access to capital, but also in societal empathy. As a result, the society perpetuates an orientation in people to look for society's unmet needs—a skill that is critical to innovation.[74]

Despite the strong bedrock of liberal democracy and innovativeness, we need to rebuild trust between the partners in this ecosystem. Elevating common objectives and harmonizing values is just the first step to mobilizing government-venture arrangements to scale impact. Rebuilding trust will require a deeper understanding of the challenges that these partnerships will face, as well as the individual, venture, and government actions that can be taken to repair this trust. In the next five chapters, we discuss these topics in depth.

Three

A DIFFERENT COMPACT

Innovating Public–Private Partnerships

In the buildup of World War II, the United States was in trouble. The military was relatively small compared to those of other major powers, with the army ranking seventeenth in the world in terms of size and the navy fifth. Two American businessmen, one from General Motors and one from the shipbuilding industry, approached the government with an idea of how to fix the government's problem: to mobilize the "arsenal of democracy" to develop the nation's military capability. The government implemented a mobilization effort, using government contracts and financial incentives to shift private companies' production lines to focus on military equipment and incentivize innovation in production and design. In just six months, the United States military was the largest and most powerful in the world. Business leaders set aside their pursuit of profits and set out to save the world.[1]

Elevating the common objectives of the government and venture, and harmonizing the values of "what function government serves" and "who entrepreneurs are," are first steps in transforming mission to create the future we want. They are only that: first steps. Developing and working these arrangements between the government and ventures involves a number of design issues that require close attention. While collaborations between public (state) and private (business) actors have long been the focus of academics and policymakers seeking to create positive change, traditional public-private partnership frameworks fall short of addressing the needs for government-venture alignment. As noted by one experienced venture capitalist, "The most overused term in Washington, DC, is 'public-private partnership'."

In recent years, the number of public-private arrangements between the government and entrepreneurial ventures has also been increasing.[2] Amid the economic challenges of 2020, U.S. Chamber of Commerce CEO Tom Donohue noted the importance of partnerships between business and government:

> America's economic rebound is not solely in the hands of top-level leaders, but all members of the greater business community. As government and business leaders pave the way for the post-pandemic environment, businesses across the country *will* have to follow their lead.…It will take the collective strength of the thousands of members of the business community…and the millions of others who helped power our economy.…Together, we can help lead our country out of the crisis and into a brighter future.[3]

With more than $500 billion in aid being sent to entrepreneurs and small businesses in the Paycheck Protection Program, it's quite clear that ventures are seen as critical to economic recovery. And the government momentum behind ventures is also seen in the 2022 Goldman Sachs "10,000 Small Businesses Summit." This brought top entrepreneurs, members of Congress, and administration officials together with more than twenty-five-hundred small businesses (the largest gathering of any such kind in the United States).[4] The most impressive takeaway of this event? A July 20, 2022, event at Nationals Park that saw four hundred Congressional offices attend, the largest nonpartisan convening of Congressional personnel outside of the Capitol building, ever.

But it's not the first time that the government is leading innovation by partnering with the private sector. In fact, after World War II, the government relied heavily on large defense contractors and technology consulting partners to help it innovate.[5] These partners, such as Lockheed and Raytheon, and most major consulting firms, such as Accenture and Deloitte, built sizable businesses and large public-sector groups. These stories highlight the shift from a vertically integrated model of government innovation to one of an ecosystem of coordinated private-sector partnerships. It appears, however, that this model is changing again.

The current model of government-business relations is often attributed in Washington, DC, circles to a 1993 dinner held in the Pentagon for defense company executives—the so-called "last supper." Deputy Defense Secretary William Perry warned executives that the post–Cold War peace dividend meant that the Defense Department would not be able to sustain enough demand to keep all the major players in business. The result was the downsizing of the defense industrial complex through consolidation and reduction. And with it came a model of largely labor-based customized services to map to the government's requirements of tailored and proprietary technical solutions. Thus many of these companies came to construct their business models largely around working with the public sector and not the commercial sector. And as a result, the government agencies built familiarity with how to evaluate and price "teams," but as the commercial world has rapidly digitized with a shift to platforms, cloud, and SaaS-based offerings, they need to shift their purchasing and innovation approach from *teams* to *streams*.

Why does this matter? Well, it highlights a broader challenge the government faces in working with technology ventures. The services businesses (such as the long-standing Lockheed Martin AEGIS radar system), while attractive, have linear growth trajectories that are interesting to private equity firms, but historically hold less appeal as investment opportunities to venture capitalists looking for nonlinear growth in the next platform-based "home run." And this largely explains the limited venture interest in having portfolio companies working with government. As technology innovation accelerated and so did the cyber threats from adversaries, it became apparent that the government needed to rely on "dual-purpose" technology (technologies with government and commercial applications) to be able to benefit from the decreasing cost curve exemplified by Moore's Law and the rapid innovation that was being produced in the commercial sector. This transition spawned opportunities for building platform-based companies, thereby increasing interest from venture firms, and thus emerged multiple examples of success of venture-backed companies that targeted the government market, such as Palantir, Gingko Bioworks, and SpaceX. Interestingly, in many tech spaces including cybersecurity, space, data analytics, bio, energy, and quantum, the government is viewed as a thought leader, and has become a desired initial customer for venture-capital-backed companies looking to provide credibility to their commercial customers.

And recent research highlights the importance of considering partnerships and collaborations among public and private organizations. In a study of 24,096 technical problem-solving efforts in public-private R&D hybrids from 1982 to 2012, Jason Rathje, a former MIT and Stanford researcher and current director of the Office of Strategic Capital, has found that divergences in practices and goals in public and private organizations often lead to more valuable and destabilizing innovations.[6] It can be reasonably concluded that diverse approaches and objectives can lead public-private collaborations to push the boundary on innovation as partnering organizations are exposed to new and complementary information. Rathje reports that technology ventures that form a contractual relationship with a public consumer (such as NASA or the DoD) produce technologies faster and survive longer than their non-contracted peers. Thus, not only can public-private collaborations drive more impactful innovations, but government-venture collaborations are more efficient at producing these innovations.

But we really don't know the inner workings of the complexities that these relationships may face. For every successful venture that has partnered with the government there are a handful of not-so-fortunate others. Expectedly, given the obvious differences in large corporations and new ventures, the complexities of these arrangements will vary from those in traditional government-corporate partnerships. To fully understand the shortcomings of these traditional public-private partnership frameworks and why they are limited in addressing the need for government-venture alignment, we must first unpack the differences in organizing principles between public and private actors. From there, we can begin to identify a set of uncertainties that confound public-private partnerships but are exacerbated in circumstances when the private firm is a venture. Only then can we begin to identify successful blueprints for and rebuild trust among mission-driven partnerships.

UNPACKING "PUBLIC," "PRIVATE," AND "PARTNERSHIP"

Ultimately, the core differences between public and private organizations can be traced to their funding structure and their production function.[7] Public agencies are state-owned and funded by taxpayer funds, which are aggregated, budgeted, and allocated across different groups in the government. Private enterprises, in contrast, are typically owned by nonstate actors and are sustained through voluntary market exchange. An agency's reliance on funding via budgeting makes it less oriented toward profit creation through its operational activities. While agencies sometimes charge a fee for the service they provide (for example, paying a toll to cross the Golden Gate bridge or buying a subway ticket in New York City), they are neither structured nor required to operate on a commercial basis.

The funding structure—as taxation based or profit based—also has significant implications on the processes agencies employ to conduct their operations. Because public agencies are not subject to the same market and competitive forces and shareholder pressure, they are subject to greater controls to prevent abuses of power. While public agents are elected through bureaucratic or democratic processes, which can pressurize them to conform to prescribed behavior, long election cycles and bureaucratic layers mean that this pressure is not nearly as strong as the pressure managers in commercial organizations face. As a result, public agencies typically have stricter transparency requirements involving the disclosure of their activities and procedures (a factor we would be remiss to overlook as a key driver of public trust in these agencies).[8]

The second major difference between the public and private firms is the production function. Public agencies create public goods, monopolistically.[9] This means that they are exclusively responsible for the creation of a public good or service with no competition. Consider the transportation infrastructure along the east coast of the United States. The Department of Transportation alone is responsible for the funding, creation, and maintenance of roads and bridges, such as those along the I-95 corridor. The roads are open to any user in the region, regardless of whether or not they actually paid for it (think of a European tourist on a U.S. road trip from New Jersey to Rhode Island). This makes the good provided by the department "nonexcludable." Also, with the exception of tolled roads or traffic congestion, the roads are widely available to everyone at any time, irrespective of the number of people driving on it. This makes the good "nonrival." Public agencies exist to create, maintain, and promote these public goods. Private enterprise alone cannot create these goods as there is no financial incentive for doing so. Because people cannot be excluded from using the public good (nonexcludable) and there is not a finite supply of the good dependent on demand (nonrival), there is no mechanism to charge money to earn profits from users.

Public goods are inherently immeasurable, meaning that public organizations have difficulty measuring their performance.[10] In comparison, private enterprise produces forms of economic goods that can be valued tangibly and intangibly with relatively high degrees of accuracy (based on the dimensions of excludability and rivalry). For example, while a private enterprise could easily measure the volume of profitable passenger traffic on a bridge (a metric of, say, the amount of profit or loss on each user's toll payment versus maintenance costs), this measure of passenger volume is incomplete for a public agency. Agencies tasked with building public infrastructure operate not with a goal of profitability, but with a goal of creating public good—meaning that these projects often have the goal of promoting other outcomes, such as local economic development, or in this case, linking communities and families together across natural barriers, such as a river. Tracing the increase in economic activity due to a new bridge is wholly more difficult than measuring profitability.

This produces accountability problems that are exclusive to public organizations; we cannot evaluate the effectiveness of agency action as we can of a high-performing or struggling business. Given that the outcomes of government agencies are hard to capture, their operational processes and decision-making behaviors are often under the heaviest scrutiny.[11] For example, the impact of building a new bridge may be difficult to value. People's homes may need to be demolished to make room, but the bridge could create jobs and open up economic opportunities in hard-to-reach places. A public servant confronting this decision consults experts and community members to ensure that their decision-making process factors in as many of these considerations as possible. As the impact of the decision *per se* is difficult to evaluate, it is the decision-making process that is often the most scrutinized element, a reason why many debates among politicians are centered around their plans to act and justifications for previous actions, versus the actual outcomes of their decisions.

This has the effect of making public-sector employees feel "under the microscope" and become significantly more risk averse than employees in private firms.[12] This risk aversion manifests itself most prominently in a proclivity to maintain the status quo and avoid adoption of new routines without consulting powerful stakeholders. An unwillingness of public managers is not due to their bureaucratic nature, but because of their belief that "red tape" is created for them by legislative and political superiors.[13]

This discourse accentuates a deeper discussion, which academics and practitioners have long noted, about the barriers of partnerships between public and private enterprise originating from the funding, function, and formalization of these organizations. We summarize these differences in organizing principles between these firms in Table 3.1.

The differences in organizing principles create uncertainties for public-private collaborations. While these uncertainties can also be seen in private-private and public-public partnerships, they are more salient and central to coordinating partnerships between public and private firms.[14]

The differences in goals between public and private organizations creates an uncertainty in the incentives of how to *actually* go about achieving goals in a partnership. Because public organizations tend to pursue nonfinancial social goals (think of their inability to measure public outcomes and their reliance on budgeting) and private organi-

Organizing Principles	Public Sector Organizations	Private Firms
Goals	Community focused, driven primarily by social objectives. Serve a defined social need, even when this may not be economically viable or advantageous.	Market focused, driven primarily by commercial objectives. Seek to maximize the organization's value for the benefit of shareholders.
Measurement	Performance measurements are problematic as public goods are by definition nonexcludable, meaning that a simple bottom-line analysis is inappropriate.	Performance can be reasonably measured through social and financial metrics.
Assets	Unique resources are capacity to disseminate information to citizens and NGOs, and to regulate, adjudicate, and legislate.	Designed to increase efficiency in capital allocation and labor division.
Formalization	Subject to controls to prevent abuses of power through transparency requirements. Display much greater formalization of procedures than private firms.	The due process requirements applicable to agencies amply exceed those of corporate entities (e.g., disclosure and monitoring by the board of directors under the Sarbanes-Oxley Act in the US).
Risk	Intense "under the microscope" scrutiny makes agency managers and staff more risk averse than managers in private firms.	Due to market pressures and the commercial basis of operations, managers are often incentivized and rewarded for innovating and risk taking.
Time	They uphold long-standing infrastructure assets, and officials often face minimal short-term pressures (only for the period prior to election).	Incentivized to meet short-term financial targets.

TABLE 3.1. Differences in Organizing Principles Between Public and Private Actors. Source: Authors.

zations pursue financial objectives, there is an inherent tension in the compatibility of their goals. For example, the City of New York issued a $9.6 million social bond for prisoner rehabilitation to be run by The Osborne Association. Goldman Sachs purchased the bond, from which they will profit if recidivism (repeat offenses) decreases. However, the city is only liable for some capital if the program is successful, and years later, there has been no reduction in recidivism.[15] While valiant in its pursuit, it's quite clear that the City of New York had no real financial incentive to demonstrate any reduction, which highlights the financial misalignment of this relationship.

Next, the measurement challenge of public organizations makes the outcomes of public-private partnerships difficult to evaluate. Specifically, the multiple and interactive nature of public goods makes it challenging to quantify the value created by the partnership. Moreover, it is complicated to determine which partner (both the public and private) and which social groups will capture the value created (claimancy rights). Consider Spain's Castor Natural Gas Submarine Storage project. These offshore gas storage plants were located in the Mediterranean Sea twenty-two kilometers off the coast of Vinaros and were designed to complement the Spanish natural gas requirements in the event of shortages and import problems. Ultimately, the project was halted after the firm's gas injection into the reservoir led to a series of a thousand earthquakes,[16] costing the public over €3 billion. The private firm failed to forecast the public risk and potential damage of its operations that were based on inadequate impact estimates.

When organizations have idiosyncratic resource bases or specificity and complexity in assets they hold, it makes it challenging for them to work together. Partnerships that create value are constructed on resources that are complementary for achieving the partnerships' objectives. When idiosyncratic resources are not complementary, the potential value creation by the partnership is limited. And when assets are specific and complex, it creates challenges for the organizations in coordinating their task objectives and value-creating routines. This is because the cost of information sharing in the case of such assets is high, as the ability for a partner to understand these assets relies on tacit knowledge, which is difficult to share and transfer. Even in situations when assets are not wholly complex, it may be difficult for partnering parties to properly understand the condition and value of assets. This is best seen in the City of Chicago's budgetary crisis in 2005, which forced the city to enter multiple asset monetization deals. Because the city hastily signed deals with multinational institutional investors, it vastly underpriced the value of the assets in these deals, costing the exchequer hundreds of millions in lost potential value.[17]

Public agencies have a higher degree of formalization in their routines due to the procedural transparency and stakeholder consultation needed for their functioning. In contrast, private organizations tend to have more flexibility in their operations to adapt to environmental changes and market pressure. This raises the question of how public-private partnerships structure the processes of their relationship. Notably, the decision-making processes behind these partnerships are likely to be seen as either imprudent or exclusive. When government agencies push formal routines and greater stakeholder involvement and consultation, private enterprises are likely to pursue more process flexibility and less stakeholder involvement. This challenge is best seen in the Three Gorges Dam project on the Yangtze River in China. Because the local communities were not involved in the consultation process of the dam's construction and location, villagers were excluded from flood zone discussions. Ultimately, the construction of the dam caused a displacement of at least 1.3 million people, destroyed countless rare archaeological sites, and increased the number of landslides and earthquakes in the region.[18]

Public-private partnerships also face a significant degree of relational uncertainty in their arrangements due to differences in the risk tolerance capabilities of public and private organizations. Because private organizations are often rewarded for strategic risks while public organizations face enhanced scrutiny for any risk-taking, the coordination costs of public-private partnerships are high. These projects often face challenges in achieving appropriate levels of risk for both partners, and in distributing it effectively among the partnering organizations. This is evidenced in the building of the Karolinska Hospital in Stockholm,

Sweden. The government contracted out the construction of the hospital to a private firm. Because the firm was hastily constructing the facility, quality control problems emerged and the partners needed to hire external consultants to resolve them, resulting in increased costs of the partnership.[19]

Finally, the time horizon differences for public agencies and private firms creates a degree of temporal uncertainty for them. Public agencies, dependent on budgets as a source of financing, are more comfortable with pursuing long-term objectives. In contrast, private firms, faced with shareholder pressure, must demonstrate short-term viability, even if pursuing long-term objectives. In public-private partnerships, the transparency requirements and formalization of routines in public agencies can create strains on private organizations seeking to meet short-term costs and performance expectations. Similarly, setbacks and shortcomings on the part of private firms can strain public agencies that may not have budgeted for increased project costs. This is evidenced in the construction of the I-69 interstate highway in Indiana, which experienced delays in construction and ultimately cost state taxpayers nearly $500 million.[20]

These uncertainties exist in all partnerships, both among public-private partnerships and among only private firms and only public organizations. Building from recent academic work on intersectoral partnerships in the face of grand challenges,[21] in Table 3.2, we list the design problems faced in public-private collaborations because of the differences among public and private organizations.

TABLE 3.2. (opposite page) Uncertainties in Public-Private Collaborations. Source: Derived from Gerard George, Thomas J. Fewer, Sergio Lazzarini, Anita McGahan, and Phanish Puranam, "Partnering for Grand Challenges: A Review of Organizational Design Considerations in Public-Private Collaborations," *Journal of Management* (2023).

Organizing Principles	Nature of Tensions Between Public and Private Actors	Nature of Uncertainty in Public-Private Collaborations
Goals	• Social and financial goal incongruence. • Individual conflicts of interests.	**Incentive Uncertainty** when the goals of the partnership are unclear, the incentives to achieve them are likely to be misaligned.
Measurement	• Multiplicity and interactivity of sources in value creation and quantifying the public, social, and/or ecological value. • How groups can capture the value created by the partnership (claimancy rights).	**Outcome Uncertainty** when performance measurements are difficult to be articulated, the value capture of the partnership is likely to be impaired.
Formalization	• Flexibility • Procedural transparency and explicitness in specification of task criteria. • Stakeholder consultation ("red tape"). • Boundaries and memberships, and the division and allocation of tasks.	**Process Uncertainty** when roles and procedures are ambiguous, the decision-making processes are likely to be imprudent and exclusive.
Risk	• Ex ante anticipation of partnership coordination costs and policy changes. • Tolerance (aversion vs. acceptance) and distribution (shared vs. transferrable) of partnership risks.	**Relational Uncertainty** when project risk is poorly evaluated and partners have low familiarity, the costs of coordinating the relationship are likely to increase.
Time	• Temporal horizons and focus. • Payment and funding structures.	**Temporal Uncertainty** when the timeframes relevant to each partner are misaligned and the objectives are not updated to reflect unplanned contingencies, the costs of the partnership are likely to increase.

A NEW PARADIGM OF GOVERNMENT-
VENTURE ARRANGEMENTS

The uncertainties within partnerships reveal the design problems stemming from differences in funding, function, and formalization of public and private organizations. However, they also accentuate a more pressing issue, the lack of understanding of these design problems in a relationship between the government and an entrepreneurial venture. Traditionally, public-private partnerships mainly have been practiced and explored between the government and large corporations, such as privatizations of infrastructure projects with multibillion-dollar price tags.

But these relationships are notably distinct from public-private partnerships between the government and smaller enterprises, which we term here as *government-venture arrangements*. For clarity, we use "government-venture arrangements" to capture a breadth of different governance arrangements, including service contracts, in which the government sources services from the private sector; concessions contracts, in which the private sector is involved in the design and construction of public goods and services; purchaser contracts, in which the government purchases innovative products from the private sector; and more. In contrast to the traditional forms of public-private partnerships, government-venture arrangements also offer an opportunity for technology developed in the public sector to be commercialized through startups. The emergence of the commercial space market in particular was heavily tied to the ability for space ventures to capitalize and construct businesses around innovations in the public sector.

The lack of understanding of government-venture arrangements is a pressing concern given the prominence by which ventures have been working with the government. In the 1980s and 1990s, when public-private partnerships were being introduced and state governments legislated for such arrangements, an overwhelming majority of these collaborations were between governments and large corporations.[22] Simultaneously, new actors have emerged as the locus of research and development, creating alternatives to universities, national laboratories, and established industry. In many fields, startup firms are where the most cutting-edge technology development is occurring. Venture-capital-backed public companies, not major industry leaders, accounted for nearly half of the total U.S. business R&D spending across government, academic, and private companies in 2019.[23] Looking only at the overall picture would lead one to believe that the situation is healthy. However, a closer look suggests that is not the case. Similarly, the rise of VC firms as a primary source of commercial innovation funding has further jolted the funding landscape. Yet venture capital's focus on relatively shorter-term returns has meant that, to date, it has largely stayed away from deep tech and commercialization of basic R&D—both of which require patience and appetite for risk. Dr. Vannevar Bush, who led the former U.S. Office of Scientific Research and Development and dubbed science "The Endless Frontier," wrote in 1945, "There are areas of science in which the public interest is acute but which are likely to be cultivated inadequately if left without more support than will come from private sources."[24] To master this new geometry of innovation, the U.S. government will have to do more than return to its role as the primary funder of basic science and procurer of military technologies. It must revise how it incentivizes research and development, reforming not only how it allocates funding but to whom, to where, and how often.

In this trend toward ventures and government working together, it remains to be seen how and when the challenges associated with traditional government-corporate partnerships manifest in government-venture arrangements. According to Professor Howard Stevenson at Harvard Business School, there are eight key dimensions to entrepreneurial management:[25]

Strategic orientation	Driven by perception of opportunity
Commitment to opportunities	Revolutionary with short duration

Commitment of resources	Many stages with minimal exposure at each stage
Control of resources	Episodic use or rent of required resources
Management structure	Flat, with multiple informal networks
Reward philosophy	Based on value creation
Growth orientation	Rapid growth is top priority; risk accepted to achieve growth
Entrepreneurial culture	Promoting broad search for opportunities

These dimensions of entrepreneurial management style highlight additional frictions for ventures collaborating with government compared with those of larger private or multinational corporations. For example, the "strategic orientation" of ventures enables them to be flexible and adaptable to the perception of opportunity with a government partner, in contrast with larger corporate or multinational corporations, which tend to be slower to deviate from the initial partnership arrangement. In addition, a venture's "commitment to opportunities" and "commitment of resources" rely on milestone-based financing from investors. Such financing makes ventures more vulnerable to delays with government procurement and payment cycles than larger corporations that have resources allocated to weather extended program delays and uncertainty. Ventures' constrained "control of resources" and fluid "management structure" can be a disadvantage in government partnerships, given the limited history of the teams working together and past performance of the venture with customers or end-users within government. Larger corporations may boast years of collaboration with an agency, as a prime contractor, with much of the same executive team being together for the duration of the partnership.

Finally, the "reward philosophy," "growth orientation," and "entrepreneurial culture" of ventures support taking on additional risk by testing and learning in the search for new opportunities that drive growth and value. In contrast, larger companies may tend to focus on minimizing failures when partnering with government. While ventures focus on increasing the reward potential (alpha) as new entrants in their relationship with government, larger corporations focus on reducing the risk of projects (beta) with government so that they may maintain their incumbency. Growth ventures differ from large corporations that are better endowed with financial and human capital resources, but the size and complexity of these businesses create commensurate constraints—they are less nimble, tend to be more process-driven, and are less experimental with their pivots toward new opportunities and solutions.

In light of this broader discourse of mission-driven venturing, what are features of the uncertainties that government-venture arrangements face? To answer this question, we go right to the heart of those working in this space.

ALIGNING GOALS, RECONCILING MOTIVES

> "Oh, East is East, and West is West, and never the twain
> shall meet,
> Till Earth and Sky stand presently at God's great Judgment
> Seat;
> But there is neither East nor West, Border, nor Breed, nor
> Birth,
> When two strong men stand face to face, though they come
> from the ends of the earth!"
>
> **—RUDYARD KIPLING, "THE BALLAD OF EAST AND
> WEST" (1889)**

The first line of Kipling's poem, never the twain shall meet, is often wrongly quoted to showcase irreconcilable differences. But subsequent lines reveal more, that when two equals come together with mutual respect for each other's character, capability, and integrity, that alone becomes the criteria for judging and accepting one another. Taking Kipling's cue, perhaps the tension between government and venture is not irreconcilable but rather one requiring effort to align goals and motives. Goals are the outcomes each party wants to achieve, while motives underpin the rationale for why we pursue those goals. The tensions between government and venture stem from this misalignment of goals and motives—of why we do what we do. It's the underlying motives that become incentives to galvanize actions. Often, we discuss this as "finding your purpose." In recent scholarly work, the authors note that *framing* and *formalizing* purpose within the organization can serve as the driver of concerted action to achieve common objectives.[26] The challenge is to get into a mindset in which we recognize that our ultimate purpose is the same, even if our mindsets, our processes, and our approaches differ.

Entrepreneurs over the past two decades are said to have developed a distinctively venture (or Silicon Valley) mindset—think big, take risks, and grow fast. Silicon Valley is the leading startup ecosystem in the world for high-technology innovations. And today, it is seen as the technological center of the private sector. While it is easy to draw the obvious conclusion that the region was a by-product of brave and venture-minded entrepreneurs pursuing the American dream, it would be unwise to overlook the lesser known, and equally important role of the U.S. government. The navy had a long-established presence in the Bay Area. Its needs, such as a radio communication system in the early twentieth century, and radar development and aeronautics later, led to technology firms establishing their roots to capitalize on government funding and contracts.[27] Together with proximate universities such as the University of California and Stanford University, the government was able to create a hub of research and innovation.

However, the recent clashes between major companies such as Google, Meta, and others have shown that the government and technology ventures have increasingly diverged on their beliefs related to data privacy, national security, and consumer protection. In some instances, they also have conflicting views about monopolistic practices in the technology space. As a result, we can see that the venture mindset may be less conducive to an effective working relationship with the government. And specifically, there appears to be a slight lack of empathy for the government's mission in the venture mindset. Unfortunately, many technology ventures have continually shied away from recognizing that technological innovations can influence the lives of billions of users, with government's concerns about these innovations going unaddressed or acknowledged too late.

The notion that ventures and entrepreneurs have all the answers and can address our most pressing problems is flawed—a fact highlighted by Amy Zegart, a senior fellow at the Hoover Institution and the Freeman Spogli Institute at Stanford University, and the author of *Spies, Lies, and Algorithms: The History and Future of American Intelligence*. Zegart sees a massive divide between how the venture community and the government operate. "I call it the suit-hoodie divide. Here in the Valley, people even dress differently than they dress in Washington. They speak a different language. They have a different culture. There's a different orientation. That's not to say it's unbridgeable, but it is in many ways bringing together two foreign cultures. I have said this to my friends in the Pentagon, stop coming to Silicon Valley and using all of your D words. Military officials love to come here and they use words like, destroy, dominate, degrade, defeat. These are very popular words in the military. They are terrifying words in the Valley. In the Valley, they like to use C words, create, collaborate, change, and culture. And so even if they're aligned interests to protect the nation or advance the national interest, it's often hard for these two cultures to even understand each other to find common ground."[28]

In spite of the growing political polarization, former National Economic Council chairman Keith Hennessey points out, "Democrats and Republicans share a growing alarm over the return of great-power conflict. China and Russia are challenging American interests, alliances, and values—through territorial aggression; strong-arm tactics and unfair practices in global trade; cyber theft and information warfare; and massive military buildups. In Washington, alarm bells are ringing. Here in Silicon Valley, not so much. Ask people to finish the sentence, 'China is a ____ of the United States'. Policy makers from both parties are likely to answer with 'competitor,' 'strategic rival,' or even 'adversary,' while Silicon Valley leaders will probably tell you China is a 'supplier,' 'investor,' and especially 'market.'"[29]

As discussed earlier, empathy is a critical value of entrepreneurship, and even more important when we consider how entrepreneurs can create actionable solutions at scale in tandem with the government. Entrepreneurs seeking to make an impact need to consider that government is truly an enabler, and not a disabler of social change and innovation. And for ventures, this extends beyond the government's mission at the start of the twentieth century. The federal government not only invests in developing innovative organizations within it, but also funds a substantial amount of the country's total R&D expenditures. According to the National Center for Science and Engineering Statistics, in 2019, while the federal government performed about $60 billion of R&D work, it allocated nearly $140 billion for R&D to higher education, nonprofits, and businesses.[30] Clearly, as put by researchers at the *MIT Science Policy Review*, "federal R&D funding is the bedrock of national innovation and plays an irreplaceable role in steering scientific progress towards the betterment of society."[31]

The venture mindset presents a unique challenge to our discussion of mission-driven venturing. A lack of empathy in this regard presents a clear uncertainty of the incentives behind a potential government-venture agreement, with ventures pushing for rapid innovation and impact and government pushing for public interests. Although venture is increasingly recognizing the importance of public well-being, it is quite clear that the mission goals of the government remain underprioritized among many in the venture community, and at times, entirely disregarded by the fastest-growing and most influential ventures in the United States. This raises the question, why is the mission of government often disregarded or underprioritized by the ventures? It is likely that it's not a lack of desire to pursue these objectives, but simply a lack of visibility of successful for-profit businesses operating in this space. Government and entrepreneurship follow two seemingly different paths, and bringing them together creates unique challenges of aligning goals and reconciling their motives. Yet both together, as equals, have the power to foster transformative innovation.

HITTING AN INVISIBLE TARGET

Public agencies and private ventures place different emphases on outcomes. The government tends to be significantly more focused on the processes of resolving problems than on the outcomes themselves. This is due to a number of reasons. Governments are primarily driven by social objectives, and serve a defined social need, even when this may not be economically viable or advantageous. Moreover, because governments are vulnerable to abuses of power, and cannot be controlled through the same equity and governance levers as the private actors, they are subject to transparency requirements that lead to focusing more on formalization of procedures. Consequently, government feedback systems (for example, investigative agencies) are asymmetrically focused on identifying any deviation from established processes rather than on measuring the desired outcomes from these deviations.

The focus on process versus outcome has an impact on government-venture arrangements because ventures may not stay with the original plan if there is a better path forward or the current plan is not achieving the desired goals. Ventures are culturally and organizationally designed to pivot to optimize resource allocation and probability for successful outcomes. These pivots are timely but unforeseen, usually driven by a test-and-learn mindset and informed by direct market feedback. The ability for ventures to pivot in a timely manner while partnering with the government is critical for long-term success and continued innovation. In fact, ventures should and can be the "safe sandbox" for the government to test and learn various solutions without being penalized by the existing feedback systems.

Nate Mook, the CEO of World Central Kitchen (WCK), a nonprofit founded by renowned chef José Andrés that provides meals in response to humanitarian, climate, and community crises, knows the challenges of matching the government's processes. World Central Kitchen was founded in 2010 to prepare food in Haiti following the devastating earthquake. The model of the nonprofit is to be a first responder to humanitarian crises and then to work with state and national governments and galvanize solutions with local chefs and restaurants to solve hunger problems. Since the conception of the nongovernmental organization, WCK has organized meals in a number of locations across North and Central America, the Caribbean, Africa, Asia, and Europe. Most recently, WCK has set up operations in border areas along the Ukraine-Poland border to distribute meals during the 2022 Russian invasion of Ukraine. For these efforts, WCK has been highly recognized, with founder José Andrés being named one of the world's hundred most influential people by *Time* magazine in 2018.

Mook points out the difference from how the Federal Emergency Management Agency (FEMA) responds to crises, "FEMA has a long tradition of overseeing crises in the United States. It was created in 1979 and initially responded to emergencies like the Three Mile Island accident, evolving to lead all natural and manmade disaster response. Following major disasters like Superstorm Sandy and hurricanes Harvey, Irma, and Maria, José, the team, and I looked at the model of FEMA and thought, there has to be a more effective way to respond to these crises. We saw how FEMA was responding to these disasters—parachuting in from the outside and bringing a bunch of food, usually MREs made for our military. We thought there has to be a better way to mobilize the resources that were already there. We wanted to build a model around being software and not hardware. It's not like all of the food and ingredients and chefs and kitchens disappeared overnight." So how does this relate to the process-focus of the government? "The government comes in with a playbook, whether or not it is optimal for the context, and they stick to it—they trust their process," says Mook.

In contrast, ventures are almost exclusively outcome focused. Early stage businesses that do not have a long history of performance need to define and redefine their metrics and milestones of performance. Funding organizations evaluate the venture's performance against benchmarks to decide whether to invest or reinvest in the organization or not. Focusing on revenue and growth in evaluating early stage investments, investors tend to scrutinize predefined metrics such as market share, profitability, retention rate, and burn rate.

And imagine if government agencies had to testify in front of Congress for not innovating enough. The culture of these agencies would likely shift from being concerned about only making mistakes and focusing on processes to being focused on innovating fast enough and producing innovation outcomes.

Dan Tangherlini, managing director at Emerson Collective and governor of the United States Postal Service, sees the importance of agencies themselves managing this innovation initiative. Tangherlini suggests that there needs to be an "innovation general," akin to the inspector general but ensuring that agencies are innovating enough: "I understand the value of the Inspector General [IG] corps and the need to provide oversight and transparency. But the work they do comes out of their organizational origin as auditors, so it is naturally retrospective and often takes the form of, 'This is what you did wrong.' As a result, leadership is particularly nervous about a negative IG report and the follow-on need to try to respond or justify an agency's action. IG reports can generate Congressional hearings or bad news stories, so the natural inclination is to avoid taking any action that risks generating a report. It would be great if there were a countervailing force for change and experimentation; maybe we could call them Innovation Generals? These…would encourage risk-taking and innovation by giving agencies a hard time for *not* trying new technology, methods, or systems. Maybe Innovation Generals could create a new form of bureaucratic pressure for change, modernization, and efficiency."

In addition, the government's opaque and unpredictable procurement process introduces outcome uncertainty that has an acute impact on venture partnerships. Specifically, resource allocation for any venture is always a high priority, given that financing is usually tied to achieving key milestones—revenue generation, product development, partnerships, and so on. Consequently, for a venture a "fast no" is strongly preferred over a "slow maybe." It is better for a venture to know up front if the partnership has no chance of success or that it may take two years to decide, versus being in a situation in which they are in a "rolling six months" decision-making process. This is true especially for deals that require significant dedicated resources from the venture, which otherwise could be repurposed for other opportunities. In a large public-private partnership, the investments into the relationship rarely put the private company at risk, given the scale of the business. In a venture, however, the outcome uncertainty can put the venture at risk.

In contrast, a "fast no" provides the venture near-term clarity and enables it to allocate resources accordingly. Even being told that a process may take two years allows a venture and its investors to decide how best to fund the company to provide the government-venture relationship the best chance of success. In both scenarios, trust and credibility are maintained between the venture and government.

The "rolling six months" scenario is the worst case for any venture collaborating with the government. In such a scenario, the senior executives of a venture report to their board, including investors, that they have had a great meeting with an agency, and believe there might be a decision for a large deal in six months. However, oftentimes this deadline may pass with no decision yet made. During this time, the board starts to question whether the management team is correctly assessing the feedback from government partners or they are being overly optimistic in their reporting to the board. Unlike the commercial deals that the ventures may be collaborating on, it is difficult for investors to get the desired transparency, given the security clearance constraints and hence the limited information that government can and will share with outside parties. During this period, precious cash resources are being depleted, and the venture can be put at real financial risk. This creates a negative feedback loop for government-venture partnerships.

The differences in focus toward outcomes between government and ventures biases the behaviors of these groups, which is problematic for any working arrangement. An inability to quantify important outcomes for government and the importance of performance metrics for ventures leads to greater outcome uncertainty for these relationships. Established organizations may accept the outcome uncertainty of working with governments to satisfy particular stakeholder needs and interests, or build legitimacy with the public constituency. But ventures, which are reliant on knowing-and-showing their performance, tend to be incompatible with such arrangements.

BESPOKE NEEDS AND STANDARDIZED SOLUTIONS

Consider the importance of growth for startups—and how these businesses get there. Traditional linear growth models suggest that to increase revenues, businesses must increase costs too. This means increasing the number of employees, offices, and other inputs. However, nonlinear growth models point to the importance of operating leverage to scaling a business. Here, businesses can drive growth by incurring only incremental costs. In the technology space, because the value of the business often lies in the already developed technology, scaling is the ability to reach additional untapped markets and drive sales and customer engagement there.

When the government releases a contract for the development of a technology or a service, they tend to seek a bespoke solution—a specific software, service, or product—as an answer to a specific problem. This "make it custom" approach may not necessarily be scalable for private enterprise, in which the general public's needs are significantly less customized. While product or service customization may yield a higher price tag, it produces a number of problems for both the venture and government, in terms of scalability and cost.

For the venture, customization limits scalability. When the government has specific product requirements, it restricts the venture from being able to generate widespread adoption in the commercial sector. As customization incorporates specific customer needs, it prevents businesses from being able to lower costs by increasing economies of scale. Standardization enables the venture to achieve consistency in content creation and delivery. Not only are products created at a lower cost and faster speed, but the monitoring processes to ensure their quality and consistency are also significantly more effective due to the repetitive nature of production.

Customization is also problematic if the needs of venture to scale in the commercial market conflict with the national security needs of government to retain highly sensitive technologies. A successful government-venture compact recognizes that both ventures and governments have needs to be considered. The Department of Defense does allow, in many instances, ventures to develop software and then release it in the commercial market, so long as it is not classified or restricted by the International Traffic in Arms Regulation or Export Administration Regulation or patent and trademark law.[32] However, if government is to realize a venture's need of commercial function, it has to shift from bespoke solutions to platforms that have an element of scalability.

Custom solutions may also lead to greater lifetime costs. Adopting a legacy system—such as a custom communication network for employees in the DoD—gets exponentially more expensive over time. A dual-purpose commercial product, by definition, will offer less customization for a government agency versus single-purpose solutions. While the government may evaluate the feature differences at time of adoption, the significant cost differences between the two systems are seen in the maintenance of the system. If the government adopts the custom solution, the cost of owning the solution increases exponentially over time. The people who created the system may move out of their roles, meaning that any updates to the system will require investments in training employees—a cost that is likely to be shifted to the government. The government workers who adopted the system may also move out of their roles, and thus the organizational knowledge of the system may deteriorate significantly and therefore the efficiency with which updates may be adopted is constrained. Also, the rate of technological innovation suggests that there is a major opportunity cost in using technology that may be outdated compared to state-of-the-art technologies.

An inherent tension exists between venture's proclivity to grow via product standardization and the government's desire to procure and employ customized products. This represents a form of process uncertainty, as the operational processes of entrepreneurial ventures are oriented toward creating products and services at commercial scale, while the desired resources of government are oriented toward customizability. Trae Stephens, chairman and cofounder of Anduril Industries, a defense tech company, and partner at Founders Fund, suggests a third alternative, "that the Department of Defense buy defense-specific items using the same streamlined procedures as it applies to dual use. These items would be built, priced, and sold using a commercial market approach. But they would be single-use defense items. This would incentivize a new breed of commercial entrants into the defense market that do not look like legacy contractors, and that put their DoD customers first instead of last, as with dual-use tech companies."

In addition to the operational tensions of process uncertainty, human capital differences bring another form of process uncertainty in government-venture arrangements. People are a key component of any organization, and the culture of two organizations plays a key role in their ability to establish and maintain a successful interorganizational relationship. The cultural processes of an organization are not abstractly created and instilled, but are a product of the individual employees, their social interactions, and the collective values and identities of the group.[33] These cultural processes also socialize new employees into the organization, orienting them to what the appropriate organizational procedures are and the relevant frameworks for decision making.

Why does this matter? "People are what truly matters in the intersection of business and government," says Phaedra Chrousos, chief strategy officer at the Libra Group and former technology transformation commissioner for President Barack Obama. "Technology is easy. You can understand a technology, its purpose, its processes, its functioning, all with relative ease. You can make different technologies speak the same language and serve complementary roles in the pursuit of a mission. But people, people are hard. People have different wants and needs. They have different expectations. They have different backgrounds and experiences. They have different cultures and languages. Getting people to work together can be hard. That is the real challenge in these government-venture arrangements. People," Chrousos emphasizes.

Government's approach to people is different from that of ventures. The bureaucratic layers of government coupled with the heightened focus to procedural transparency are manifested in rigid hiring practices based on educational qualifications. Specifically, government hiring policies are built around degree requirements as opposed to capability requirements. Many federal jobs at the entry-grade levels (GS-05 or GS-07 grade levels) accept baccalaureate degrees, while candidates with just a high-school diploma qualify only for clerical or assistant positions

(GS-02 level).[34] This hiring practice has been shown to handicap not only the ability to recruit from a larger talent pool, but also the ability to recruit the *right* applicants.

Government's policy of requiring a college degree is also a stark contrast to the makeup of most entrepreneurs. A CNBC small business survey found that only 44 percent of entrepreneurs actually completed a four-year college degree before starting their business.[35] And even more interestingly, only 9 percent completed a bachelor's degree in business.[36] As Mark Zuckerberg famously pronounced to the 2017 graduating class of Harvard, "Let's face it, you accomplished something I never could."[37] While 44 percent is still a higher percentage than the one in the general adult population of the United States (around one in three adults has a four-year college degree[38]), it is still significantly less than the percentage of nonclerical government employees with a college degree. Moreover, over 30 percent of the federal government's employees have a master's degree or above, compared to less than 18 percent of entrepreneurs.[39]

It is quite clear that entrepreneurship stresses human capability more than scholarship, an approach different from that of the federal government. It considers personal attributes of the individual that have value and applicability across outcomes, sectors, and domains, such as creativity, perseverance, and dedication. It also values the tactical knowledge that is required in specific situations to achieve targeted outcomes, such as domain-specific experience and expertise.

The government's reliance on educational background as an indicator of individual capacity creates an additional layer of process uncertainty, as it is in contrast with entrepreneurial emphasis on capability. A reliance on hiring procedures that are growing increasingly incompatible with hiring trends limits the pool of capable individuals with entrepreneurial mindsets from joining public agencies and even from receiving government contracts. In addition, competing philosophies about what makes someone qualified to perform a specific task or job draws questions on the boundaries of partnership task responsibility. When cultures clash, this can promote distrust, micromanagement, reduced transparency, and employee disengagement, all of which underpin greater process uncertainty.

RISK-TAKING AND REWARD-SHARING IN RELATIONSHIPS

How risks and rewards are allocated among government and ventures presents a unique lens to observe how innovative labor is divided, how success and failure are perceived, and what the expected returns of the project are among these groups. With this in mind, an obvious conclusion can be reached—*the government tends to socialize risk while ventures privatize upside.*[40]

Consider the 2008 financial crisis. When the economy was in shambles, who was asked to step in? Not the corporations—but government. In this view, government's role is to facilitate the processes of fixing market failures. And despite the major role of financial institutions in creating this crisis, only businesses are seen as creating value. This belief is rooted in how we define value as a matter of exchange. Goods and services with a price tag drive the nation's gross domestic product, and in turn, policymakers construct terms of the deal around the private sector upside. Only when this upside isn't achieved, or worse, creates detrimental economic consequences, is the government expected to demonstrate value by stepping in.

But this conceptualization of value simply isn't accurate. Consider a palm oil plantation farmer in Indonesia who uses controlled fires to burn down forest land to create space for palm oil plantations. This palm oil drive created the largest fires in Southeast Asia in 2015, where the health risks of the smog affected Indonesia, Malaysia, and Singapore. The 2015 fires caused the largest economic losses associated with health impacts (US$7.3 billion), with $5.7 billion losses for Indonesia, $1.3 billion for Malaysia, and $0.3 billion for Singapore. In other years, the total health-related economic losses were US$1.8–3 billion.[41] From the palm oil plantation perspective, it increases the GDP, and so it is valued by this definition. But the costs to offset the natural environment and health impacts are not considered or valued. Only the government, and not the private sector, is expected to bear the burden of this cost and restore the ecosystem.

Clearly, this definition of market-exchange-based value is too narrow. Governments create value every day for citizens and businesses without utilizing market-based exchange levers. Transportation infrastructure, technological advancements, and national security are three examples of government-created value that are not captured by this definition. Considering that many of the greatest innovations were produced by government funding and then handed off to the private sector for upside, the government currently burdens the weight of the risk of these innovations, with limited upside.[42]

Michael Morell, former CIA director, speaks about this problem. "The CIA, NSA, and a handful of other intelligence organizations are the only organizations I know where IT security people get a veto over what the CEO wants. And it all comes down to the security risk of the technologies. The incentives to bring technologies in are far overshadowed by the incentives not to bring them in. People don't get punished for not bringing a new technology in, but they definitely will be under scrutiny if they do and it fails. And not only are these agencies more averse to taking on risk, but they also handcuff the entrepreneur's ability to scale their product. They often want to make subtle changes to it, which can be significant for a venture, costing a lot of money and taking their focus off of other markets."

This may explain the divergent, and at times contrasting risk profiles of government and entrepreneurs. With a limited upside to innovation and a significant downside, it is unsurprising that the government tends to be significantly more risk averse than entrepreneurs. In many instances, the risk aversion of the government is a necessary and valuable attribute for the nation. It would be difficult to see the value of a risk-taking government operating in the geopolitical space, one making egregious and potentially harmful decisions in regard to foreign policy that could antagonize relationships with foreign nations. Also consider how a risk-tolerant government may approach deteriorating transportation infrastructure. Decisions to remodel or rebuild an older bridge may be delayed by a government that is comfortable with absorbing the safety concerns.

However, in the context of innovation, this risk aversion presents significant challenges. Innovation is inherently a trial-and-error process. Organizations that avoid making any errors or are fearful of making mistakes are limited in their ability to be agile and innovative. Making mistakes is a critical part of the innovation process, as the new knowledge gained from past failures is integrated into the next steps of the process. Innovation does not ask an organization to avoid making mistakes, but to embrace the value acquired from them. Counterintuitively, avoiding making any mistakes in pursuit of innovation also increases the organization's exposure to risk. A false sense of security that comes with the status quo ignores the fact that the status quo is the current state of the present. An uncertain and rapidly changing future is quite different from the current state of the world. By avoiding innovation, we are creating more distance between where we are and where the world is going.

Innovation also has a direct impact on the productivity of the workforce, and we can see the gap in efficiency grow between the public and private sectors as a result. In a fifteen-year span from 1997 to 2012 alone (a time period characterized by the introduction of the digital age and the internet), output per job grew by 24 percent in the private-sector services, but by only 9 percent in public-sector services.[43] All signs are pointing to the need for a federal government that's more innovative. But how can it be done?

In our discussion, we have mentioned the importance of trial-and-error for innovation. For entrepreneurs, failing is a critical and necessary step in the journey to innovate. From failure comes learning, iteration, adaptation, and the building of new models. Researchers in the University of Virginia Darden School of Business found that 90 percent of innovative organizations see failure as a necessity in the pursuit of innovation.[44] How does this compare to the government's view of failure in innovation? A survey of twelve thousand young adults found that the average risk tolerance of entrepreneurial individuals is 21.3 percent *higher* than that of public employees.[45] But, it's unsurprising.

Consider Solyndra, a clean-energy startup that was believed to revolutionize solar technology. However, broken promises and poor management led the company to go bankrupt in 2011, but not before receiving nearly $500 million in federal funding. This failure in innovation was considered so egregious that it was even a political talking point in the 2012 presidential campaign,[46] despite the fact that the Department of Energy (which was never designed to be a money-making organization) was able by 2014 to turn a surplus by making investments in clean-energy technologies through its U.S. Energy Loan Program.[47] Yet it is easy to see how the failure of Solyndra can be criticized for poor due diligence and improper budget allocation.

We can also see the value in other innovations, such as the Interstate Highway System, drugs to treat a host of ailments, and thousands of products developed from NASA research, such as aircraft de-icing systems and cell phones. Much like the investment in Solyndra, none of these innovations were guaranteed to work. All of them cost considerable money.[48] And they demonstrate that the government should not be judged on its "worst deal," but on the success of its portfolio, just like VC.

The incentives for taking risk are not there for public service employees. Pulling off a major improvement in a service delivery does nothing for government employees. They likely will not be compensated, promoted, or recognized for this achievement. However, any hiccup in the design and implementation of the improvement could lead to heavy criticism from the public. In contrast, we see an ethos in tech companies in Silicon Valley to "fail fast." People are encouraged to take risks, and successes lead to huge payoffs.[49] While government needs to champion innovation—for itself, for corporations, and for ventures—the incentives to assume risk when partnering with other organizations are not aligned with the cause.

The discrepancy in the upside and downside of risk-taking behavior between public agencies and ventures is substantial. Because innovations are borne out of a propensity to take risks, this discrepancy manifests as substantial relational uncertainty between these groups. Moreover, with ventures willing to assume higher risk than the established organizations that have constructed competencies around existing routines and practices, there is even greater relational uncertainty for the government as it is harder to evaluate the risk associated with the venture's operations. Again, this highlights the importance of trust. Without it, ventures have little indication of the commitment of government in their products and the government is unlikely to assume risk in lesser-known companies and products.

THE VALLEY OF DEATH

Back in 1991, Geoffrey Moore, an organizational theorist, authored the book *Crossing the Chasm*, which detailed to the startup community how to jump over the gap between early adopters and early majority customers and was re-released in two later editions.[50] For government-venture arrangements, this gap has different meanings, and it is a key topic among these circles. Among government officials and commercial software executives, this gap is commonly called the "valley of death." To the government, the valley of death refers to a transition from a research and development project to a program of record—the application that the government envisioned when the original small business innovation research program was funded. For ventures, the valley of death refers to a transition from a pilot program to a deeper and larger engagement with the government and other customers, and the rounds to enhance financing.

In-Q-Tel (IQT), which sources, conducts diligence, and executes investments in early stage enterprise software, cyber, biotechnology, and other companies that offer commercial products with applicability to national security missions, deals with the valley of death problem quite frequently. IQT is a not-for-profit strategic capital investor for the U.S. government based in Arlington, Virginia, that invests in high-technology companies to aid in the mission of equipping the CIA and other intelligence agencies with the latest information technology capability. IQT is an independent organization interestingly sitting outside of the CIA or any other government agency; however, IQT is bound by a charter agreement and annual contract with the agency. To aid in their collaboration, IQT works closely with a standing office within the government (In-Q-Tel Interface Center) which facilitates communications and relationships between IQT and the various government intelligence organizations. The relationship is perhaps best summarized by former CIA director George Tenet: "The CIA identifies pressing problems, and In-Q-Tel provides the technology to address them. The In-Q-Tel alliance has put the Agency back at the leading edge of technology."[51]

Since its founding in 1999 (under the name "Peleus"), IQT has become the gold standard of mission-driven VC investing. The average dollar invested by IQT in 2016 attracted fifteen dollars from other investors.[52] It is believed that the company now holds around three to four hundred different investments in an array of industries such as augmented and virtual reality, biotechnology, power and energy, space, and critical infrastructure.[53]

There is an inherent time horizon conflict between ventures and government. Ventures are usually funded for achievement of key milestones over a period of eighteen to twenty-four months. Therefore, it is important for ventures to show progress in three-to-six-month windows rather than the longer cycle and procurement times of government, which may last two to three years. The lengthy temporal uncertainty favors the existing incumbents, given that the government is inherently risk averse and even more so with new partners. The up-front costs to ensure compliance—such as the FedRAMP program[54]—can be a deterrent for ventures to collaborate with the government given the added investment and time required to even be in position to compete for key programs.

The valley of death has its name for a reason. It refers to products and services being solicited or purchased by the government. However, during the process, the expectations of new concepts and technologies can undermine the commitment of the government to adopt the new capabilities in the long term. As a result, initial investments made by the government do not materialize into operational products and solutions. This is perhaps best seen in the approach of the Pentagon to artificial intelligence, which some say has been in a never-ending cycle of investment and failure.[55]

Ted Davies, the president and CEO for Altamira Technologies Corporation, is also a senior advisor at Attain Capital, a VC fund that invests in growth-stage companies in the knowledge economy and partners with firms that deliver high-value technology-enabled solutions to businesses, government, and education clients. Davies deals with the valley of death problem frequently in both his executive role and advisory role. He says, "The government is looking for young companies to bring new and innovative products and services to meet constantly evolving missions. Multibillion-dollar government contractors obviously play a role in supplying some key solutions, but these companies are just not viewed as truly innovative. But smaller, newer entrants to the market can often have financing problems in the long cycles of working with the government. Their innovative products and services can lose their shine for the government if they fall victim to long government procurement cycles, and they can experience their own hiccups complying with unique government requirements. It's been said that the best job at a new entrant to this highly competitive marketplace is to be the second sales leader, as they can reap the benefits of a long market penetration process undertaken by the first sales leader."

Research and development drives new technology into the marketplace, often accompanied by market "hype" around the technology's ability to solve legacy problems. During this time, government or private funding occurs. The product undergoes some customization to meet the requirements of the government, while the venture foregoes some level of opportunity in the commercialization of the product. This is because the government may require bureaucratic stipulations and regulations around intellectual property rules, price controls, and contract auditing requirements. However, government officials, in turn, may lose interest in the product or service, thereby trapping and killing the innovation in the valley of death.

So how do these temporal differences affect the government? The recent resignation of Preston Dunlap, a senior official responsible for driving innovation in the DoD, highlights the problem. Dunlap, the first person in the DoD to fulfill the role of chief architect officer, says in his resignation letter, "By the time the Government manages to produce something, it's too often obsolete, much more must be done if DoD is going to regrow its thinning technological edge."[56]

A temporal uncertainty is perceived due to the misalignment between the long and cumbersome procurement process of government and the short-term financing requirements and product cycles of ventures. Because the funding structure of the government in these ventures is not intermittent, initial investment often is not enough to sustain the short-term needs of the venture.

DESIGN CHALLENGE OF GOVERNMENT-VENTURE ARRANGEMENTS

With these observations in mind, we present in Table 3.3 a roadmap of the design challenges that government-venture arrangements face. To summarize, incentive uncertainty manifests as the inability of entrepreneurs to empathize with the government's public mission. Outcome uncertainty is seen in the entrepreneurial need for flexibility versus the government's relative inflexibility of formalization. Process uncertainty occurs as the entrepreneurial ventures require standardization for growth in contrast with the government's need for customization. Relational uncertainty arises in the incentives for assuming risk, often seen as a prerequisite for ventures while damaging for the government. Finally, temporal uncertainty arises due to the valley of death phenomenon, which can drain the financial and time resources of new ventures.

So how do we overcome these seemingly insurmountable challenges? Through vision and alignment, says In-Q-Tel CEO Chris Darby in his "2022 Summit Speech":

> We must start by focusing on an affirmative vision, a vision that sees us collectively solve for Health, Education, Energy, Production, including food, Security, and finally Happiness, all by 2040. There's probably a word for it, but if "happiness" was good enough for the Founding Fathers, who am I to argue. Smarter people can probably come up with a better list, but for me, this is a good starting point. It would be a starting point that reasonable people around the world, in the public and private sectors, could rally around.
>
> From that starting point, we then must work backwards to our national tech strategies and craft an aligned public/private investment roadmap to, over time, achieve our aspirational goals and realize our vision. Technology can be transformative. Fusion, quantum, bio, autonomy, AR and VR; these technologies will change our world, and in this transformation, America must stand for something bigger than itself, because in doing so we will triumph in the new era of great power competition, the competition for ideals.
>
> Execution of our vision can only be achieved through alignment. We must align a long-term national vision with the ongoing public

Types of Uncertainty	Design Challenges in Government-Venture Arrangements
Incentive Uncertainty When the goals of the partnership are unclear, the incentives to achieve them are likely to be misaligned.	**Aligning Goals, Reconciling Motives** The compatibility of the venture mindset and the mission mindset highlights lack of empathy for the government's "no-fail" public mission and the venture's "growth and strategic orientation" to accept risks to scale innovation.
Outcome Uncertainty When performance measurements are difficult to articulate, the value capture of the partnership is likely to be impaired.	**Hitting an Invisible Target** The government's inability to cultivate ventures based on vision and quantified future public outcomes, and the challenges of creating and observing venture performance metrics lead to uncertainty. Government prioritizes following formalized processes whereas ventures focus on value capture outcomes based on "reward philosophy" and "entrepreneurial management structure."
Process Uncertainty When roles and procedures are ambiguous, the decision-making processes are likely to be imprudent and exclusive.	**Bespoke Needs and Standardized Solutions** Government's traditional desire for custom solutions for bespoke needs with specialized uses is in contrast with the venture's need to build standardized product offerings that can achieve repeatable sales in consumer markets to achieve its "growth orientation" and support its "entrepreneurial culture."
Relational Uncertainty When project risk is poorly evaluated and partners have low familiarity, the costs of coordinating the relationship are likely to increase.	**Risk-Taking and Reward-Sharing in Relationships** The government tends to socialize risk while ventures privatize upside of risk. Discrepancy and lack of familiarity in organizational cultures increases the cost of coordinating the relationship, as the government faces disproportionate downside if new technology fails in contrast with ventures, for whom the "commitment to opportunities" and "growth orientation" drives them to assume risk, to experiment, and to fail quickly in order to rapidly innovate.
Temporal Uncertainty When the timeframes relevant to each partner are misaligned and the objectives are not updated to reflect unplanned contingencies, the costs of the partnership are likely to increase.	**The Valley of Death** Bridging the gap of early stage research to be commercialized and later-stage products to be procured by the government in a timely and predictable manner can be difficult. Venture's stage-based "resource allocation" and "control of resources" present acute challenges when timeframes are misaligned.

TABLE 3.3. Design Challenges in Government-Venture Arrangements. Source: Authors.

sector tech investments necessary to realize the vision. We must align our Allies and partners with ideals that underpin our vision and enlist their support. We must then align the public sector tech investments with our private sector investments to work in a complementary fashion to support our shared national vision. Government cannot do this alone.

We must align our nation's tech investments, R&D through commercialization, with global commercial markets, not just domestic markets, because we need our private sector to flourish on the global stage.[57]

Four

MISSION VENTURING

*How Entrepreneurs Partner with Government
to Create Value and Scale Impact*

"There's never been a better time to build companies that support the national interest and solve critical problems for the country.... *Mission*-driven and civic-minded founders often build companies that transcend verticals and business models in their quest to solve important national problems. These companies view the government as a customer, competitor or key stakeholder—and the success of these companies supports the flourishing of all Americans."

**—AMERICAN DYNAMISM INVESTMENTS,
ANDREESSEN HOROWITZ**[1]

The design constraints of a government-venture agreement surrounding mission venturing highlight the urgent need to revisit the entrepreneurial model and reconstruct it such that these ventures can successfully support the mission of government. In Chapter 2, we reviewed the barriers to action, among other things evoking the important need to personalize entrepreneurship. So, what are the actions that ventures can take to help with this idea of personalizing entrepreneurship in the aim of rebuilding people's and government's trust in venture?

To answer this question, we turn to the concept of public value. University College London economics professor Mariana Mazzucato distinguishes public value from public goods as broader and less limiting, as public value is not created exclusively inside or outside of either the public- or private-sector markets, but rather by both as a whole.[2] Mazzucato recalls how AT&T created Bell Labs out of a demand by the government that the company invest its profits versus hoarding cash. And the company began investing in areas in which it would create the greatest amount of public value. We need to challenge the private sector to begin to engage in a fair share of public value-creating activities. Far too often, the private sector has been focused on creating consumer value, raising both the intrinsic and extrinsic worth of their products and services. But public value means that the private sector must begin to focus on creating societal surplus. In this chapter, we discuss how ventures can work toward creating societal surplus by resolving some of the design challenges of government-venture arrangements.

MISSION MULTIPLIES PROFIT

Understanding and appreciating the mission of government is central to government-venture arrangements. The mission of government can serve as a beacon by which ventures can not only construct their broader sense of purpose and fulfill intrinsic meaning but also guide their economic function. By aligning the goals of the venture with the mission of government, the incentives for an effective partnership are likely to be stronger.

"This understanding is critical," argues Ken Krieg, head of Samford Global Strategies and former U.S. Under Secretary of Defense for Acquisition, Technology, and Logistics. Krieg says, "I think we're at a point where we are truly risking dividing the waters on all of these big problems that we need to solve. Politics has divided us, and we need an integration of thinking and not a separation of thinking. Big tech has not only failed to rise to these challenges, but also has caused a lot of problems, and they alone are not going to be solving them. Also, if you think that government alone is where things will get done, you're sorely mistaken. We need to figure out how to harness industry, how to move interesting things in the right direction to do the things that the government cannot. And that only happens with a mission mindset. The government should not be seen as a hobby. No matter how interesting your product is, it has to match the mission of the government."

Expanding the model of venturing to one in which an entrepreneur collaborates with government to serve the government's mission is a challenging, but not impossible, task. Several examples of successful ventures and financiers have proven that there is a different recipe to building the foundation of a solid partnership. A first key difference these successful ventures have is in their understanding of the "no-fail mission" of government. When ventures fail, customers and investors may be disappointed but the effects stop there; when a government partnership fails, the impacts are often debilitating.

Linda Zecher, operating partner at C5 Capital and former head of Microsoft Global Public Sector, has built a career around the government's mission. Zecher says, "It's critically important that we understand the government, and actually come to accept that sometimes they're far ahead of the commercial sector in terms of research. The most important thing is showing the government that they can be comfortable with you, and this happens by achieving something that's of value to the customer, which really only occurs if you understand the mission sets that they have." So what is this mission? Zecher explains, "One of my most impactful trips was traveling into Iraq with armed services to experience the seriousness of how the government was using products and services. Witnessing firsthand that if technologies fail on the battlefield, it could be the difference between life and death for a soldier, changed me as an executive and made me a stronger advocate with my companies. Any corner cutting could result in public catastrophes."

And this is exactly where national security venture firms such as Lux Capital, Shield Capital, Blue Delta, Capitol Meridian, and Razor's Edge try to help. These dedicated national-security-focused venture firms have emerged to target investing in ventures at the intersection of national security and commercial enterprise. National security venture firm C5 Capital states that it "targets high-growth companies that are transforming the future of critical infrastructure including cybersecurity, space and energy sectors,"[3] while Razor's Edge states their mission: "We work tirelessly to identify disruptive technologies and capabilities that can solve critical mission needs and deliver them to government and commercial customers who need them."[4] The strategic empathy and trusted understanding of the governments mission enable these firms to identify, invest, and scale the next generation of capabilities needed to support the government's mission.

Teresa Carlson, who founded Amazon's Web Services Public Sector business in 2010, credits the importance of developing trusted relationships with government customers and private-sector partners working to serve the government as an important driver to the exponential growth of the AWS Public Sector business during her eleven-year tenure. Having worked with Linda Zecher at Microsoft earlier in her career, Teresa applied the lessons learned to appreciate the uniqueness of the government's mission to shift to a new technology platform. Through building trust, their team at AWS was able to facilitate the transition government agencies to a cloud platform, eventually making AWS a major player in the public-sector cloud market after landing the CIA's $600 million Commercial Cloud Services contract in 2013—which at the time was a tipping point in government cloud adoption for other agencies to subsequently pursue cloud migrations to the AWS platform. In less than ten years, they had created a multibillion-dollar business.

Anand Shah, a partner at The Asia Group, has built a career working with international mission-focused ventures, having founded a strategic innovation firm in India that helped companies align their business with public good. Shah advises, "I would ask these businesses one simple question: How do their business interests align with the interests of the public? You can't succeed only by getting people to buy what you're selling. In the long game, a business needs to show that it is providing public value. Businesses we admire the most succeed when they are contributing to the world. And in no case is this clearer than when you're working with the government." Shah goes on to say, "The government can be very wary of the private sector. The best way to overcome this is to show an ability to understand their mission. Startups that start with mission and approach the government by identifying what the government needs, rather than what the business needs, often build the reputational credit that makes it much easier to actually do work alongside the government."

A second key difference about these ventures is in how they identify the source of profit opportunities. Oftentimes, ventures pick opportunities that serve existing segments of society that are reasonably well served with alternative services. But ventures with a public or common good mission signal to their government partner that the enterprise is committed to issues that are neglected and/or often seen as intractable. Tom Davidson, the founder and CEO of Washington, DC-based EVERFI, knows the value that a social mission can bring to a partnership with government.

After starting EVERFI in 2008, Davidson has led the organization to comprise over five hundred employees and thirty-three-hundred customers that include several major corporations, financial institutions, and colleges and universities nationwide. The venture constructed a business around making learning more scalable and impact more measurable. It offers digital curricula for learners ranging from kindergarten to retirement, on a number of topics, including financial education and workplace financing, diversity and ethics training, and mental health and digital wellness education. The model has been so successful that in January of 2022, EVERFI was acquired by Blackbaud (a software and services provider) for $750 million.[5]

So where did the idea come from? Davidson says, "It was during my tenure in the state legislature that I realized the powerful role the private sector can play in tackling issues affecting the public sector—specifically education. I created EVERFI because I wanted to balance the opportunities for students in low-to-moderate income communities. These students didn't have a fair shot, and it didn't seem like the government really knew how to solve this problem." What's Davidson's key takeaway in constructing a mission that aligns with the government? According to him, "You just have to capitalize businesses that show respect for the problems that actually exist. It's really that simple."

Third, examples have also emerged of companies creating win-win solutions to the government's problems, when the venture and government are both able to capitalize on an opportunity. Will Porteous, general partner and COO of RRE Ventures, sees how the Russian invasion of Ukraine presented an opportunity for ventures and government to build their capability around the government's mission. Founded in 1994, RRE Ventures has grown to become one of the oldest and largest venture capital firms in New York City. With $2.5 billion across ten funds, RRE has invested in over four hundred companies, targeting early stage, technology-enabled companies across all sectors and across the country.[6] While the firm does not have an explicitly government-facing or "public value" focus, RRE is investing in critical sectors such as climate technology and space. Bowery Farming, for example, is a consumer technology company that uses automation technologies to monitor plant growth. By conserving resource usage, this company demonstrates a commitment to public value creation. Since its 2015 founding, the venture was valued at $2.3 billion after attracting large institutional investors.[7]

Porteous says, "The thing that really got my attention was the transformation of the satellite sector. The creation of all these new companies has become intensely relevant in the context of the Ukraine crisis. If you take a step back, the satellite industry has basically existed to serve customers in the telecom industry, oil and gas and insurance customers, and the defense and intelligence community. And the perspective of this last customer base is historically rooted in the Cuban missile crisis, where the government had great overhead reconnaissance, which showed exactly what was on the ground at the event time. Since then, the industry has been building big expensive satellites to take the most perfect picture that it can from space. The legacy commercial reconnaissance companies are focused on delivering the most perfect picture possible. But generally, a pretty good picture in as little time as possible is actually good enough. The people who go to work at these companies often have a strong sense of national mission, and they recognize that their principal customers are typically the defense and intelligence community."

Porteous goes on to say how this historical relationship shaped a role of ventures into the twenty-first-century geopolitical chess match between NATO and Russia. "Because Ukraine sits outside of NATO, when the Ukrainian government went looking for good overhead re-connaissance, they couldn't get it from the U.S. government. They also couldn't get it from many of the major contractors affiliated with the U.S. government." So how did they get their imagery? Porteous points out, "A coalition of commercial space companies stepped in to fill the gap. Both large-scale commercial and emerging startup teams in optical and radar imagery analysis were dealing directly with the Ukrainian government. In some cases, they stood up twenty-four-hour crisis cov-erage desks to allow them to turn requests for imagery to support the Ukrainian government hour by hour. The employees working on these initiatives were incredibly motivated by the importance of the mission, and we know that their work saved lives."

Months into the Russian invasion of Ukraine, Alex Karp, the CEO of Palantir, sent out an email that demonstrates the tight coupling of emerging technologies and government needs: "The power of advanced algorithmic warfare systems is now so great that it equates to having tactical nuclear weapons against an adversary with only conventional ones. The general public tends to underestimate this. Our adversaries no longer do."[8]

BUILD THE EASY BUTTON

Imagine your team being approached by your boss with an ambigu-ous, yet critical assignment: make our customers more satisfied. It's not difficult to see how ambiguity may constrain your ability to formulate an action plan. Your team begins to panic and asks questions such as, How do we measure satisfaction? Who are the customers that we should target? What makes them satisfied? This ambiguity more than likely opens the door to disagreement on what constitutes satisfaction and whose satisfaction actually matters.

The difficulty in being able to articulate outcomes can constrain the ability of partners to work together toward a common goal. The ambi-guity leaves room for interpretation, and the interpretation can breed conflict, which is a hindrance to any collaborative objective. As ventures often find it challenging to quantify important outcomes for government, namely the public or common good, how can they approach the problem of outcome uncertainty in working with the government? By building an "easy button."

Imagine if there was a button that you could push to solve all the problems of government, an easy button. A button that makes it easier for the government to deliver its service to citizens (and for citizens to access and benefit from it). That service could be reducing energy consumption, mitigating climate change, improving access to education for upskilling displaced jobs, or protecting national security against cyberwarfare. The venture's job is to build that easy button which focuses on selling outcomes (not processes).

Trae Stephens recalls the importance of the easy button while working for the government. "We were approached by a company that was offering a product that would save me a whole day of work every week. It would make me 20 percent more productive, and all I had to do was access the software. I pushed and pushed and, finally, there was an email that went out from the tech director that said, 'Someone please tell Trae to get back in the box.'" Frustrated, Trae eventually left the government to work for Palantir Technologies, a public American software company that specializes in big data analytics. But as Trae moved into Palantir, he remembered the importance of this moment. "Being able to bring something like that to the government, something that would make the government's job easier, stuck with me. It became my guiding principle of how to sell products to the government—by having a deep understanding of how the product is being used. It helped clarify the outcomes we were trying to achieve."

Now, Trae is a partner at Founders Fund, a venture capital firm founded in San Francisco in 2005. Founders Fund was organized by PayPal cofounders Peter Thiel, Ken Howery, and Luke Nosek. With over $11 billion in aggregate capital under management in 2022, Founders Fund has a proven record of investing in companies that have made the government's job easier. For example, Founders Fund was the first institutional investor in both SpaceX and Palantir Technologies, which have both grown on their ability to solve key government needs in space and software technologies, respectively. And "building the easy button" for the government remains a key focus of Trae's approach to government-interfacing ventures.

Joshua Wilson, a former U.S. Army officer who served two overseas tours in Iraq and is current senior executive officer of LMI, observes the importance of ventures that are able to build an easy button while working with the government. Wilson says, "The common theme I see with every venture that is able to break through and work with the government is that they are building an easy button—they make government challenges disappear." He adds, "As opposed to some private-sector companies, which can get away with delivering value around some niche aspect of a larger problem where the government is still left to figure out how to solve that larger problem, or they offer some incremental cost savings...that typically just isn't enough to get them to jump through the hoops of bringing you into the federal ecosystem. Focus on problems that matter. And the easy button here is really unique to this market. The bottom line is not typically the biggest priority. It's time to impact. You have to look at what the government needs, see what capabilities you are bringing to the table and how you can best meet those needs. And when everyone has the same mission in mind, the easy button approach really becomes a unifying concept to rally behind. Solving the government's problems is really the biggest driver of who makes it and who doesn't."

Ken Krieg brings a different perspective on how to build the easy button, by knowing the problem *and* the people using it. He says, "The government doesn't always do the best job of explaining what their problems are, and this can make it difficult to spot how to create solutions. But knowing the people who need the solutions helps. Building those relationships can expose you to more information about their problems." Krieg's advice? "Know the people, follow the money that is flowing into the agency, and solve 100 percent of a specific problem versus 80 percent of a larger problem."

EVERFI shortened the time for showing the government and corporate sponsors the value of the platform. Their research-backed education curriculum has served a clear purpose for the government's broader mission of public education. By quickly integrating into existing data systems, it is easy to see how EVERFI has built the easy button, allowing them to scale, activate, and create real-world solutions for twenty-first-century learners. It has collected an impressive repository of student learning data to prove our thesis of impact—that reaching students at a young age can drive ecosystems of change. It has aggregated data from the millions of learners who have taken their educational courses, and will now be sharing this data to inspire a fresh look at how education on critical skills can benefit students in the long run.[9]

Flock Safety took an interesting path toward constructing an easy button for the government. Founded in 2017, this Atlanta-based technology surveillance company began by selling automated license plate recognition technology to neighborhood associations.[10] These associations, who were trying to maintain the safety of their neighborhoods, found utility in the ability of Flock's cameras to track vehicles coming in and out of neighborhoods. Whether for vandalism or theft, Flock's technology can quickly and objectively identify a suspect's vehicle— and if a crime does occur, Flock can alert law enforcement. Eventually, the Flock product had utility in other residential and commercial settings, including both schools and businesses. However, they identified the ability of their product to solve a major issue for law enforcement: crime deterrence and response time. Andreessen Horowitz notes that "the majority of crimes in the U.S. go unresolved" and "only 46% of violent crimes are fully resolved and that number is staggeringly low (17%) for property crime."[11] Using the objectivity of their system, Flock could detect and deliver valuable crime leads to local law enforcement officials. For example, after only two months with the Flock system, the police department in Wichita, Kansas, recovered fifty-six stolen license plates and returned $1.1 million in stolen property. Flock's latest product serves to aid in local law enforcement's mission even more: a gunshot audio detector. One of the earliest customers in Flock technologies in Atlanta put it best: "Flock is the single most effective tool we have ever used." Quite simply, Flock Safety was able to build the government's easy button by reimagining their product's usage in the public sector.[12]

Each of these ventures was able to break through and work with the government because it was focused upon a very specific problem and delivered a comprehensive solution that helps make that problem go away, or less painful. These companies aren't part of the solution, they are the "easy button." They also hold a total understanding of that agency's mission, current technical ecosystem, and customers.

CUSTOMIZE FOR THE UNKNOWN

Governments want customized solutions. While commercial or "off the shelf" solutions may be more affordable for solving simple government problems, only a few of its problems can actually be classified as a simple problem. The complexity of problems government deals with coupled with the red tape of the regulatory environment means that custom solutions are more effective for government agencies. Also, governments face unforeseen and rapidly changing circumstances. Customized and adaptable products help public agencies adjust to these changes with agility.[13]

This poses a major problem for ventures that are seeking to grow via standardization, as customization makes the enterprises forfeit the opportunity to scale economies. Commercial products are designed to offer the greatest functionality to the largest number of users for the least amount of money. As a result, the generic nature of these products requires users to compromise their requirements, add on to the products, or adapt their processes to fit the product. But how can ventures achieve scale through standardization while fulfilling the customization for government? Having a grasp of the "ecosystem" of government-related products and services will help ventures understand how their products can retain some degree of standardization while offering certain customized features.

National Resilience, a new biotechnology company created in San Diego in the wake of the 2020 COVID-19 pandemic, has tapped into this magic recipe for success. "COVID-19 has exposed critical vulnerabilities in medical supply chains, and today's manufacturing can't keep up with scientific innovation, medical discovery, and the need to rapidly produce and distribute critically important drugs at scale," said Robert Nelsen, cofounder and chairman of National Resilience's board.[14] "We are committed to tackling these huge problems with a whole new business model," he added. National Resilience launched in November 2020 with over $800 million in funding from venture capital firms, including National Enterprise Associates and ARCH Venture Partners, a clear indication that investors not only see the utility of their business model but are also interested in the company's mission. National Resilience's stated purpose is to create the processes and platforms that will allow for scientists to make novel therapeutics quickly, safely, and at scale. Since the company's 2020 founding, it has raised more than $2 billion in venture capital funding and millions more from government and industry contracts.[15]

National Resilience has a number of different product offerings, including Biologics, which enables antibody discovery companies, early stage biopharma companies, and other biologics research teams to rapidly reach first-in-human studies; cell and gene therapy, which aims to solve critical industry challenges—including productivity, scalability, and robustness, along with a simplified supply chain—all to increase the velocity and quality of manufactured products; and vaccines, which uses a modular approach to next-generation vaccine manufacturing to integrate novel biological, analytical, or process-related technologies and pull the industry forward.[16] Ultimately, National Resilience aimed to address many of the challenges plaguing the biomanufacturing industry, including the challenge of creating custom and scalable solutions, increasing the ability to handle surge capacity, and delivering high-quality and cost-efficient products. National Resilience not only has tapped into government's interest in public good but also has been one of the most successful ventures in garnering both investors' and government's attention. The company has been highly effective in creating a commercial as well as a government presence, all by constructing a business model that allows for both standardization and customization.

Rahul Singhvi, cofounder and CEO of the company, traces the business idea to the problems that the company is trying to solve. "To do this work, you need to be humble enough to say, we don't know what the next pandemic is going to be. We need to be able to have products which are customizable to fit the next outbreak. So, how do you create a custom solution for an unknown enemy? You have to reform the way you think about how to put together vaccine development processes, as compared to how the FDA currently approves drugs. And this goes to the core of a very simple idea of our business model: you need to have components."

Singhvi shares, "Our company is built around the idea that we can standardize components and customize solutions. Normally, in our industry, every single time you want to make a solution for a new drug, you start from scratch. It's like a cottage industry. We see this as lengthy and inefficient. We are building standard components that can be stitched together to create solutions. We don't have to reinvent the wheel every time a pandemic breaks out or we need to quickly respond to a biological disaster. Think of our company this way. If you wanted to build five different things with ten Lego blocks, you just rearrange the blocks, the bricks don't change."

Singhvi sees this modular business model as the optimal solution for dealing with the custom needs of the government, and a key factor behind the company's competitiveness in the commercial space. He points out, "You need to build a company that is sustainable. You cannot have a company that is one hundred percent dependent on government work. You have to be able to exercise your troops in between the government needs. A venture needs to be able to sustain itself based on market forces. Modularity helps sustainability."

How did National Resilience form their connection with the government? Not by looking for a handout. Singhvi says, "We started to socialize with the government to let them know that, 'Hey, we are here.' We didn't ask them for anything. We didn't go to them with any specific ask. We basically just approached them to tell them about our mission, about our story. This gave us credibility and more importantly, trust with the government. I have seen companies which only approached the government when they needed government money, and it is obvious. The government can sniff that out and it does not form the foundation for a good relationship."

More important, meeting with the government ahead of when it

needs anything gives the venture time to build trust with the government. As government clients are able to watch and monitor the progress
of the venture, the venture gains credibility and trust when it successfully meets its stated goals. This trust and credibility in many cases re-
places the past performance qualifications that larger incumbents use
to compete for government contracts. "We didn't need the government
money. We had a plan to support the government in the event of a pandemic, and that was part of our mission. So, we just let them know,
'Look, we are building this venture purely through private financing.
If you need something, we are here for you. We are here to help your
mission. Call us when you need us," shares Singhvi.

Sometimes customizing for the unknown is not the outcome itself,
but rather the uncertainty with the processes by which the government
attains its mission outcomes. Sonu Singh, the founder and CEO of
1901 Group, a leading provider of innovative cloud, cybersecurity, and
enterprise-scale managed services, has constructed a business model
around the limitations of government's hiring practices. Founded in
2009 by Virginia Tech engineering graduates, this Virginia-based company offers IT products for both commercial markets and the public
sector, having served organizations like the United States Department
of Agriculture, United States Department of Commerce, and United
States Small Business Administration. Since 2009, the 1901 Group has
been recognized as one of Virginia's fifty fastest-growing businesses.[17]
Having created over three hundred tech jobs in southwest Virginia prior
to being acquired by Leidos, Singh's venture is estimated to eventually
lead to around three thousand new jobs in Virginia alone.[18]

The recipe for 1901's success, Singh says, lies somewhat in realizing
the inefficiency in how the government was looking for talent. "When
recruiting, the government is so focused on hiring people with specific
education credentials that they really limit their potential pool of applicants. We decided that we can hire anybody and train them. We didn't
have to just hire people based on specific labor categories. We were going
to open the aperture. We hired people from community colleges and
trade schools and emphasized workforce development. The students that
wanted to be in state-of-the-art technology and manufacturing didn't

have to leave for Silicon Valley." So, how did they approach workforce development? Singh explains, "We focused on technical and business certifications for our workforce. We wanted to help people build their careers by investing in them. We pay for every certification, so we were just constantly spending money on building the workforce." In doing so, 1901 shifted the typical government service model from providing professional service teams on the basis of a collection of labor categories to teams focused on providing managed services that are based on business outcomes. By eliminating labor categories, this managed service model opened the labor pool 1901 hired from and shifted government measurement of success from outputs of labor hours to outcomes in terms of business and technical performance.

Having grown up in Blacksburg, Virginia, Singh identified the value of untapped talent in rural areas of the country. "I looked at Blacksburg and thought, there's a unique opportunity for talent here. There's a very advantageous cost of living, a great quality of life, and there's talent because of the universities and local manufacturing facilities. Virginia Tech has a great engineering program, Radford is an up-and-coming regional school with a fantastic computer science department, and the community colleges are very strong. This enabled us to employ many people who were the first to go to college in their families." In addition, Singh points out that the government's hiring practices, at times, appear incompatible with a mission of workforce development. Singh says, "In many areas, the government misses out on a significant pool of talent because of qualifications requirements based on labor categories. As opposed to distilling the qualifications of individuals into a simple labor category, the government should emphasize more upon the quality of the service they, as part of a larger team, can deliver. The government should focus on investments in upskilling employees and shaping contracts based on service-delivery service-level agreements rather than labor category certifications. These seemingly small changes to requests for proposals around labor categories for government contract work would dramatically change the available labor pool for tech talent and allow the government to meet its technical and security requirements while stimulating specific segments of the workforce." And this is something that we see playing out in the public and private sectors as the labor pool becomes increasingly tight. In Maryland, for example, Governor Larry Hogan announced the launch of a workforce development initiative to formally eliminate the four-year college degree requirement from thousands of state jobs, working instead to recruit job seekers who are "Skilled Through Alternative Routes (STARs)."[19] In the private sector, Google, Delta Airlines, IBM, and other companies have announced they are reducing the college degree requirements for some positions amidst the tight and competitive labor market.[20]

To expand upon the importance of this workforce transformation, geography is emerging as an important theme around mission-driven ventures. "I haven't been to New York or the Valley in months," says a general partner at a leading venture capital firm. "And it's not that we are avoiding these places, we are just seeing more and more of these public-impact ventures popping up all over the country. And it's largely tied to the localization of different problems, which require a more specialized focus of showing respect for the problem."

One such example of a company, the partner says, is Remora.[21] This 2020 Detroit-based startup kept with the "motor city" roots of Detroit and invented a device that captures carbon emissions from semi-trucks, which are hard to electrify and account for 5 percent of all U.S. carbon emissions. Remora's technology is designed to bolt onto nearly any tractor-trailer combination to capture around 80 percent of emissions from the truck's tailpipe, which is more energy efficient than removing carbon from the atmosphere. From there, the carbon is stored in an on-board vehicle and then offloaded for concrete producers or other end users. The company estimates only three-and-a-half years to pay back the system from the carbon revenue, which has impressed many and helped them gain the support of investors and partners such as Ryder and ArcBest. The "clustering" of automotive manufacturers in Detroit and Remora's choice of founding location shows how the localization of certain skill and problem sets is leading to geographic diversity in ventures with mission.

LEARN THE LANGUAGE OF GOVERNMENT

Public and private firms speak different languages. Not literally, of course, but the terminology employed by the public and private sectors differs. Language in this sense is highly tied to organizational culture, as most businesses use terminology that relates to the stated purpose of the organization. As the purpose and function of the organization takes new forms, the language is updated. Terms and concepts take on new meaning.

But language takes on a broader meaning in the context of partnerships. A common question asked before entering any partnership is, "Are we speaking the same language?" Cultural conflicts, divergent meanings, and opposing ontologies compound the complexities of working together. When organizations have similar cultures and a shared understanding of terms and their meanings, an architecture that provides support to each other in pursuit of common goals can be more easily created. The understanding of language reduces the complexity of working together. Ken Krieg equates this compatibility in language with entrepreneurial integrity. He says, "Of all the things that are taught in business school, the most important, in my opinion, to working with the government is having integrity. No matter how you value your attributes, you should never value your integrity as less than something else. Protect your integrity and do good things. That will help you when you're trying to carry out the mission of the government."

Jack Kerrigan, cofounder and general partner at Razor's Edge Ventures, sees value in having a focus on the government's mission and not on making money. He emphasizes, "A mission orientation is key to a venture's ability to work with the government. If you focus on the right mission and the right people, you realize that it's not just about the money. The money comes when you show value in the mission. And if you focus only on money, you aren't making mission-driven decisions." When evaluating the mission of new ventures, Kerrigan goes on to say, "An entrepreneur's mission-focus is a critical predictor of their success in working with the government. The great part about this business is that stakes are super high. You're supporting really important national security missions. If we hear an entrepreneur pitching their idea to us, and we hear their pride in the mission and see their enthusiasm for it in their body language, it tells us that they are confident in trying to save the world every day. And it tells us that they will be successful in understanding what the government is trying to do."

Having a common "language" around mission serves to build trust—a key component to any professional or personal relationship. Trust can be defined as "a psychological state comprising the intention to accept vulnerability based upon the positive expectations of the intentions or behavior of another"[22] and therefore "alleviates the fear that one's exchange partner will act opportunistically."[23] When businesses understand their partner, it aids in smoothing out their interactions and serves as the foundation of trust.

Consider the 1975 Apollo-Soyuz Test Project, a collaboration between NASA and the Soviet Space Agency with the objective of docking spacecraft in orbit. At surface level, one would expect the collaboration to be filled with mistrust, stemming from the deep political divide and mutual hostility between Americans and Soviets. And, in the initial stages of the collaboration, it was. Only by learning the language of their counterparts, both literally and interpersonally, could they lay the foundation for an effective partnership.[24] Remarking on working with the Russians, NASA astronaut Jeffrey Williams said, "We are working together as well as we have at any time in the program, and that has been dependent on the relationships built. We know each other personally. We can trust each other personally, and we know the constraints that each of us has, and we try to work together to manage those constraints. I think that will be the legacy of the program."[25]

So how can ventures learn the language of government to build this trust? First, this relationship requires an understanding that the Valley and government speak different languages. To make this relationship work, ventures don't have to change their language, they need to recognize the government's language. They need to understand why the government works the way that it does—it could be better—but it works that way for good reasons. This understanding of government is exactly what In-Q-Tel has so successfully achieved to build a bridge of trust with the government. Understanding the government's mission, In-Q-Tel invests in visionary, commercially focused companies and identifies the opportunity to build a long-term partnership between those companies and government partners. By being "a careful, selective, strategic investor," In-Q-Tel invests in companies and technologies that have real utility and potential to deliver national interests. The strategic capital investor for the U.S. government has a clear understanding of the government's mission, while emphasizing its ability to drive product commercialization:

> In-Q-Tel identifies and adapts "ready-soon" technologies and products near the final stages of commercialization [that] do not require long-term development from the ground up. This means we find and deliver to our U.S. government partners critical, innovative technology quickly and cost-effectively to strengthen national security through new technologies.[26]

Second, this relationship requires that ventures build mission-focused teams. Typically, ventures don't really consider "mission." They might consider it among a broader set of applicant attributes in their hiring process, but rarely is it central to whether a person gets hired. Building a mission-oriented team is critical to learning the language of government.

Rebellion Defense is a mission-focused developer of artificial intelligence products for the United States, the United Kingdom, and their allies' national security and defense needs. It was founded in July 2019 by Chris Lynch, Nicole Camarillo, and Oliver Lewis, all of whom had extensive experience in working for the government.[27] With headquarters in Washington, DC, and employing 175 employees across two countries, the company currently sells three types of products: comprehensive battlespace awareness, autonomous mission execution, and cyber readiness. Each software is adaptable and interoperable, providing each contracted customer with the ability to use the system for their particular needs. The company's early success led it to "unicorn status" with investors Insight Partners, Venrock, Innovation Endeavors, Declaration Partners, and Lupa Systems. Rebellion Defense has received millions in awards from the Department of Defense for the technology's cross-domain solutions.[28] Their software is mostly being used in the Air Force and to detect cyber vulnerability risk during missions.

Nicole Camarillo, one of the cofounders of Rebellion Defense, is a licensed attorney and accomplished strategist who has led several cultural and management reforms across the private, public, and nonprofit sectors. When discussing how the company approaches hiring around mission, Camarillo recalls the initial discussions the founders had. "We had these meetings on hiring and our main question was, 'How do you get people who are very successful in the private sector to take time to come and work for government?' We decided to look for people who felt the same sense of mission and purpose that we felt. At the end of the day, we're working on projects that would ultimately save lives. We were working on things that matter to the nation. We looked for people who wanted to make a difference and serve a bigger purpose." Camarillo describes the "stickiness" of mission and purpose as the company grew its workforce. "I've watched a lot of colleagues try to go back to the private sector and then spin right back out to us, to Rebellion Defense. It's because we just built this really fantastic team of super-talented people with a sense of mission. People realize that there is an opportunity to make impact here."

"But we don't only hire from the private sector. We invest in people who have an interest and expertise in the government's mission because they worked for the government. To have a shot at working successfully with the government, you cannot go into it with the same approaches that you have used in the commercial sector, they simply will not work. To have the expertise in this space, you have to play by the rules, and you have to have credibility. You need to have an understanding and empathy for the government, and that's very specific knowledge. We built an advantage here because we hired people from inside the government at senior levels. They have a deeper understanding of the ins and outs of government. The frustrations and the complexities. Not only were we better able to identify the government's problems, but when we hit obstacles in working together, we were able to quickly overcome them. That's only because we have the right people on our team. People who understand and embody the government's mission."

We can also consider how individuals are serving as bridges to translate the language of government to the private sector and students. Nick Sinai, the former Deputy Chief Technology Officer of the United States, senior advisor at Insight Partners, and lecturer in public policy at the Harvard Kennedy School has done exactly that. While in government, Sinai led President Obama's Open Data Initiatives, coauthored President Obama's 2013 executive order making open and machine-readable the default for new government information, led the relaunch of Data. gov, and co-led the Open Government Initiative to ensure the federal government is more transparent, participatory, and collaborative. Sinai also helped start and grow the Presidential Innovation Fellows program, a twelve-month program, during which a fellow works on innovation projects across federal agencies. Using his experience in government, Sinai authored *Hack Your Bureaucracy*, a book about making a lasting impact in public and private organizations, identifying the strategies that can be used to succeed in transforming any bureaucracy—public or private. Sinai also has used his experience in government at Insight Partners, where he is helping bridge interest in government needs with venture technology companies. In addition, in the Harvard Kennedy School, Sinai is teaching students about the peculiarities of technology and innovation in government. From Sinai's career experience, he has been able to create valuable bridges from the public sector to the private sector and academia.

BUILD FOR THE LONG HAUL

It is easy to get lost in the weeds of time when working with the government. The slow bureaucratic processes mean that the sales cycles are twelve to eighteen months at their fastest, as the government follows strict procurement processes. Firm employees, too, may need to receive security clearances to comply with government regulations. But it isn't only the stagnancy of government processes that makes it difficult for ventures to match the pace of government. Civil servants frequently rotate in and out of positions, which constrains the ability for ventures to maintain a singular and centralized communication channel. In addition, poor visibility of approval processes makes ventures feel as though they are in the dark of government timelines.

Clearly, ventures need to prepare for the uncertainty of working with the government's timelines. The first thing they can do to prepare for this uncertainty is build up cash reserves. Rahul Singhvi of National Resilience recognized the importance of this. "You need to have a lot of money. This is a capital-intensive business. That was the understanding of how we went from raising $50 million in one month to $750 million in the next three months. We were able to mobilize capital around purpose. Investors acknowledged our mission and this extra capital buffered us from any uncertainties."

The challenges of working with government timelines can also swing in the opposite direction. Government's function to protect the public can sometimes require a swift and urgent response. The COVID-19 pandemic showed how government needs can rush the timelines of government-venture arrangements. Here, the long and drawn-out procurement process flips and requires ventures to hasten production. So, how can ventures meet the temporal uncertainty of rapid needs? By building surge capacity. Singhvi says, "Surge capacity is something that all ventures have to look at, but hardly address. The black swan events can require a lot of capacity in a short period of time. So how do you do that in a sustainable business? We have built a network of facilities that we use as a portfolio. At any given time, we can scale up and adapt our network to meet the unforeseen needs of government, particularly in vaccine manufacturing."

Singhvi goes on to say, "The same skill set we develop in our commercial operations is what we can use to address surge from government needs. Then we have an army of employees who are always exercised, but not exercised on handouts from the government but exercised on the basis of doing work that is needed to make a profit. So now you've created a sustainable business that can immediately be pivoted into surge capacity for the nation. And because you have a network, you can accommodate your customers somehow without disappointing them, while also serving the government."

But what if you have no familiarity with the government's timelines, as most entrepreneurs hoping to move in this space will face? Create partnerships with VC firms, says Joshua Wilson of LMI, a consultancy dedicated to powering a future-ready, high-performing government by drawing from expertise in digital and analytic solutions, logistics, and management advisory services. LMI reduced temporal uncertainties for ventures by helping ventures to construct relationships. Wilson shares, "It became pretty clear to me that the key driver of success here was all about time to value. And if you want to reduce your time to value you have to be tied to the venture capital community." Developing these relationships enabled LMI to establish an ecosystem that helps private sectors overcome the temporal challenges of working with government.

"We started building a lot of partnerships with academia and start-ups. When customers would come to our building with a problem, I would have entrepreneurs and academics in the room, because it was about our ecosystem delivering value, not necessarily LMI always having to deliver all the value. We could guide the venture through the timeline and tap into different funding sources where needed. And that's been tremendous. It's been fun to see these companies grow and see how the ecosystem could provide value here. Building relationships is a critical step in the process. It's beyond the connections, it's about learning these unfamiliar processes and procedures. The cycles of working with the government can be long and cumbersome, and the best ventures are those that can keep the excitement, that can keep the momentum going, throughout even the most difficult of times," emphasizes Wilson.

NEW MINDSET, NEW BUSINESS MODELS, NEW TEAMS

The private sector needs to pursue public value creation. For too long the burden of public value has fallen heavily upon the government and other public actors, while the private sector reaps substantive rewards. But public and private value creation are not decoupled. Venture Meets Mission capitalizes on this harmony of purpose and profit. The expert accounts and exemplar enterprises provided in this chapter detail the

TYPES OF UNCERTAINTY	ACTIONABLE STRATEGIES FOR VENTURES

Incentive
Aligning goals, reconciling motives

Mission Multiplies Profit
- *The government is not a hobby, match the mission*
- *Show that you're adding public value*

Outcome
Hitting an invisible target

Build the Easy Button
- *Deep understanding of the problems, provides clarity of product outcomes*
- *Solve 100% of a specific problem versus 80% of a larger problem*

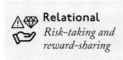

Process
Bespoke needs, standardized solutions

Customize for the Unknown
- *Standardize the components and customize solutions*
- *Develop new business models and processes that tap geographic and labor diversity*

Relational
Risk-taking and reward-sharing

Learn the Language of Government
- *Common language around mission builds trust*
- *Build intersectional teams of diverse experience and shared mission*

Temporal
The valley of death

Build for the Long Haul
- *Resource for the unexpected*
- *Focus on time to value for government*

FIGURE 4.1. Venture Actions to Overcome the Uncertainties of Government-Venture Arrangements. Source: Authors.

way that ventures can begin to create societal surplus, by rebuilding trust and overcoming the challenges of working with the government. From the uncertainties identified in Chapter 3, we distill the essence of the actionable solutions in Figure 4.1.

Our goal is not to provide a comprehensive list of solutions that these ventures adopt. Instead, we wanted to bring a flavor of the creative actions and approaches by which these ventures manage the uncertainties that characterize public-private collaborations, more broadly, and government-venture arrangements, specifically. Perhaps Trae Stephens of Anduril sums it up best: "It's not entrepreneurship as usual. It's an entirely different mindset. We need new business models and a different kind of team to make this work. It is challenging to partner with the government, but all partnerships are unique. What's important here is that we both know why we are in this venture. Mission. What we do saves lives. We are in it together."

Five

A "VENTURE MEETS MISSION" ECOSYSTEM

How Government Can Catalyze Innovation

The government is an engine of innovation, having funded much of the R&D for our modern technological marvels. In the previous chapter, we detailed actions that ventures could take to help rebuild trust and create public value by resolving some of the design challenges of government-venture arrangements. With the government increasingly relying on the private sector for technological innovations, trust indeed is a critical first step toward constructing a "Venture Meets Mission" ecosystem. And perhaps even more important is rebuilding trust in our governing institutions and bringing back an optimism in the government as a force for positive change. To begin that journey, the government can take bridging actions that further build upon its shared values with ventures. This chapter presents these important initiatives in light of the various roles of government.

ENABLING TRUST

Trust is the key enabler for an ecosystem to flourish. The Organization for Economic Cooperation and Development (OECD) tracks trust-in-government data across countries. Switzerland and Norway are among the most trusted governments, measured in 2021 at 84 percent and 77 percent of their populations, respectively, with Germany and Canada at 61 percent and compared to the United States and United Kingdom at 40 percent.[1] Trust is fundamental to the development of ventures in any market economy. Francis Fukuyama makes this clear by stating that "no entrepreneur will risk money in a business if he or she thinks that it will be expropriated the following year by a government, business competitors, or a criminal organization."[2] So where can the government look to rebuild trust and become an enabler of impact for mission-driven ventures?

The first step for rebuilding trust is by redefining interests. This is linked to what is often popularized among business scholars as the principal-agent problem. This occurs when a person (agent) is able to make decisions and or take actions on behalf of another (principal). Moral hazard arises in circumstances when agents are motivated to act in their own best interests, which are contrary to those of their principals. The fear of conflict of interest can be overcome only if the principal is able to trust that the agent is acting with their best interests in mind.

While the principal-agent problem is heavily applied in business context to explain how to safeguard against the perils of self-interested behavior of executives, it has applicability in any situations when a person is acting on behalf of another. The principal-agent problem can be seen when the ambitions and goals of public authorities and politicians diverge from each other, or from the public at large. For example, public administrators may want to implement a national social welfare policy program but political figures may have other personal interests such as local infrastructure development to appeal to their constituencies. An upcoming election can prevent a political figure from pursuing legislation that has negative short-term consequences but significant positive long-term impact. Business and the public rely on the government for making policy decisions on behalf of their interests. The principal-agent problem in government results in lack of implementation of public policies, an overall waste of public resources, and the foregoing of public value creation.

Governments can become enablers of impact by rebuilding trust that they're creating public value, and this comes by highlighting good public service behaviors. Max Stier, the founding president and CEO of the Partnership for Public Service, talks about the importance of recognition in incentivizing public servants. He says, "Everyone is counting on the government to address critical problems ranging from foreign threats to poverty. If we want best performance from our government, we need to do much more to recognize and reward the tremendous outcomes we are receiving but are usually hidden from view. Stier goes on to say, "We also need to hold accountable our government leaders, both political and career, for being stewards of the public good." In addition, we can look internationally for examples of how governments are showing their willingness to support the public good. In Taiwan and South Korea, for example, government agencies signal their commitment to the public's interest by continuously gathering data and information from the private sector and using it to update their own goals and policies over time.[3] Redefining interests as less self-centered and more collective-focused can enable the government to signal its commitment to creating public value.

We also see the growing importance of "people" being recognized in the public sector. Look at the need for workforce development for cybersecurity, for example. There is an estimated shortage of around forty thousand cybersecurity professionals in the public sector.[4] Accordingly, to ensure that their recruitment efforts reflect their operational priorities and to coordinate with the private sector, the Cybersecurity and Infrastructure Security Agency (CISA) decided to hire a "Chief People Officer" in 2022. Jen Easterly, the director of CISA, also noted the importance of bringing more women into the cybersecurity industry. Currently, only 24 percent of the cybersecurity workforce is women.[5] Easterly notes the importance of having a diverse, collaborative, and empowered workforce, as "nothing's more important than having a good foundational culture to build an excellent team," because "this is the future of cybersecurity." National Cyber Director Chris Inglis echoes the importance of hiring good people in government, saying that "culture eats organization for breakfast, so we need to make sure we establish a positive, compelling culture that, essentially, outlasts us."[6]

The second step for rebuilding trust in government is by redefining and reiterating the mission of government. By finding and cultivating this mission, we can reduce the action-intention barriers for public officials. Let's be clear: mission is different from ambition. Ambition starts with what you want, while a mission starts with what others need. We tend to associate ambition with money and status, and a mission with the intrinsic worth of tasks. Developing a mission shows a dedication to the larger needs of others, while developing an ambition shows a pursuit of the narrower needs of self. Having mission, and not just ambition, means that the public sector is acting upon values that care for the interests and needs of others. Having a mission and being guided by these values in turn helps overcome the psychological inertia that reinforces the status quo, the same inertia we discussed in Chapter 2.

Leslie Smith, a retired army lieutenant general who served as the Inspector General of the Army from 2018 to 2021, believes that mission can guide meaningful action. Regarding one of the missions of the army, Smith says, "as a vice president at the Association of the United States Army, we really have the mission to educate, inform, and connect people. We educate people inside and outside the army on the mission we pursue. We inform our stakeholders about the problems that we are facing. And we connect people inside and outside the service to help solve the big problems."

Smith goes on to talk about how the mission of the army is a key feature of the service members and influences impactful work in their careers after service. He says, "As leaders, we have the responsibility to train our young people to thrive in a world after their service. To continue to pursue their sense of mission from different perspectives, either in the public or private sector. For the young people that serve, who develop and fulfill that sense of purpose during their enlistment, we try to give them the skills to be successful in all careers. And this is mostly in training them to be a fair leader, in whatever they are doing." And how does this training relate back to the "triangle of trust" between government, venture, and civil society? "Good leaders—fair leaders—they build trust in the organization. In the army, trust is the bedrock of our profession. The American people want to have faith that the army will serve the nation in the right way—ethically, effectively, and efficiently. If we can build leaders in other spaces, including entrepreneurs, who display the same sense of mission and values of fairness, we know we can trust them. Those are the people that we want to be working with. Those that demonstrate that level of trust."

Another measure for rebuilding trust in the government is by redefining the governing processes and making them more transparent. Transparency is frequently evoked when discussing building trust, and has often been hailed as an important first step. In the words of Jack Welch, former CEO of GE, "Trust happens when leaders are transparent."[7] Transparency can be thought of as being open and honest, and expressing opinions with genuineness and directness.

Transparency is key to producing trust in a government. A functioning democracy and market economy require governments to be open and transparent. Transparency is the government's willingness and obligation to share information with its citizens and hold officials accountable for their public conduct. Hailed as a key component of building institutional trust, transparency and open government were the subjects of President Obama's first memorandum for the heads of state.[8] Agencies such as the Government Accountability Office or programs like the Federal Information Technology Acquisition Reform Act scorecard have demonstrated that the government can self-regulate conduct and maintain accountability to itself. Also, there are open government strategies and initiatives, such as those related to Data.Gov. In May 2013, President Obama signed an executive order that made open data the new default for government information. The principle is that transparency of government data enables scaling up of efforts across the health, energy, climate, education, finance, public safety, and global development sectors.[9] As of December 2022, Data.gov contains two-hundred-and-fifty-thousand datasets for researchers, entrepreneurs, and citizens to access, ranging from topics like federal student loan program data; monthly housing prices indexes; and manufacturing, inventories, and sales.[10]

Another example of transparency is detailed by the OECD aim to promote transparency, participation, and stakeholder collaboration.[11] Spain's open government initiative identified two key areas for public value creation, which led the nation to adopt several policies to improve transparency. In 2013, Spain passed a law that contained a series of obligations regarding the publication of public information, allowing citizens to see how administrators make decisions that affect them, including how public funds are distributed and what performance criteria are used to judge public authorities. In 2015, Spain introduced legislation that regulates the reuse of public information, including the process and publication of this information and its structuring, formatting, and security. This legislation further opened the door to an array of applications, including how doctors treat patients, how farmers manage farms, and how citizens access free internet.[12] Spanish trust in government has since improved from a low of 18 percent in 2013 to 37 percent in 2021.[13]

Multinational initiatives have also spawned around opening up government data to the public. The Open Government Partnership (OGP), launched by governments and civil society leaders in 2011, seeks to make government more accessible, more responsive, and more accountable to citizens.[14] Currently, seventy-eight countries and 106 local governments (which represent more than two billion people) are partners in the OGP and have co-created more than forty-five hundred commitments across three hundred action plans. The OGP decisively embraced the principles of classical liberalism of protecting individual rights and freedoms that underpin democracy, ensuring commitments from the United States and its allies, including Germany, Israel, Korea, and Sweden. Currently, the partnership is pursuing policy area issues related to justice, gender and inclusion, digital governance, public service delivery, right to information, protection of civic space and natural resources, and corruption.

The final step for rebuilding trust is by creating intersectional sandboxes for the different players to collaborate with the government. In Chapters 1 and 2, we discussed the economic, social, and political polarization as well as the divergent and incompatible perceptions about who and what entrepreneurs and government are. While these may seem like disparate observations, their underlying causes are quite similar—a lack of interaction among different groups. The benefits from creating this intersectional sandbox extend beyond facilitating collaboration. These interactions will also actively undermine the biases and preconceived incompatibilities between the government and ventures. Social psychologists have labeled this broader phenomenon as "intergroup contact hypothesis" and argue that positive interactions across social groups facilitate learning, reduce fear and anxiety, and increase people's ability to empathize.[15] The government's ability to rebuild trust will rely on its capacity to foster positive interactions among the key players of the ecosystem. An intellectual sandbox enabled by the government, one in which people, ventures, and public officials can come together to have these interactions, will aid in the destruction of siloed groups and preconceived incompatibilities. Engaging with people and ventures will better expose the mission of government and its role as an enabler of innovation. By becoming exposed to the different perspectives and strengths of players in the ecosystem, government too will be in a better position to tap into the capacities of these players.

Governments can indeed enable a Venture Meets Mission ecosystem. To do so, the government needs to reiterate and redefine collective interest around mission, public officials need to pursue mission along with ambition, and the government needs to improve transparency and openness and foster positive interactions to break down any preconceived biases and incompatibilities.

ORCHESTRATING MISSION

While governments globally have had varied levels of success in creating a "startup friendly" environment that enables entrepreneurs to even pursue opportunities within critical government industries, the model needs updating. Governments need to become orchestrators of mission by promoting an ecosystem perspective—a deeper understanding of the interdependence of opportunities between society's institutions: political, business, and academic. Governments can develop trust and create an environment for partners to flourish by assuming an ecosystem perspective that will help map these intersecting skill and opportunity sets, and chart a viable course of action.

In their book *Ecosystem Edge*, Professors Arnoud De Meyer and Peter Williamson rightly claim that the nature of innovation is changing from product and process innovations to more integrated solutions.[16] To deliver these solutions, companies need to access partner capabilities and draw on know-how and talent from a wide variety of related industries. Drawing from examples of large corporations that anchor and build ecosystems around them, such as Apple's network of app developers and Microsoft's legions of hardware manufacturers and software developers, De Meyer and Williamson find that creating and engaging with these ecosystems creates unique advantages, for example, network economies for scaling and innovation agility to ride out disruptive innovation. Governments can and do play similar ecosystem coordination roles by being the North Star that gives directional purpose around mission. De Meyer and Williamson suggest that developing and sharing an initial roadmap for the ecosystem and communicating the value of joining are essential strategies for ecosystem formation. Governments can become enablers of the Venture Meets Mission ecosystem by communicating that the ecosystem is a means of coordinating collective effort toward a shared goal.

In-Q-Tel has identified and constructed an ecosystem-based business model around the government's mission: connecting cutting-edge technology and strategic investments to enhance national security for the United States and its allies. However, the firm has demonstrated the importance of government-venture relationships for society's challenges as well, investing in an array of climate and biotechnology companies.[17] Chris Darby, CEO of In-Q-Tel, knows what it takes for a valuable business-government compact. According to Darby, "This alliance requires systems thinking. Our company has that philosophy: let's start with the problem the government is trying to solve, let's map the architecture of the problem, and get the government to agree on the components of the architecture. Then, we can go to the venture community and see if they have a component that might fit in the architecture. We then focus on integration with other components." Darby points out that this systems-thinking starts with the government embracing an architectural approach. "Government needs to set a 'vision' and the private sector needs to have a flexible business model, adapting their products as necessary and ultimately being comfortable with what they know and what they don't know. Successful emerging companies find their 'niche' with government. They won't go for the 'enterprise' solution out of the gate. They go for a component and then try to expand from there." It is about finding how your technology venture can contribute a piece into the larger mosaic.

Recent scholarly work also highlights the importance of the government setting the "vision" and allowing the private sector to mobilize within the ecosystem around this. Howell, Rathje, Van Reenen, and Wong study the outcomes of the U.S. Air Force's Open and Conventional innovation competitions in 2018.[18] They find that open awards serve to positively affect the outcomes that the government desires in the procurement process: military benefits from the adoption of new technologies and VC funding and patenting for commercial innovations. By contrast, they find that, while specificity in conventional awards can serve to build a specific niche product, the constraints placed by customer need definition limit the creativity and innovativeness of product ideas. They observe that winning an open-topic award is associated with higher patent originality. The results point to benefits of the government specifying a larger "moonshot" and allowing players to mobilize new and flexible products within the ecosystem.

Within domestic borders, national strategies define the pathways for competitiveness for countries and map out players in an ecosystem. For example, Singapore's Future Economy Council drives the growth and transformation of Singapore's economy.[19] The council created the Alliances for Action initiative, industry-led coalitions in partnership with the government, to prototype ideas to address common challenges or avail areas of opportunity for Singapore. In recent years, Singapore has invested heavily in digital, data, and technology. It has taken a holistic digital-society approach by investing in their digital infrastructure, developing private-sector digital capability, and setting aspirational digital government agendas. Following early success in the wake of the COVID-19 pandemic, the initiative is planned to be institutionalized as an additional tool for public-private collaboration. The objective is to enable transformative economic growth and spur collaboration on creative ideas across economic clusters such as advanced manufacturing, connectivity, health, urban systems, and sustainability. The success of Singapore's model should serve as an example of the importance of adopting an ecosystem perspective in regard to mobilizing mission and capital.

And these strategic initiatives have allowed countries to become technological leaders on the global stage. The Netherlands, a country that has always been exceptional at water management due to one-third of its land being below sea level, has used strategic technological development in farming and land management to become a global leader in food exports. Only slightly larger than the state of Maryland, it produces twice as much food as its population with half as many resources as comparable countries. Guided by state-led innovation initiatives, the Netherlands has become the world's second-largest exporter of agricultural products by value behind the United States, and among the largest exporters of agricultural technology, including cell-cultured meat, vertical farming, seed technology, and robotics in milking and harvesting.[20] By orchestrating the mission around agriculture technologies, the Netherlands has assumed a key geopolitical position.

Much of the discourse surrounding the government and technology sees the government as a consumer or scaler of technology. However, as governments are pushing open-data initiatives, they are increasingly assuming the role of a data partner for private enterprises. Singapore's Data Collaboratives Programme[21] shows the government's commitment to support businesses that explore how to implement and manage mechanisms that allow for safe and economically sustainable data sharing. Businesses that are interested in data sharing for meaningful innovation can work through the Data Regulatory Sandbox and explore innovative use of data in a "safe environment." The government creates this sandbox and facilitates data sharing among businesses, startups, and government agencies. This approach shows the government's role as that of creating an ecosystem in data sharing and creating public value.

In the United States, the government has helped create mission-driven organizations by seeding them with data that advances government objectives. CareJourney, a company cofounded in 2014 by Sanju Bansal, Aneesh Chopra, and Dan Ross, started with the mission to deliver better-quality health care at lower cost. This founding team includes the cofounder of MicroStrategy, a big data pioneer, and the former federal chief technology officer, who has health care expertise. CareJourney licensed terabytes of Medicare & Medicaid claims data from the U.S. government, raised private capital to build a modern data refinery, and then invested nearly $50 million in research and product development. Today, CareJourney creates a variety of analytic products that provide detailed insight into the inner workings of the U.S. health care system. It has created the first-of-its-kind Provider Rating System, which transparently benchmarks and ranks nearly one million U.S. doctors on cost and quality, and allows anyone with a web browser to view this data.[22] These analytic products help hundreds of health care providers and payers build higher-performing physician networks, expand into underserved markets, and intelligently enter into pay-for-performance programs. In doing so, CareJourney has combined government data, cutting-edge research, and private capital and entrepreneurial talent to build a self-sustaining scalable venture that advances the government's mission of improving health care services and lowering costs.[23]

Governments also work across borders to define global needs and identify opportunities. With that logic, frameworks exist to develop a foundation for this perspective on ecosystems. Multilateral systems, such as the United Nations Sustainable Development Goals and the World Sustainable Business Development Council have not only mapped out the grand challenges for governments to pursue, but also highlighted critical pathways that for-profit businesses should be encouraged to tread, in order to solve these challenges.

Indeed, governments globally are now partnering with each other to create and share ecosystems across countries. For example, in 2022, the

UK Government Digital Service, a global leader in government digital platform ecosystems, renewed their partnership with Singapore that was originally signed in 2019. Both the United Kingdom and Singapore are widely recognized as digital leaders and take an active role in shaping international standards and discussions in the digital government space. Their partnership will cover know-how sharing and capability development with a shared goal of building more effective, efficient, and economical government digital services in the long term.[24]

The U.S. government appears to be recognizing the importance of the ecosystems approach to impact. In late 2021, the White House Office of Science and Technology, along with federal agencies and domestic and international stakeholders, announced the launch of the International Grand Challenges on Democracy-Affirming Technologies for the Summit for Democracy. These initiatives have a stated goal of "bringing together innovators, investors, researchers, and entrepreneurs from across governments and societies toward the goal of advancing technologies with democratic values embedded at every stage of development and use.[25]

The ideals of a liberal democracy are essential to the functioning of the Venture Meets Mission ecosystem. "We can and should harness innovation to advance technologies that have the potential to further our shared democratic values, including privacy, freedom of expression, access to information, transparency, fairness, inclusion, and equity," says Dr. Eric Lander, the president's science advisor and former director of the White House Office of Science and Technology Policy.[26] He adds, "It's not a guarantee that any given technology will support democratic values. It takes constant vigilance, and constant commitment; we, the people, have to make sure that technology is developed and used responsibly. That is our solemn obligation." Thus, in the pursuit of transforming mission into impact, the ecosystem must not only capitalize on the value of liberal democracy, but also embody and reinforce its values.

And these considerations are largely present in how technology policy is created. Michael Kratsios, former chief technology officer of the United States appointed by President Trump, sees national tech policy falling into two buckets: promote and protect. "Policy needs to promote the coordination of federal funds across dozens of agencies and areas of national importance, the training of the American workforce for jobs of the future, the removal of barriers to tech innovation so these technologies can make safe, meaningful impacts for the country, and the partnering with allies to drive democratic leadership in these emerging technologies." Kratsios argues, "Policy should protect intellectual property through the use of a variety of tools, including export controls and restriction lists. These tools are in place to protect our citizens and domestic market." Most important, he says, is that national strategy be created for specific technologies to tailor these promotion and protection efforts.

The importance of a national strategy cannot be understated. Thomas Kalil, the chief innovation officer at Schmidt Futures, has experienced firsthand the importance of government as an orchestrator of mission. According to Kalil, for this ecosystem to thrive the government must recognize the importance of providing strategic direction to the ecosystem. In an interview with the *Stanford Social Innovation Review*, Kalil says, "I think it is particularly powerful to link the attainment of a compelling goal with a 'why now' story. In some cases, something has changed about the world (e.g., technological progress, fundamental scientific advance, institutional or business model innovation) that makes the previously impossible, possible."[27] Kalil goes on to point out the importance of identifying the domains of impact—such as health, education, energy, and space exploration—and the coalitions of actors that could contribute to these goals—such as companies, research universities, nonprofits, private investors, and government agencies.

But without direction, the ecosystem will be rudderless, facilitating the need for a vision of pursuing technological "moonshots"—or highly ambitious, but entirely achievable goals that will have a sizable social impact. Kalil suggests a list of "what if?" as one such framework by which the government can align the Venture Meets Mission ecosystem. In tackling climate change, for example, Kalil asks, "What if non-food crops can be used to produce liquid fuels, electricity, animal feed products, and industrial materials anywhere in the country, tailored for each local area?" To address challenges related to trust in public institutions and innovation in government, Kalil asks, "What if thousands of Americans with expertise in areas such as digital services, human-centered design, and data science successfully complete 'tours of duty' in the government, and more than 90 percent would recommend it to their friends and colleagues?" Even relating these "moonshots" to national competitiveness, Kalil asks, "What if teams of workers and robots allow American companies to beat the 'China price' for many manufactured products?"

The University of Chicago's Development Innovation Lab Market Shaping Accelerator has brought together leading scholars to advance an understanding of the effective use of market shaping to solve grand challenges. Through market-shaping mechanisms, governments can promote targeted innovation by focusing the creativity of the private sector toward specific challenges. In contrast to traditional "push" funding inputs such as research grants, market shaping uses "pull" funding that rewards outputs and outcomes. Sponsoring several competitions around climate mitigation and pandemic preparedness, the accelerator has helped mobilize private-sector interest around these grand challenges.[28] According to Kalil and the Market Shaping Accelerator, we can create our own set of modern "moonshots" that guide the Venture Meets Mission ecosystem toward meaningful societal impact.

But what does the ecosystem's approach truly look like? Taking cues from both the Singapore Together Alliances for Action model[29] and the recent White House Office of Science and Technology initiative, the ecosystem means that the government recognizes the larger system in which a community of organizations, both for-profit and nonprofit, big and small, domestic and foreign, are all working together for impact. Pathways for development are not isolated to individual players, but fostered between ventures and larger corporations, between ventures and their domestic governments, and between ventures and multilateral institutions. By setting national objectives, mapping out partnering organizations, and scaling impact, an ecosystems perspective helps create a uniform plan for change.

The ecosystem perspective means that organizations, big and small, will have a shared understanding of the government's mission and priorities. This directed action helps target change by pushing the wave of products and services, human capital, and investments in the direction of change while creating a force multiplier for innovation with the private sector. Adopting a systems perspective of how all of our paths intersect can help develop a more virtuous system of change in which the government defines trajectories, ventures partner and map pathways of innovation, and individuals and academia develop skills. Much like what Chris Darby remarked in his 2022 Summit Speech (see Chapter 3), we must not only develop a national vision for the country's most pressing missions, but craft an aligned public-private investment roadmap to, over time, achieve our aspirational goals and realize our vision.

DEVELOPING TALENT

Critical to any ecosystem, natural or social, are the living parts of the ecosystem. The Venture Meets Mission ecosystem is no different. Human talent, both as the driver of mission and the people who make up this ecosystem, is one of the most critical considerations in creating trust in the ecosystem. And specifically, the government's ability to attract talent in the form of subject matter experts is of utmost importance. The expertise of the American people is one of the most valuable resources for the government to help make more informed and better decisions. Thus, without a coordinated approach to human capital, the ecosystem will not thrive to its full potential. For the government, this means not only investing in innovation, but investing in people too.

Let's consider how a typical citizen develops skills and experiences. Most commonly, professional development of a citizen begins in the academic sector, when that person is a student. The government plays a critical role here in the development of this human capital, by funding public education from kindergarten onward. For many, government-sponsored education continues through to college and university, as these institutions receive over a quarter of their funding from federal government grants.[30] Today, over 60 percent of high school graduates go to college—a trend likely to increase. Since 1960, the rate of enrollment among high school graduates has increased by 46.8 percent (0.8 percent annually).[31]

For the critical and formative years of adolescent education, the government has assumed a primary role in developing human capital. But following university graduation, the human capital development for the government begins to hit speed bumps, with students increasingly moving to the private sector. For example, in 2014, the federal government found that only around 10 percent of college graduates were even considering a career in government, and this percentage was rapidly shrinking.[32] Even among graduate students pursuing a master's degree in public policy, the group most expected to take a position in the public sector, a decreasing number of students are choosing careers with government. The same study finds that between 2001 and 2017, the number of students opting for government jobs dropped by 15 percent to only 34 percent of all graduates. And the most unlikely college major group to consider working in government is business majors, at 3.4 percent.[33] See the problem? Not only are students in general becoming less inclined to join government, but those who undertake professional careers most proximate to ventures are also significantly less likely to consider a career in government. The government invests heavily in students who have no interest in working in the public sector, and the group called upon to address the government's biggest challenges are the least likely to answer this call to service. It's quite evident where the dichotomy between the public and private sectors arises and how this produces many of the cultural challenges in their potential collaboration.

It is a difficult challenge for the government to orchestrate the Venture Meets Mission ecosystem, and it warrants a closer consideration of the hurdles that governments face in organizing human capital. First, there appears to be an incompatibility between the skills needed to do the government work and those required to thrive in the private sector. Ask any private-sector manager what the public sector can learn from them, and you can expect answers such as efficiency, rigor, and delivery. But what happens if you ask them what they can learn from the public sector? The answer may not be as clear. Press Secretary for the United

Kingdom Parliament Alexander Stevenson discusses three skills that the public sector cultivates, which are useful to private-sector enterprises:[34]

1. **The art of persuasion**. Public-sector managers typically spend more time than their private-sector counterparts seeking to persuade diverse groups of people, including the public, other government officials, and the media. The exceptional leaders are adept at working with a variety of stakeholders, knowing when to compromise, and when not to, and getting things done in uncertain environments—all skills that are vital in the private sector.

2. **Complex decision making**. Public-sector managers invest considerable time making complex and far-reaching decisions in the course of their careers, whether it's making fine judgments about foreign policy or anticipating the federal assistance needs of diverse groups. Many are well-versed in identifying the stakeholders whom their decisions might affect as well as the long-term external factors that must be taken into account. Instinctively they seek out experts and interested parties to test their ideas, listen to input, and adapt their strategy accordingly.

3. **Crisis management**. Government managers spend more time managing crises than their private-sector counterparts, partly because they face more life-altering situations, and partly because they are subject to greater media scrutiny. A major crisis, such as a terrorist attack or a virus outbreak, requires swift decision making as well as careful media handling. Public managers are likely to be good at prioritizing, making sensible decisions and communicating effectively.

Stevenson's account highlights the utility of public-sector skills to the private sector. While the public and private sectors share their differences in form and function, the skills developed and needed in both spheres are neither mutually exclusive, nor incompatible.

Vivek Kundra, the first U.S. federal chief information officer and a successful technology operating executive, shares how his public-sector experience provided him the executive and operational skills to excel in the private sector. "My public-sector experience presented me with a daily set of complex problems to address across a diverse group of stakeholders—employees, agencies, and constituents. You quickly learn the importance of systems thinking, thriving in chaos, and unwavering operational leadership to get things done at scale. My public-sector experience was invaluable in preparing for senior executive roles at some of the leading growth tech companies." Kundra's public-sector journey started when he was interviewing with the County of Arlington on the morning of 9/11 and was asked to join given the imminent crisis. He later was selected as the assistant secretary of commerce and technology for the Commonwealth of Virginia before moving as the chief technology officer for the District of Columbia, and eventually in 2009 Vivek was appointed as the first United States chief information officer by President Obama. He was responsible for managing more than $80 billion in annual technology spend and credited with saving billions in taxpayer dollars, adopting game-changing technologies, strengthening the cybersecurity posture of the nation, and launching an open government movement which has been replicated around the world. Following his journey and experience of operating at scale in the public sector, Kundra joined Salesforce as executive vice president, leading growth and go-to-market for key global verticals such as financial services, health care, retail, auto, communications, and public sector in its journey from $2 billion to $8 billion-plus in revenue. He later became chief operating officer (COO) at Sprinklr, which he took public in 2020, and is now president and COO at project44. He emphasizes, "Everyone underestimates the vast experience, leadership skills, exposure to nation-scale problems, and opportunity for impact that the public sector affords young talent."

Kundra goes on to suggest that it is imperative that we foster more intersectoral collaboration, saying, "We live in historic times—facing an unprecedented global economic crisis and new threats to our national security that change daily. Used wisely, technology can help us confront these challenges, but it will require all of us—the public sector, the private sector, and academia—working together to build a brighter future and lead us to a better tomorrow." Yet a perception still remains that there's no easy career offramp from the government back to the private sector. Success stories such as Kundra's can be made more visible.

And we are beginning to see the government acknowledging the importance of creating institutional permeability. Recently, the DoD announced its 2023–2027 cyber workforce strategy, which stressed collaboration with industry and academia. As the government struggles to capture the next generation of tech-focused talent, the DoD has decided to change its talent model, creating a talent-exchange pilot project which will allow top cyber professionals to move in and out of government from industry and academia "without penalty."[35] And how can they build this offramp without being burdened by the long and intensive government hiring process? By shifting to a continuous-vetting model that updates an employee's background in real time. By innovating their hiring process, the DoD has an opportunity to rapidly close the government tech-talent gap.

One other example of the relevancy of cross-sectoral skills, Jason Matheny explains, can be seen in the White House Fellows program. "We found that, through the White House Fellows program, the skills that students and those from the private sector bring are quite relevant to what we are doing here. But it is not to be mistaken, things here aren't as easy as just joining a private-sector company. People experience culture shock when they join the government. We started giving people a 'boot camp' so they are prepared for the nuances of working in the public sector and also to explain the huge amount of good that they can do." Matheny goes on to say, "But once they clear these cultural barriers, we see just how effective their skills are in government. Two fellows managed to pass the most significant STEM immigration reforms in the last twenty years. They got to know the Department of Homeland Security and the State Department, and got the rest of the White House on board. I mean, it's historic! And they did this thanks to six months of work. And we will soon all get to see its huge impact, there's going to be tens of thousands of scientists and engineers from other countries who will now be able to immigrate to the United States, thanks to their work."

The policy Matheny is referring to is part of an update to the America COMPETES Act, or the "America Creating Opportunities for Manufacturing, Pre-Eminence in Technology and Economic Strength

Act of 2022." The White House Fellows were able to push a series of policy updates that aim to improve the ability of the United States to attract and retain STEM students and scholars from abroad, adding twenty-two new STEM fields to a program that allows students on F-1 visas to work in the U.S. for some time after graduation. These new fields include many that are critical to innovation, such as human-computer interaction and neuroscience; cloud computing and computer science; economics and mathematics; data science; visualization and analytics; and several social science fields, including industrial and organizational psychology, research methodology, and quantitative methods research.[36]

Matheny also makes a nod to diverse skill sets by overseeing one of the largest crowdsourcing experiments in history. This effort to predict world events combined the wisdom of tens of thousands of ordinary people. According to Matheny, the more diverse the teams, the better their results: "The best ideas are going to come from a more diverse group of thinkers. And what excites me about the future is that the United States is still, currently, the world's primary engine for invention. We continue to demonstrate the value of democracy and diversity by showing that they work. And we're still the destination of choice for the world's leading scientists and engineers."

The second hurdle to attracting human capital to support the government's mission is largely generational—the achievement orientation. Whether it be growing up in an era when "everyone gets a participation trophy," or under the pressure of mounting political, economic, and environmental challenges, millennials and Generation Zers value achievement more than any generation in modern history. In fact, these two generations are most likely to define themselves and their identities through their professional and educational achievements.[37] But how does this create a barrier for government in orchestrating human capital around mission? While agencies such as NASA and the FBI have always been perceived as "prestigious" government positions, this is a distinction that is waning.[38] And it likely has to do with deteriorating trust in government and growing trust in business. For example, as SpaceX and Blue Origin increasingly penetrate the commercial space market and dominate the low- and far-earth-orbit initiatives of the United States, students too are considering these roles over similar positions at NASA. In addition, Google, Apple, and other technology companies are bolstering their role in U.S. cybersecurity defense, signaling that work similar to that of the government's is available in the private sector.[39] With the decay of trust in government and growth of private-sector organizations performing various government functions and often providing larger compensation, the perceived achievement of working for the government is fading. And without a perception of public service or mission-driven work as a professional achievement, the generational gap in the government—one in which younger workers are less likely to join the government—will continue to increase.

What are potential solutions? First and foremost, the government needs to be perceived as a builder for *all* careers, and not only those that are limited to the public sector. Pockets of government, such as the White House Fellows program, have produced exceptional public servants including congresspeople and judges, and also exceptional civil citizens, including the founders of many private enterprises. Besides producing some of the most notable public servants in the federal government and military, government has also supported notable business figures, many of whom have developed companies that work closely with the government. Such programs can attract people with diverse skill sets to the Venture Meets Mission ecosystem.

However, while prestigious, these programs have become increasingly tainted with political polarization and have not demonstrated their ability to create a clear path back to the private sector following completion. The divisive state of U.S. politics means that a tour in the White House Fellows program is no longer seen as a service to the country, but as a service to a president and party—a clear hurdle to attract people seeking mission without politics. In addition, these programs have provided limited opportunities that enable top talent to engage in a "tour of duty" in government and leverage those skills back into the private sector. This tour of duty would be one during which they can build skills, get training, and have onramps back to the private sector on the basis of highly recognized and accredited fellowships. The U.S. Digital Corps is a recently created fellowship program with the goal of tapping into young tech talent hoping to leverage fellowship skills into future public- and private-sector positions. As per their website,

> The Digital Corps will invest in Fellows' career growth with a dedicated learning and development curriculum and individual performance plans, helping you mature as a technologist and sharpen the problem-solving skills that will make you more effective in creating impact in government and other large organizations. Accordingly, Fellows who meet all performance and program requirements will be eligible to be promoted to GS-11 in the second year of the program and to GS-12 at the conclusion of the fellowship.[40]

And we have also seen instances of late-career executive professionals moving from industry to government. For example, look at a recent hire by the U.S. Department of Veterans Affairs (VA). In Spring 2022, the VA hired a new chief information officer, former Microsoft executive Kurt DelBene. They hired Kurt with the goal of overhauling an in-house medical records system that was developed in the 1980s; who better than a software executive to deliver IT expertise and aid in the transformation of an agency beset by aging IT systems?[41] The VA is "the largest integrated health care and financial services infrastructure organization in the country," explains Kurt. "We also have around a thousand systems that need modernization."[42]

For those who have developed expertise in the private sector, the government presents significant opportunities to use this experience for the collective good. However, it is essential that government agencies empower these executives for success. Without institutional empowerment, no executive can be expected to succeed. Much of Kurt's success at the VA, for example, is attributed to his ability to drive change, recruit talent, and create a culture of innovation. In fact, we see the impact of this empowerment, as the VA is hoping that the recent wave of tech layoffs could help it fill around a thousand open positions in areas ranging from cybersecurity to software development. Kurt hopes that other technologists will follow his move from private to public sector, at least while industry is in a payroll downturn. "No one needs to be making a decision for the rest of their life," he says.[43]

But the challenge remains. Despite the ability of these initiatives to promote human capital development and inter-sector mobility, many agencies have limited success recruiting from college campuses, especially top tech talent. While some areas of the government have proven highly successful in their marketing campaigns, the federal government's approach to hiring does not consist of large-scale marketing campaigns Think of contemporary examples such as "the few, the proud, the marines" or historical examples such as NASA's marketing to students during the space race. In fact, it is rare to see government recruiting on college campuses the way the private-sector tech, finance, and consulting firms recruit. These firms show up with alumni painting their respective employers in the most positive light possible. They engage in making students feel important and wanted, while also highlighting the firm's culture and values. This social dynamic goes underappreciated by government during recruitment and contributes to the lack of generational enthusiasm. Without these engagements, it is growing difficult for the government to attract private-sector employees and even recruit college graduates. With massive retirements of baby boomers looming and a hollow pool of mid-career candidates remaining in government, talent in government is indeed emptying out. The investment in citizens' school and higher education is not being captured in mission-driven work.

More creative storytelling of mission-focused narrative to graduates and private-sector employees can help grow the pool of talent by inspiring prospects by the opportunity for impact. We need to make working in government cool again! Even amplifying awareness of existing opportunities would make it easy for prospects to find information in a user-friendly manner. As a standalone website, the USAJOBS site is unlikely to create any generational inspiration. Of course, trust in government has implications for how young Americans make decisions to pursue a professional career in government. The primary trust-building initiatives detailed above should be considered paramount to enabling and orchestrating the Venture Meets Mission ecosystem. By highlighting public service impact, public-sector skill development, and transferability to the private sector, the perception of public service shifts from a resume checklist item to a stepping stone in a lifelong career.

Hacking for Defense (H4D) is a university course which is confronting these challenges head-on. H4D was cocreated by Steve Blank, an entrepreneur, author, and educator at Stanford University; Joe Felter, founding director of Stanford's Gordian Knot Center for National Security Innovation and former deputy assistant secretary of defense; and Pete Newell, a retired U.S. army colonel and former director of the army's Rapid Equipping Force. The class provides students with the opportunity to work on real-world DoD and Intelligence Community challenges.[44] In this quarter- or semester-long course, students with diverse skills and expertise form into teams and mirror the experience of a startup. These interdisciplinary teams apply "lean" problem-solving methods requiring them to "get out of the building" and interview scores of experts, end-users, and other relevant stakeholders in order to better understand their problems and iteratively develop deployable solutions. The class advances a practical approach to government work as well as applied, experiential education. It was developed and first taught at Stanford University in 2016 and continues to be pedagogically supported through the Gordian Knot Center at Stanford. Students can also introduce their own ideas about DoD/IC problems that need to be solved.

Joe Felter recalls the H4D evolution. "When we developed H4D in 2016, we were unsure whether a course like this would appeal to Stanford students—whether they would want to work with the DoD and help them solve their problems. Encouragingly, students showed up in droves—we had three times the number of applicants that we could accommodate in class. In the first H4D cohort, eight teams worked on priority problems from a range of defense sponsors from Navy Special Warfare Group to the Intelligence Community. The teams all conducted over one hundred interviews in the ten-week class as part of their intense effort to develop solutions. All the teams helped their sponsors better understand the real nature of their problem, and many teams made extraordinary progress in actually solving their chosen problems. Officials from across the DoD and IC were impressed by the results of this new and disruptive class. And this created a positive feedback loop which helped us secure government funding to scale the class beyond Stanford. H4D provided students the opportunity to engage in meaningful public service while helping the government tap into a wellspring of talent committed to developing solutions to its most challenging problems. In our end-of-course surveys, nearly every student attested that the course had a significant and positive impact on their views toward those serving in the DoD and broader USG and were inspired to seek ways to serve and contribute to their important missions. It was really amazing—and gratifying—to see this transformation."

To further advance the mission, course materials are open sourced to other universities—an initiative that has brought this Stanford University class to over fifty colleges and universities through partnership between the Gordian Knot Center and the Common Mission Project, a 501c3 nonprofit. Alex Gallo, a former House Armed Services Committee senior staffer who leads the Common Mission Project as of 2023, commented, "The H4D experience has spawned similar classes across sectors such as "Hacking for Climate," "Hacking for Oceans," "Hacking for Environment," and "Hacking for Local"—among others—and is now taught in Australia and the United Kingdom with plans to expand further. We are working with the Gordian Knot Center at Stanford and other collaborators—like the NobleReach Foundation—to continue to create opportunities for our best and brightest young people to serve and help solve our most pressing problems."

While H4D represents a grassroots movement that does a great job stimulating demand on college campuses, harnessing this excitement into government is another challenge. The bridge from these campuses to the agencies in the DoD/IC such as the CIA and NSA is not easily identifiable. In addition, speaking to the achievement gap, the best students want to be part of the most prestigious programs because the social dynamic of a career cannot be underestimated. And when the top talents in technology are not told by their academic mentors and peers about the opportunities in government, these professional silos are systemically reinforced. It is critical to have interdisciplinary classes, like H4D, to make students aware of opportunities at the intersection of mission and tech. According to Steve Blank, founder of Lean Launchpad, "Today if college students want to give back to their country they think of Teach for America, the Peace Corps, or Americorps. Few consider opportunities to make the world safer with the Department of Defense, the Intelligence Community, and other government agencies. The Hacking for Defense class promotes engagement between students and the military and provides a hands-on opportunity to solve real national security problems."[45]

The limitations of government's human capital development, however, are not reserved to college campuses. Retired military personnel hold exceptionally valuable skill sets that would benefit the Venture Meets Mission ecosystem. As emphasized by Nathaniel Fick, the leadership skills, team orientation, and mission mindset reinforced by military experience were all critical in his ability to operate in mission-driven organizations.

Sumeet Shrivastava, a long-time executive in the government IT industry and CEO of Array Information Technology, is working closely with a team of executives, business leaders, and staff at George Mason University (GMU) who identified the need to leverage the position of higher education in the government-business ecosystem. They created the Center for Government Contracting at GMU to be a "neutral" convening entity for industry, government, and academia.[46] And their center is making waves in how the government accesses talent. In a 2021 meeting between the president of GMU and five CEOs of billion-dollar government contracting businesses, the issue of security clearances for students came up. As over fifty thousand of their alumni work in government and government contracting, the center noted the importance of a standing clearance-ready program for students to help them prepare for government industry work.[47] This led to a workshop titled "Trusted Workforce 2.0 and Tomorrow's Digital Workforce," which identified a number of critical steps to improve how companies and government can access security-cleared talent.

In addition to academic institutions working to transform talent development, Guild Education is an example of a for-profit company that is working to this aim. Guild works for large corporations that are looking to invest in their employee's human capital. However, they specifically target adult learners who are feeling pressure from barely livable wages and automation.[48] Guild cuts out the need for marketing degree

and certification programs, working directly with the education provider. In turn, working in long-standing relationships with the private
sector, they are able to create a tuition-free payment infrastructure that
allows these adult learners to achieve degrees and certifications without
any debt.[49] Guild's education mission supports the goal of the government: to develop talent. But it shows us that there are many different
models in which all players in the Venture Meets Mission ecosystem can
help develop talent.

MOBILIZING CAPITAL

The "valley of death" problem, discussed in Chapter 3, presents a significant financial strain to the innovation ecosystem by bleeding startups
in both time and sunk cost. For ventures, this means that pilot programs and early stage products may not successfully make the transition to a deeper and larger engagement with the government and other
customers, and to subsequent rounds of capital for enhanced financing.
So, keeping with the goal of rebuilding trust in the government, what
can the government do to help ventures? With mission and innovation
comes capital deployment, and the government can play a critical role in
this ecosystem of investors.

First, the government can deploy capital through its various initiatives. One such example is the Singapore Economic Development Board
(EDB), a government agency under the Ministry of Trade and Industry
that is responsible for strategies to enhance Singapore's position as a
global center for business, innovation, and talent.[50] In addition to facilitating investments in strategic and nascent industries, the EDB engages
with existing companies to transform operations and boost productivity.
The EDB has helped the nation diversify its economy, undergo a massive digital transformation, and attract many new businesses.[51]

In the United States, the Defense Advanced Research Projects
Agency (DARPA) has made pivotal investments in breakthrough technologies for national security for over sixty years. The genesis of the
mission of DARPA dates to the launch of the Soviet Sputnik satellite in

1957.[52] From that time forward, the U.S. commitment has been that "it would be the initiator and not the victim of strategic technological surprises." By working with innovators both inside and outside of government, DARPA has produced game-changing breakthroughs including military capabilities such as stealth technology and icons of civil society such as the Internet and Global Positioning System (GPS).[53] DARPA's ability to deploy capital into emerging and critical technologies has enabled the DoD to produce some of the most important technological breakthroughs in modern society.

NobleReach Emerge exemplifies a new initiative that is working primarily with U.S. agencies to help funded researchers get through the valley of death by breaking down the barriers between mission, tech, and entrepreneurship.[54] The initiative explicitly states that it seeks to address the massive amount of federal R&D funding that yields only untapped or under-developed capabilities by looking for entrepreneurs to help R&D make the transition from the lab into commercial markets. NobleReach Emerge fosters interactions and connections between the developers of early stage technology and entrepreneurs early in the innovation pipeline and provides commercialization guidance and support via a network of seasoned startup executives that possess the domain expertise in the targeted technology sectors. This will help achieve the goal of increasing the likelihood for commercial success in support of national security efforts. To date, results have been positive, with multiple researchers raising venture funding and building products that have the potential for dual use. This initiative fits the Venture Meets Mission ecosystem approach, by establishing and maintaining the connection between government research and the U.S. innovation economy.

In the United Kingdom, the Engineering and Physical Sciences Research Council is the primary funding body for engineering and physical sciences research. Investing in a range of fields from health care technologies to structural engineering, manufacturing, mathematics, advanced materials, and chemistry, the agency's funding has a clearly stated goal of "providing a platform for future UK prosperity by contributing to a healthy, connected, resilient, productive nation."[55] These government initiatives play a critical role in bridging the valley of death problem by connecting research to prototype to commercialization.

In addition to these strategies to promote capital mobilization around government initiatives, government investment funds have been established to promote mission-driven startups. Temasek Holdings (Singapore) and the Government Pension Fund (Norway) are two examples of sovereign wealth funds that have been successful in deploying capital with purpose. Sovereign wealth funds are state-owned funds that invest reserves or surpluses generated by the government.[56] While these development funds, also termed "strategic investment funds," can take different forms, including stabilization, savings, and buffer funds, they are established with a primary objective to fund specific projects or sectors within a nation.[57] According to PricewaterhouseCoopers, sovereign wealth funds have been found to not only help bring product development along, but also reduce inflation, lower borrowing costs, and improve governance and transparency.[58]

Temasek is a state holding company established in 1974 and owned by the government of Singapore with over US$300 billion in assets.[59] The company proclaims itself as a "generational investor seeking to make a difference with tomorrow in mind." Investing in transforming economies, growing the population of the middle-income classes, and deepening comparative advantages—Temasek is putting its money where its mouth is. Not only has the company produced 14 percent annual return since inception but it has also been lauded for its transparency and investments in sustainable development. Norway's fund (also commonly referred to as the Oil Fund) was established in 1990 to invest the surplus revenues of the Norwegian petroleum sector. With over US$1.35 trillion in assets, the fund is the largest sovereign wealth fund in the world. With a clear social mission, the fund invests only in companies that are deemed entirely ethical.[60] More recently, in 2019, the fund started an initiative to invest in renewable energy firms, in hopes of becoming environment-friendly while improving the green and renewable energy sector of the Norwegian economy.[61]

The United States does not have a sovereign wealth fund, an issue worth looking into for its future strategic competitiveness. There are

complementary funding agencies that perform a few of the related functions, such as the outward-looking International Development Finance
Corporation (DFC). The DFC partners with private-sector organizations to finance solutions to the most critical challenges in the developing world.[62] The organization invests across sectors including energy,
health care, critical infrastructure, and technology, with an objective of
making the U.S. a more competitive leader on the global development
stage. The institution differentiates itself from overseas investment corporations by focusing on initiatives that promote inclusive growth. For
example, the DFC recently has committed to providing financing and
political risk insurance to support the development of Sierra Leone's
first large-scale and independent utility power project.[63] This initiative
will promote the development of reliable education and health care institutions, contribute to future integration of renewable energy sources,
and provide a reliable counterbalance to consumers' fluctuating power
consumption on the electricity grid. This approach also differs from the
development initiatives pursued by the People's Republic of China that
has left countries riddled with debt.[64] The DFC model presents several
takeaways for a domestic U.S.-equivalent institution. Because the DFC
has been successful in catalyzing investment in specific areas abroad, it
is worth taking a look at some of the tools they hold at their disposal to
either reduce risk for private investment or increase return potential. The
aim is to create a force multiplier on government dollars with private
capital.[65]

There remains a number of initiatives that governments can pursue
to mobilize capital around mission. In 2018, President Trump autho-
rized the DFC with the BUILD Act, a development finance institution
and agency of the federal government.[66] The DFC's lending capacity includes loans and loan guarantees, equity investments, and political risk
insurance for development projects led by the private sector. Within this
is the highly viewed first loss guarantee, which means that the government can reduce the risk profile of certain deals so that the private sector
will find the risk of projects as not too unbearable. As a result, the first
loss guarantee of the DFC can be thought to reduce many of the uncertainties of government-venture arrangements by promoting among

ventures the interest to pursue public problems, showing a commitment to the venture's products and services, and reducing the financial burden for ventures.[67] A similar model can be seen in India, which provides viability gap funding. This is designed to provide capital support from the private sector to public projects, which would not otherwise be financially viable.[68]

But it isn't only the government that has shown a willingness and effectiveness to deploy capital around mission. Jay Emmanuel, a partner at NextEra Energy Investments, sees a transformation in the ability of investors to mobilize capital around purpose. Emmanuel argues that this transformation has pushed for a purposeful startup ecosystem, saying, "There's a very clear recognition across investors that government-related innovation is happening rapidly, faster than ever before. And if you look at what's in store, no one sees innovation originating primarily from inside government. There is general acknowledgment about the value startups bring to government technological innovation. And we need to have a startup ecosystem to cultivate these projects. A way of keeping eyes and ears to the ground with what's happening and what the government needs, but also absorbing techniques that make sense. Not only are we seeing success stories in ventures' ability to produce impact, but also success in the venture funds that are investing in these mission-driven companies. It has created this ecosystem where ventures, investors, and government are all serving a complementary role and are thriving."

And there remain opportunities for these intermediary firms to improve the way they are mobilizing capital around mission. The public sector should be looking to catalyze industry with dollars from the private sector to fund opportunities—by shifting away from investing and competing with venture capital firms to providing nonrecurring engineering contracts and warrants in companies that offer dual benefits of revenue along with less dilutive capital.

Deploying capital around purpose, whether through direct and agile funding of R&D or through equity investments by intermediaries or state-owned companies, is critical to creating a Venture Meets Mission ecosystem. This capital should demonstrate a commitment to society's biggest problems and the organizations that are being created for their reconciliation. Deploying capital for purpose can help rebuild trust in the government's willingness to create public value.

PROCURING VALUE

Let's say you have the next great technological innovation that is ideally suited to thrive in both commercial and public sectors. Who do you call and where do you go? In the private sector, you may go to the patent office to file for a new design, reach out to potential manufacturers, or consider reaching out to larger corporations who may be interested in licensing or purchasing the product. Well, in the public sector, it's not that easy. You have to go through the front doors of the government, which are incredibly hard to find.

Perhaps this is not surprising given the opaqueness of government institutions. This fact, the ambiguousness with which the public at large interacts with the government, is one with which public officials have grappled for years. In fact, in 2016 the federal government widely acknowledged this challenge when it launched the initiative "Federal Front Door," designed to increase citizen's satisfaction with their interactions with the government.[69] The goal is to improve user experience by improving transparency in a service, promoting information sharing among agencies, and eliminating redundancies of interactions with the government.

Having a front door is critical to the success of creating products and services for the government. "If you really want to understand what the government's problem is and see if you have a potential solution, you need to have people who can walk through the door and listen. And that doesn't mean just anyone, it has to be someone who can speak the government's language. Having these doors into government means a better understanding in the commercial sector to what the problems are," says Niloofar Razi Howe, a fellow in New America's International Security Program and an investor, executive, and entrepreneur in the technology industry for the past twenty-five years, with a focus on cybersecurity. Razi Howe goes on to say, "The front doors of government also provide…for people in the private sector, with that important sense of mission, an opportunity to approach and work with the government. Without it, it's easy to get lost in the weeds of the government, figuring out who to work with, what the processes are, and how to best position your company.

"You want organizations that are genuinely trying to go out and partner with technology companies and come in and create a testing ground for the best solutions to be able to pull them in, understanding that they've been a super hard agency to work with," Razi Howe says. "In many cases where we have seen a clunky procurement process, some of these front doors have seriously benefited our nation. I have seen cases where there's a great commercial technology that the U.S. government should be procuring but the request for proposal process makes it impossible to do that. The process is too long and painful for the manufacturer. So, they end up going with a larger vendor who makes a custom-built version of the technology. The front doors can help in getting the right technology into the hands of the government."

Front doors are also for people. "People are skeptical of the government. This is really no surprise for anyone who has turned on the news lately," says Jason Matheny. He adds, "And they should be. Governments can do terrible things. But what is the best way to stop these things? By joining the government. There's no better way to ultimately reduce the harm and increase the benefits of government than by joining the government." But according to Matheny, government is not any different from most organizations, as it also hopes to attract talent with integrity. He goes on to say, "There is no perfect organization on the planet. Every major company that you can think of likely has at least one moral objection to what they are doing. The simple fact is that there are dangerous activities everywhere, but you need safety breaks in these organizations to reduce this harm. The best way to improve government is to just walk in the front door and start fixing things."

In August 2021, the Biden administration helped create one such front door for people looking to join the government's mission, the U.S. Digital Corps. This collaboration between the General Services

Administration, Office of Personnel Management, the Cybersecurity and Infrastructure Security Agency, and the White House Office of Science and Technology Policy created a cross-government fellowship that sought to bring entry-level technologists into the government. As referenced in Chapter 1, the federal government has a clear technologist deficit, which the U.S. Digital Corps is aiming to fill. The U.S. Digital Corps is a paid, full-time, two-year fellowship that has the opportunity to convert into a full-time career position after successful completion of the program.[70]

Chris Kuang, a cofounder of the U.S. Digital Corps, recalls the inspiration for this initiative. "When I was a college student, I remember searching USAJOBS for an entry-level position that combined two of my passions: technology and public service. Imagine how I felt when the only result that came back was an unpaid position installing basic software! That experience set me on a path of creating more opportunities for students and recent graduates in public interest technology, which is why I am so excited that we were able to launch the U.S. Digital Corps."[71] Creating the U.S. Digital Corps was a natural extension of Chris's prior work as a cofounder of Coding it Forward, a nonprofit by and for students creating opportunities and pathways into social impact and civic tech. "Cofounding and helping lead Coding it Forward while engaging with so many passionate students and young people from across the country—and around the world—was an incredible privilege and opportunity. At its roots, I have always seen Coding it Forward's work as aspirational. Our work as an organization and a broader civic tech movement will have won a victory when using tech, data, and design skills in service of the public interest is considered the gold standard—the "dream job"—and perhaps even an expectation. But our work will not be done until there are enough opportunities inside and outside of government to meet and truly take advantage of this growing supply of mission-driven talent." Chris's work in the U.S. Digital Corps and Coding it Forward show his commitment to making more front doors for those seeking to work for the government.

Government initiatives to create more front doors are critical to creating trust in government. For ventures, this means the government is giving a better understanding of where to identify opportunities for products and services. For individuals, this means the government is providing an opportunity to better understand where they can look for impactful and mission-driven work. But while the government initiatives to create front doors are valiant efforts to overcome the difficulty of working with the government as a purchaser or consumer of venture and citizens' goods and services, the idea of too many front doors is quite concerning. For example, the recent focus on innovation to foster creative problem solving in the U.S. government has produced a number of exceptional programs meant to foster partnerships with the private sector, including Challenge.gov (a platform for prize competitions in federal agencies), CitizenScience.gov (a resource designed to accelerate the use of crowdsourcing and citizen science across the government), and NASA Solve prize competitions and crowdsourcing.

But sorting through these initiatives and identifying which are the most appropriate for specific products and services can be daunting, hence, the challenge of "too many doors." "Look no farther than the Department of Defense," says Trae Stephens, a partner at Founders Fund, who invests across sectors with a particular interest in startups operating in the government space. "There are over a hundred different innovation organizations and software factories inside the Department of Defense. Over a hundred! It's impossible for an outsider to know where to start."

CATALYZING THE ECOSYSTEM

While the government maintains a key role in the Venture Meets Mission ecosystem, we would be remiss to overlook the critical role of social enterprises in aiding impact. We take a more expansive view of social enterprises as existing in many forms, as foundations, triple-bottom-line firms, and nonprofits. These organizations help testbed ideas and new business models that can be scaled by government, provide risk capital through foundations to develop mission enterprise, and serve as an intersectional convener that can bridge trust across government, the private sector, and academia. Simply put, nonprofits are an ecosystem catalyst.

The president and CEO of the World Wildlife Foundation, Carter Roberts, acknowledges this, stating, "People look to WWF and its leadership to bring imagination and perseverance to the important work of conservation, and to build bridges between government, civil society and business in devising solutions at the scale of the challenges we face. The world demands no less of us."[72] As we look to other nonprofits, we see the role of these organizations in driving change around mission-driven work.

The recent work of Dr. Eric Schmidt, the former CEO of Google who recently announced the launch of the Special Competitive Studies Project (SCSP), is one example of a social enterprise aiding the government's impact and facilitating the government's mission. This initiative will make recommendations to strengthen America's long-term global competitiveness for a future in which artificial intelligence and other emerging technologies would reshape national security, economy, and society.[73] It is quite similar to the Rockefeller Special Studies Project launched in 1956 by Nelson Rockefeller. In the midst of the Cold War, Rockefeller brought together some of the nation's leading thinkers to study the major problems and opportunities confronting the country to chart a path to revitalize American society.[74]

Interestingly, Schmidt's decision to form the SCSP comes from a feeling of empowerment to support the mission of government. "Federal government support launched my career," says Schmidt. He elaborates, "My graduate work in computer science in the 1970s and 1980s was funded in part by the National Science Foundation and the Defense Advanced Research Projects Agency. Five years ago, I was fortunate to be able to start giving back when then-Secretary of Defense Ash Carter asked me to serve on the Department of Defense's Defense Innovation Board, and then three years ago, Congress asked me to chair the National Security Commission on Artificial Intelligence. Both of these roles convinced me that the U.S. needs to think, organize and compete in significantly new ways. No serious nation can ignore the impacts of emerging technologies on all aspects of our national life. Our government cannot be a passive actor, but it needs help. For this reason, I am starting the Special Competitive Studies Project...to study these critical

issues alongside my friends and colleagues."[75] And the SCSP is successfully aiding the government in identifying and coordinating new tech
for long-term global competitiveness, as seen most recently in a new
project on human-machine teaming in military operations.[76]

Another organization helping to enable impact is youth-led social
enterprise unBox, cofounded by Isa Foster and Charlie Hoffs. This organization is working to empower younger generations to fight food insecurity, by connecting these individuals with "the tools, training, and
networks needed to transform US food policy through research, policy
advocacy, and activism."[77] Recently, unBox collaborated with the government on addressing nutrition and food security issues in legislation.
Working with Senator Richard Durbin on legislation S. 4202, "Expanding SNAP Options Act of 2020," unBox was invited to review the legislation as it was being drafted and offer suggestions on what should
be included to overcome existing policy barriers. By bringing together
research, subject matter experts, and other organizations, unBox was
able to help the government understand the true nature of the problem
in their drafting of legislation, enabling better impact.

All Tech Is Human is another organization helping orchestrate the
government's mission. This nonprofit group maintains that the future
of technology is intertwined with the future of democracy, and that a
"responsible technology ecosystem" is critical to a functioning democracy.[78] This group, as many scholarly works have underscored, argues
that an entanglement of technology with social, political, and economic
systems that are inherently unjust means that advances in technology are
hindered from being a public and planetary good. All Tech Is Human
is seeking to instill the ideals of a liberal democracy in new technologies through multistakeholder convening, intersectional education, and
diversifying the pipeline of talent with more backgrounds and experiences.[79] By working with the government to ensure that technological
trajectories and development are aligned with the public interest, All
Tech Is Human is helping the government orchestrate its mission. Such
social enterprises also provide a chance for new models of engagement
to be tested, and later scaled with government assistance.

And while the government is struggling to attract talent to the ecosystem, we are seeing examples of how nonprofits can help develop talent. Teach for America, a nonprofit organization whose stated mission is to "enlist, develop, and mobilize as many as possible of our nation's most promising future leaders to grow and strengthen the movement for educational equity and excellence,"[80] is a great initiative that has produced exceptional public servants, successful entrepreneurs, and business leaders. Activate Global is a nonprofit that partners with research institutions and U.S.-based funding organizations to support fellows in an "entrepreneurial fellowship model." The organization sits between the government and the private sector to help transform scientists into entrepreneurs through a fellowship that guides them through the journey. Their 142 fellows have generated $1.3 billion in follow-on funding and created over twelve hundred jobs.[81] And MissionLink.Next is a nonprofit trade association that is helping to train CEOs on opportunities to leverage their company's technologies to address emerging mission-critical opportunities.[82] These are recognizable models that have been able to draw an array of talent from different backgrounds and interests, and cross-fertilize the public sector with private-sector talent. Thus a solution to attracting talent into the Venture Meets Mission ecosystem may be through nonprofit organizations that sit outside of government and promote public service.

And finally, social enterprises are helping to mobilize capital around the government's mission. The Elemental Excelerator, a not-for-profit platform of the Emerson Collective, is committed to mobilizing capital around mission-driven work. They hold a portfolio of for-profit companies in energy, sustainability, water, agriculture, transportation, finance, and cybersecurity. Since 2009, the nonprofit platform has invested in over 150 companies, celebrated over twenty-five exits, and funded more than a hundred technology projects.[83] Among their accomplishments was the significant impact they made to these ventures, with their portfolio leveraging Elemental's dollars 100x and raising over $3.8 billion in follow-on funding.[84] Even more impressive is the origin story of the organization, which brought together renewable energy and military capability in the form of a $30 million award from the DoD's Office of Naval Research to scale their program impact and support the navy's climate initiatives. The Gates Foundation is an example of philanthropy

THE GOVERNMENT AS AN ENABLER OF TRUST

- *Celebrate the success stories of mission driven workers, ventures, and citizens.*
- *Articulate and reiterate the missions of government.*
- *Cultivate an environment of transparency.*

THE GOVERNMENT AS AN ORCHESTRATOR OF MISSION

- *Promote the ecosystems approach to mission.*
- *Expand the roles of ecosystem engagement.*
- *Align vision across the ecosystem.*

THE GOVERNMENT AS A DEVELOPER OF TALENT

- *Change perceptions of the gap between skill development in the public sector and private sector.*
- *Broaden the aperture for talent, consider capability over credentials.*
- *Make the government a career enhancer for young talent.*

THE GOVERNMENT AS A MOBILIZER OF CAPITAL

- *Harness research investments for moonshot opportunities.*
- *Set ambition to help align and converge teams and capital.*
- *Create capital stacks which pool family office, nonprofit, government and private financing.*

THE GOVERNMENT AS A PROCURER OF VALUE

- *Make the government front doors more visible and accessible.*
- *Build entry points into government for talent, ventures, and products and services.*
- *Facilitate better intersectoral communication.*

FIGURE 5.1. Government Actions to Enable a Venture Meets Mission Ecosystem. Source: Authors.

for mission-driven ventures and innovations. Created by Bill and Melinda Gates, this nearly $50 billion endowment provides funding to organizations in order to achieve measurable impacts in the fight against poverty, disease, and inequity around the world.[85] This base of philanthropic capital mobilizing around mission-driven ventures certainly aids in providing critical funding to the ecosystem, as these social enterprises risk capital to develop the mission enterprise. In the Venture Meets Mission ecosystem, nonprofit organizations play a key role in catalyzing the ability for governments and ventures to scale their impact.

INTEGRATING THE VENTURE MEETS MISSION ECOSYSTEM

We summarize the key roles of government as an enabler of trust, orchestrator of mission, developer of talent, mobilizer of capital, and procurer of value (Figure 5.1). To rebuild trust, governments need to assume their role as an enabler by continuing to act with a commitment to the public interest in a transparent manner. By articulating mission and celebrating success stories, governments can be an enabler of impact. To orchestrate collaboration, governments can adopt an ecosystems approach to mission—rallying people around societal problems, expanding the roles of engagement, and aligning ecosystem vision with key participants. As a developer of talent, the government can reduce perceptions of incompatible skills in the public and private sectors, broaden their talent search, and make the government a career enhancer for young talent. The government can also play a key role in the mobilization of capital around mission through various agency initiatives and wealth funds, creating capital stacks that leverage government spending and reduce the financial risks of government investments. The government can enhance its role as a procurer of public value by making it easier to work with and for the government in support of its larger mission and to cultivate an outcome-focused marketplace. Finally, social enterprises are critical in the Venture Meets Mission ecosystem, by serving as testbeds for new models, finding new sources of funding, and convening participants across sectors to rebuild trust.

Six

RESOLVE TO ACT

Making a Bigger Impact with Your Career

The Venture Meets Mission ecosystem can thrive. In this chapter, we shift our focus to the individual—you. We interviewed recent graduates, rising stars, and accomplished leaders to highlight how we can surmount the intention-action barrier that we discussed in Chapter 2, but thrive by doing so. One theme that emerged across our interviews, whether it was in venture or in government, is that there need not be a dichotomy between making money and having impact. Our stories confirm that building a career does not require a trade-off between doing good and doing well. Quite the contrary. And better yet, there is no right stage of career or types of experience or age. Many find a career in this mission ecosystem with the powerful motivator that it is never too early or too late. We reflect on these individuals' career strategies to help you map your own journey, and our vignettes are intended to help you reflect on becoming an impactful changemaker.

LEADERSHIP AT THE INTERSECTIONALITY

Leadership is a process of applying social influence to maximize the efforts of others for achieving a common goal.[1] Intersectionality is often used to describe the relationships between individuals and social categories (such as generation, occupation, nationality), and concepts that fall into more than one category. In the Venture Meets Mission ecosystem, leadership skills emerge from experience in operating at the interface of public and private, first, through developing a working knowledge of how to operate and succeed in both environments, and second, through understanding the differences in motivating and influencing in very different contexts. To thrive in a mission ecosystem, we need to develop a new set of intersectional leadership skills.

In the summer of 1998, following his junior year at Dartmouth University, Nate Fick attended the United States Marine Corps Officer Candidates School and was commissioned as second lieutenant upon graduating. The Baltimore native then became an officer in the Amphibious Ready Group of the 15th Marine Expeditionary Unit, training with the Australian Army for humanitarian operations deployment to East Timor. However, following the September 11 attacks in 2001, Nate led his platoon into Afghanistan for Operation Enduring Freedom and eventually, in 2003, into Iraq during Operation Iraqi Freedom.

"I was really unsure of what I was going to do after serving," says Nate. "As I thought about my military experience, I found that I liked building and leading teams. And I wanted to find a way to keep doing that. So, I went to business school. And candidly, I went to business school because it seemed like a socially acceptable way to tread water and figure out what I wanted to do with the rest of my life." He used the GI Bill to attend Harvard Business School and the Harvard Kennedy School. Nate recounts his experience: "I had this nontraditional background. I was a classics major and an infantry officer, I could not build a financial model in my life. I found myself sitting there, in business school, surrounded by all these kids that came out of Goldman and McKinsey. It was a totally eye-opening experience. I loved it in hindsight." Nate goes on to say, "The most valuable thing that I got out of business school was, when things were really hard running a business, and it felt like everything was falling apart, I never once laid in bed at night staring at the ceiling thinking, 'If only I had an MBA I would know what to do.' And I don't mean that to be faint praise—I think, actually the sort of self-confidence that comes with saying 'Hey, I've been exposed to a bunch of situations via the case method. I've seen a lot of stuff vicariously and, sometimes, this is just hard.' That really helped me, more than anything." In case you need even more reason to be impressed with Nate, he also wrote a *New York Times* bestseller, *One Bullet Away: The Making of a Marine Officer.*

After business school, Nate was recruited to a nonprofit organization that helps develop national security and defense policies, CNAS, but the decision was not understood by most of his business school classmates who were pursuing traditional banking and consulting jobs. He says, "As a leader, it was a terrific training ground. Because in for-profit companies, you have the resources to motivate people with stock options, cash, and all kinds of stuff. But in the nonprofit, all you have is mission, vision, values, and culture. That's all you got. And there are no shortcuts. My dad used to tell me, 'You can't take the elevator, you have to take the stairs,' and I feel like that's an important message, in nonprofit management you're walking up the freakin' stairs."

Years later, Nate started working in for-profit, mission-oriented organizations such as Endgame. He served as the CEO of a cybersecurity software company from 2012 through its acquisition in 2019. Nate recalls the importance of his journey. "That was the arc of how I got here. Military leadership, nonprofit leadership, venture and private-equity-backed leadership. And all the while a focus on mission and technology. And what did I learn? They're all the same in a lot of ways—they're all human organizations looking for the same things. I learned that businesses can be a powerful force for society."

In September 2022, he was sworn in as the U.S. State Department's first Ambassador at Large for Cyberspace and Digital Policy.[2] Reflecting upon his experiences and achievements, Nate says, "My career only made sense looking backwards, it didn't make sense looking forwards." Nate's story highlights the importance of "leadership at the intersectionality." It means having a mission mindset, above all else. Having a mission mindset means that you understand that all players in this ecosystem have a similar purpose—a larger mission. At the same time, it means that you realize the differences in goals and incentives of various players in the ecosystem. Government agencies, businesses, academic institutions, and the individuals that make up these groups all have varying preferences for risk and different incentives for taking risks. This shapes the different goals of each of these groups, whether to safely promote the public good, to invest in innovation, to train tomorrow's leaders, or to provide for a family. A leader in this ecosystem recognizes how to advance the interests of each of these groups without compromising the well-being of any of them or the mission at large. Forming this bridge helps address some of the incentive uncertainty in motivating mission-driven action.

Nate Fick's leadership experience also highlights a different role— one of a translator and facilitator. Experts in the government-venture arrangements frequently remark that traditional public-private partnership models constrain the players from fully capturing the plurality of relationships that can occur in the Venture Meets Mission ecosystem. Whereas traditional public-private partnerships see bilateral coordination between the business and the government, the Venture Meets Mission ecosystem brings together multiple groups in pursuit of one mission: government agencies, nonprofits, ventures, investment funds, and academic institutions. Nate's journey through all of these institutions enables him to have a "leg up" in understanding the challenges they face when working together. In Chapter 4, we identified the importance of "learning the language of the government." Becoming a leader in the intersection of government and venture can aid in learning and developing the communication practices of their relationship, a key feature in overcoming some of the process uncertainties of government-venture arrangements.

Finally, Nate Fick embodies the values of intersectional thinking. Trust has been a concept frequently evoked in this book, and for good reason. Trust reduces the risk and costs of partnering, and it increases a willingness to act and to act in good faith. Trust maintains a focus and commitment to agreed-upon goals and outcomes. Nate's realization of the partnership among the various parties, all supporting one larger mission, accents the importance of building strong bridges among these groups to provide a foundation for trust. Trust is the currency of collaboration. Intersectional leadership skills that elevate common objectives and harmonize values will build this trust.

Another leader at the intersection is Stacey Dixon, the principal deputy director of National Intelligence in the Biden administration since August 2021. Starting as an intern at Nokia Bell Labs and later earning a doctorate in mechanical engineering from Georgia Tech, Dixon thought she had her path laid out: pursue a career in industry and then academia. Following the 2009 financial crisis, she explored opportunities within government and came across an opportunity to join the CIA. After reaching out to some contacts in the intel community, she could see the passion and fulfillment these individuals had protecting national security. She decided to take the job and pivot to the public sector, later rising through the ranks of the Intelligence Community and eventually becoming the second-highest ranking intelligence officer in the United States, and the highest-ranking Black woman in the Intelligence Community. Dixon's takeaway—STEM backgrounds can make a great impact on the nation and the world through analytical thinking, complex problem solving, and building and refining operational processes. And there's enough breadth of government work needed for every skill set.

INTENT AND THE RIVER OF CONFORMITY

The opposite of leadership is conformity. To change our own attitudes, we need to break conformity. Hebert Kelman, emeritus professor of social ethics at Harvard University, says that there are three different processes of social influence: compliance, identification, and internalization.[3] We comply when we want to get a favorable reaction or avoid disapproval from our peers. We identify with others when we want to reinforce our belonging and similarity to our peers. We internalize when we find our actions rewarding and they reinforce affirmation from our peers. These three processes make our current peers, whether at work, at school, or at home, exert a social influence on us to "conform to the norm." The norm in a business school context may be to enter a consulting or finance career if you are pursuing an MBA degree. Peers, advisors, mentors, seniors, and buzz surrounding certain jobs may all reinforce conformity to the norm. Parents too reinforce this mentality with an initial risk aversion that often leads them to assume the role of a guarantor formally or informally on their child's financial commitments. Social influence is a metaphorical river of conformity—it is so powerful that we drift along or are washed away. But leadership at the intersectionality for the Venture Meets Mission ecosystem requires breaking the norm—it requires intent.

"I was born in the heart of the Middle East, in Beirut, Lebanon," said Tiffany Saade, a student at Stanford University. "I grew up in a country that has been plagued by historic consociationalism and corruption, resulting in civil wars, economic recessions, and ethnosectarian divides. The dream of a democratic Lebanon has traced both my academic and professional journeys." Saade, who became an intern for former U.S. Ambassador to Lebanon and Under Secretary of State David Hale during the Stanford in Washington program, goes on to say, "I was also fortunate to enroll in the Valley Meets Mission class taught by Professor Gupta. I underestimated the potential and power at the intersection of tech and politics. This class showed me that this intersection is the solid foundation for peacebuilding and cooperation on common barriers like climate change, nuclear proliferation, and democratic erosion. My experience in DC has revealed to me a new path for reform and reconstruction for Lebanon, one that can allow the people to flourish. The collaboration of the private and public sectors are one of the pillars of a stable democracy, and can usher in a new period of Lebanon with a secure state and a united nation."

Daniel Sabzehzar, a managing partner at Tesserakt Ventures, also found a sense of mission from his international roots. Sabzehzar decided to launch a VC fund with friends during his years at the University of California, with a "mission to make the world's data useful so people can live healthier, wealthier, happier lives." Sabzehar recalls "feeling an importance of continuing my parents' immigrant journey. My father is from Iran and my mother is from El Salvador. Both came from developing countries to pursue the American dream. And, growing up here I always believed that this was the greatest country on earth to make a difference. There's nowhere else in the world that you can make this scale of impact." In only three years, Sabzehzar's Tesserakt Ventures has helped fifteen early stage deep tech and climate tech companies raise over $300 million. Most recently, this was in a nearly $50 million Series A funding of Verdant Robotics, a company with a unique robot that can simultaneously weed, fertilize, and treat plants for pests and diseases while gathering data on the plants, allowing for key farming decisions in real time.[4]

Arun Gupta's "Valley Meets Mission" class at Stanford University was an eye-opener. The class, which builds from many of the same tenets as in this book, introduces students to the world of mission-driven entrepreneurship. Through cases and career exemplars, students are exposed to this exciting, and critical, space. Here are sample snippets of student accounts of the class:

> "My biggest revelation is that I don't have to choose between the 'private' and 'public' sectors to pursue my ultimate mission impact. I realized that there is even more work to be done and so many opportunities to do it. I realized that I have so many more pathways to explore my mission so that I can truly be an effective public servant."—*computer science major, Class of '24.*

> "I have always wanted to do something 'more.' There is no 'straight line' in one's career journey and there are many exciting ways to combine interests in technology, security, entrepreneurship, etcetera With public service and impact."—*public policy and international policy studies major, Class of '18.*

> "Many students feel pressure to go down the route of being a software engineer or working at a big tech company. However, I learned that it is okay to go down nontraditional routes, but also that these routes

are often more impactful and more exciting. I wanted to ensure that at every step along the way I was pursuing jobs that involved meaningful and impactful work."—*economics and computer science major, Class of '24.*

"I came to Stanford five years into a public service career burnt out. The Valley Meets Mission class provided me a path for solving problems through entrepreneurship. I am now exploring starting an entrepreneurial venture in Africa in collaboration with local government to scale climate adaptation solutions in agriculture, which I believe will be a crucial part of offsetting the security risks that will come with climate displacement."—*international policy major, Class of '23.*

Each of these early career and student accounts presents a key lesson in how students constructed their careers with *intentionality*. In Chapter 2, we discussed the barriers to action associated with perceptions of business and government as incompatible partners serving different roles, and the subsequent importance of elevating common (mission) objectives. These student accounts discuss the importance of being guided by these objectives and pursuing careers with intentionality. While these students may not have always held the most accurate perceptions of the government or of ventures, at various stages, their perception of what the government stands for, and what businesses can do for society, changed. In addition, many students' accounts discussed the social conformance pressure to pursue traditional and less risky career paths. This brings us back to the importance of shared values and, specifically, empathy. Each student was motivated by their desire to pursue mission-driven work. And as a result, they were able to find and hold empathy for all of the roles in the Venture Meets Mission ecosystem, which led them to adopt different positions in growth ventures, venture capital, the public sector, and nonprofit firms. Increasingly young people are pursuing their larger sense of purpose with the power of venture.

However, perceptions of intersectional careers as riskier than traditional ones are entrenched in the minds of most. But this notion is also changing. Millennials and Generation Zers, now the largest class of workers in the United States, are moving between jobs at rates never seen before. According to CareerBuilder, for Generation Zers (age six through twenty-four) the average length of time spent at a job is two years and three months. For millennials (twenty-five through forty) that figure is two years and nine months, while for Generation Xers (forty-one through fifty-six) it is five years and two months, and for baby boomers (fifty-seven through seventy-five) it is eight years and three months. This explains the fact that Generation Xers and baby boomers are likely the longest-tenured employees in any organization. A 2016 Gallup report on millennials found them to job-hop more than all other groups. Twenty-one percent of millennials said they've changed jobs within the past year—more than three times the number of nonmillennials who reported the same.[5]

What explains these recent trends? Well, it appears that students are overcoming the social conformance pressures to switch jobs and careers. Millennials are increasingly looking for careers that allow them purpose, growth opportunities, workplace flexibility, and engagement. Rather than remaining with an employer that fails to offer these opportunities, millennials are switching positions. It also appears that the financial concerns of changing jobs are lowering. Forbes found that employees who stay with a company for longer than two years make 50 percent less than those who move between jobs.[6] Thus it appears that the professional risk from conforming is higher than the risk from diversity of experience.

The norm is to adopt traditional career trajectories due to social conformity. To overcome these forces, you must have intent. A clear and unadulterated intent provides the power to cross the river of social conformance—intent for developing a rich and varied experience, skill set, and passion to operate in the interface of mission and venture. All toward the common mission.

FUNNELING

In addition to social conformance pressures and the lack or presence of clear intent, structural forces also "funnel" or channel students into career trajectories. Colleges in particular play a key role in funneling students into known and well-trodden career pathways. This is because of the ease of recruitment and placement these structures have. By establishing relationships with companies and industries, colleges have become more efficient and successful in placing students into traditional jobs. Intersectionality is sacrificed for academic efficiency and efficacy. In corporate America, formalized recruiting patterns and the process of extending job offers means that recruiters are frequently tapping into the same pipeline of talent, with similar attributes among candidates. In addition, the speed of recruitment is quicker, more streamlined, and more structured in corporations than in startups and government agencies. A smoother process means that people are more likely to consistently accept what's familiar—and easier—for them. Similar to the river of conformity from social pressures, structural forces too funnel us to traditional careers.

"I felt like I had to climb the corporate ladder in a traditional career," says Angela Chen, a master's student in international policy at Stanford. She points out, "I completed my undergrad at the University of Pennsylvania and the Wharton School of Business, and it felt like I had to become either a consultant or an investment banker. These were really the only options that were presented to me in this setting. And once I started consulting, I gradually realized that I was doing something that I didn't fully have my heart in. Even though I loved the act of consulting—helping others to solve their stickiest challenges—I wasn't fond of the idea that your impact depended on whether your clients implemented your recommendations. I also didn't enjoy the promotion-driven work environment. I felt that many peers around me were working to be promoted, rather than to learn, grow, and actually help our clients. It began to affect my way of thinking too. So, I started exploring different career paths. And I was drawn to the exponential change-making potential of entrepreneurship. At first, I faced a lot of resistance from my parents, who didn't understand why I wanted to leave behind a clearly defined, high-earning career for something where success isn't guaranteed. I understand where they are coming from—they sacrificed a lot immigrating to Canada to create a better and easier life for me and they saw entrepreneurship as abandoning a safe harbor for stormy waters.

Thankfully, they realized that innovating and solving sticky challenges makes me happy, so they gave me their blessing to become a founder. But I never would have imagined this as a viable career path when I was initially looking for a job out of college."

Chen, an entrepreneur interested in EdTech who has prior experience working as an AI policy advisor, recalls the structural inertia she had to overcome to become an entrepreneur. "Sure—the pressure of conformity is real. No one is explicitly saying you should be pursuing 'this' career over 'that' career, but we assume that we should be acting one way or another to achieve a certain goal—typically to be seen by others as 'successful.' But what I thought was striking was that there were so many careers that I didn't even consider coming out of undergrad. The institution was so set up for placing students into well-paying jobs that it pressured students to overlook opportunities to do work with a deeper mission." Chen goes on to offer students some advice. "Instead of thinking about what path I *need* to be on, I started thinking about what path I *want* to be on. Day by day, I started figuring out and gaining confidence about who I truly want to become."

Funneling forces students into specific career "buckets"; one would expect that this model of human capital development is more valuable for employees and their organizations. But research has found the opposite. Academic research in the field of innovation management frequently evokes concepts of generalists and specialists, in which generalists have skills that are varied across domains and applications and specialists have particular skill sets relevant to specific fields of study. Both specialists and generalists play critical and complementary roles in organizations. While specialists tend to have domain expertise, generalists are typically seen as having leadership attributes for organizations, as they accumulate broader knowledge of issues and problems and approach their solutions with "big picture" and "out of the box" thinking.

An opportunity lies in how universities form and maintain relationships with recruiters. For universities, established corporations present a safety net to ensure their graduates are employed by the time of commencement, a key metric to attract more and higher-quality applicants. In addition, consulting jobs present an opportunity for the business schools to elevate their rankings, which are largely based upon graduate salaries. And as a result, we often see that colleges and universities form and rely heavily on relationships with corporate America and consulting companies.

This is a surmountable obstacle for the Venture Meets Mission ecosystem's ability to attract talent, but also for the universities, which must recognize that these models are neither sustainable, nor the most impactful. Consider two career paths for a recent graduate. Either take a well-paying job with little promotion potential and only a 33 percent chance of staying in it for more than two years, or take a job that pays slightly less, but with a much higher chance of building a lasting career and becoming a leader. The current university model funnels students into the first path with options such as consulting and investment banking. While this raises the program rankings in terms of graduate pay, it actually leaves the student with a riskier and less optimistic outlook in the longer run. The second path that offers the option to work in a venture does not mean that the student is taking a job in a garage startup with little funding. Growth ventures present a number of opportunities to learn while maintaining a market salary. Universities seeking to be a player in the ecosystem can address their role in funneling by including alternative metrics of graduate placement and success such as placement tenure, promotions, and even impact narratives. Increasing awareness of Venture Meets Mission opportunities on college campuses will tap into the generational shift for mission-oriented employment without sacrificing career opportunities.

For the Venture Meets Mission ecosystem to thrive, career trajectories need to be constructed around intersectionality—and we are seeing that there are more opportunities to do so now than ever before. For individuals seeking to build intersectionality, the government also presents an opportunity. Perhaps one way of looking at this is as a "tour of duty" in public service. Just as we look at Teach for America for the brightest kids, here is an opportunity to rethink service for the public good, while building critical skills for impact. Having experienced the challenge of acquiring technology personnel in government, former CIA director Michael Morell sees the tour of duty as one excellent way for the federal government to attract young talent.

Morell says, "The agency culture clearly needs to change, from hiring people right out of school essentially and having them spend a career with you to having people come and go at different parts of their career. Young people just aren't approaching their careers the same way, and we need to adapt to that. I think it's a really good idea to consider having more internship and fellowship development programs. Every year, the White House brings into government a significant number of White House fellows, and they put them in different parts of the government, and these are the best and brightest that the country has to offer. This program gets much interest because it is prestigious. And either you get these best and brightest for at least a year, or what actually happens is many of them decide to stay on because they find the mission so compelling. It's one way to give young people an opportunity to pursue mission while revolutionizing the agency. And, if they leave, hopefully, they'll start a company that will do something significant for us."

The structural forces of funneling present major barriers to bringing talent into the ecosystem. We are seeing the younger generations break the mold with how they construct their careers. But this discourse highlights the urgent need for our primary cultivators of talent—government and academia—to reconsider their models of placing students in careers. They need to consider targeted efforts at bringing the best talent to solve our biggest challenges ahead.

FIND THE DIAGONAL

While government bodies with a robust resource base are powerful agents for impact, history has proven their bureaucratic features to be quite rigid and inflexible—not exactly the ideal traits of an agent meant to bend and shift in response to a changing environment. It soon becomes apparent that those best suited to thrive in the face of uncertainty and tackle large systemic problems are those whose experience draws from diverse perspectives. We underscore diversity as a powerful driver of flexibility and innovativeness in the problem-solving process. Academics have shown that diversity of thought, experience, background, and culture improves the quality of decisions during trying times, and that diverse teams tend to have higher-quality decision-making routines and innovative outcomes.[7] We need to embrace the view that those who are able to draw from a breadth of experience and perspective to think outside the box are the ones who thrive in an increasingly uncertain future.

This begs a natural ensuing discussion on how you can build your own individual diversity. While the national, cultural, ethnic, and social forces that have shaped your background and perspectives are determined by chance at birth, professional diversity, in contrast, is not. Professional diversity is largely an individual choice that reflects career paths along the diagonal in which people follow their passions and broaden their skills and knowledge through various roles across different industries and sectors.

Toni Townes-Whitley, former president of U.S. Sales for Regulated Industries at Microsoft, shares, "I'm a military brat, so I really have been moving around my whole life, and I think that really shaped how my professional life unfolded." Townes-Whitley, who now sits on the boards of organizations such as NASDAQ, PNC, United Way Worldwide, and Johns Hopkins Medicine, recalls her professional beginnings. "When I graduated from Princeton with an economics degree, at a time when everyone who graduated was going to graduate school, I decided to join the Peace Corps, in hopes that I could apply my economics and business principles right there on the ground. I went to several countries along the equator and started building schools, learning different cultures, and exposing myself to new situations and experiences. And when I came back from the Peace Corps I decided that I wanted to join the government. I went right into the GAO—the Government Accounting Office, which has since been renamed—and I started working with three- and four-star officers in the military and State Department trying to find fraud, waste, and abuse across the government. It was a great way to see the government from the inside."

She goes on to say, "My next move was over to the private sector into Arthur Andersen as a tech consultant and then later to Microsoft with the goal of running their public-sector technology interface on a global scale. And I was able to see how the private sector really interacts with the state and federal governments in regards to how new and emerging technologies shape and can address societal and national challenges. For example, we had many discussions on issues of responsible AI, Microsoft's role in the health care industry as a HIPAA-certified platform, and the role of technology in educational equity. The company really began to focus on the UN sustainable development goals and ESG targets while working with the government and trying to understand the intersection of civics and technology. And in some cases, I actually felt like I was working for the DoD, as we were shaping policy as technologists that the government was not equipped to easily understand."

Townes-Whitley's greatest piece of advice: "*Find the diagonal*. The broader and more diverse your scatter plot, the better your regression line is in terms of your own career. For me, I created a pretty broad scatter plot. I did public- and private-sector work, and I found that the learnings are important to apply across the two. Look for the vertical opportunities to learn something new. And then look to the horizontal opportunities to apply what you've learned. I think we've got to break down the construct that 'Oh, I'm doing A or B.' To find the diagonal— to really walk this critical path of developing skills and experiences, you have to extend your curiosity into different areas."

A lifelong hooper, Townes-Whitley is quick to make a basketball analogy about her career. "Be a triple-threat athlete. In basketball, the most valuable player on the court for any team is the player that can shoot, dribble, and pass. The triple threat. And I realized the importance of this coming out of Princeton. When I joined tech, it was the economics background and the regressions and the econometrics models that led me to see how to define the need in business innovations. And when you consider that, growing up as a kid in a public-sector family, I had this idea of volunteerism and making a difference ingrained in me. And my career was built along this premise—that being able to do public and private-sector work would allow me to do these regressions. To see where the difference needed to be made and identify the optimal ways to apply technology to do so."

And one final piece of advice from Townes-Whitley—there's no dichotomy between purpose and profit. She says, "I never felt like I ever had to make a choice between doing good or making money. While my parents were exceptional public servants, I made an amazing amount of money working at Microsoft, and yet it was my most impactful work on the globe in terms of social change. The idea that you cannot make money while making a significant and meaningful change is wrong. And even more so when you have the technology to really scale this change." Townes-Whitley is a remarkable and shining example of how to develop a skill set to thrive in the Venture Meets Mission ecosystem.

Donald Gips is another great example of finding the diagonal through blending public and private careers. Gips attended Harvard for his undergraduate degree and Yale for his master's degree and started his career in Sri Lanka, where on a fellowship he helped install water wells. He then went into politics on a senatorial reelection campaign and as a policy advisor for then New York City Mayor Ed Koch before working as an executive for McKinsey & Company, the consulting company. Gips went on to help draft *What You Can Do for Your Country*, a report of the Commission on National and Community Service. After the report became the blueprint for AmeriCorps under President Bill Clinton, Gips assisted Congress with setting up AmeriCorps. He then worked for the Federal Communications Commission for four years directing strategy and became the agency's international bureau chief. In 1997, Gips was named Vice President Al Gore's chief domestic policy advisor. He held the position for a year and focused on internet policies related to schools. Using his public service skills in corporate leadership roles, Gips became the vice president of corporate strategy at the communications technology firm Level 3 Communications. A meeting with then Illinois State Senator Barack Obama in 2004 propelled Gips into eventually becoming director of personnel for the Obama White House in 2009. President Obama appointed Gips as U.S. Ambassador to South Africa, a post he held until 2013. After leaving public service, he returned to the private sector as a venture partner at Columbia Capital, a communication and infrastructure growth venture firm and as senior counselor for Albright Stonebridge Group, a global business strategy firm, where he led African operations. In 2019, Gips was announced as the CEO of the Skoll Foundation to help the foundation increase its support for social change groups domestically and internationally.

Townes-Whitley and Gips have shown the value that a career along the "diagonal" of public and private sectors can bring, both to an individual's career and to the organization they work for. Our discussions bring us to a simple conclusion—the best people to thrive in the Venture Meets Mission ecosystem are those who have built their experiences and careers along the diagonal. Why? The answer lies in both the challenges and the opportunities that the Venture Meets Mission ecosystem presents.

Quite simply, the cultural influence of Malcolm Gladwell's concept of "outliers"—in which expertise is only achieved through ten thousand hours of training—is limiting. It reinforces a siloed world of professionals with a narrow worldview, and an even narrower social network and professional skill set. Even parents are considering the outliers argument as parenting advice, raising their kids at eight or nine years old to be specialists in one form or function. Beyond the clear implications the "outliers" argument has on the Venture Meets Mission ecosystem, which relies on intersectionality and collaboration to tackle larger missions, it may very well be also aiding in the polarization of society. In the previous chapter, we discussed the importance of diversity in interactions in breaking down hostilities and biases. Specialization, while improving depth of expertise, prevents diversity of interaction by reinforcing connections with like-minded others.

And perhaps this is why we have seen alternative approaches, such as those advanced by Georgetown University's McDonough School of Business Professor Nick Lovegrove in his book *The Mosaic Principle*.[8] He says, "Life—personally and professionally—is lived to the fullest as a mosaic, encompassing a rich and complex set of diverse experiences that provide purpose, meaning, happiness, and success. Yet, the pressures of modern society push us toward narrower focus and deeper specialization in our lives and careers. Today we have businesspeople and government officials who persistently distrust and demonize each other; a fortunate swath of society with professional and financial security, increasingly isolated from those left behind; and community leaders who struggle to relate to and connect with the communities they serve. In every walk of life, we have allowed ourselves to be pushed into self-defining cocoons from which it is difficult to break out." Lovegrove's mosaic principle builds from the premise that to succeed in an ever-changing and complex environment, diverse experiences will lead to a more rewarding and fulfilling life.

We are happy to let Townes-Whitley's and Gips's experiences speak on Lovegrove's behalf. The "find the diagonal" approach is also akin to David Epstein's "range" theory, which suggests that the real challenge everyone faces is in "how to maintain the benefits of breadth, diverse experience, interdisciplinary thinking, and delayed concentration in a world that increasingly incentivizes, even demands, hyper-specialization." Epstein compellingly argues that "[b]readth of training predicts breadth of transfer. That is, the more contexts in which something is learned, the more the learner creates abstract models, and the less they rely on any particular example. Learners become better at applying their knowledge to a situation they've never seen before, which is the essence of creativity."[9] The "outliers" approach is designed to push people into silos and reward those who have developed an area-specific skill set and knowledge base. But this is not helping people to thrive in an increasingly uncertain world.

Complex problems and a world growing more uncertain create serious concerns for our future. By building a career along the diagonal, and accumulating diverse skills and experiences, we can position ourselves to address these challenges head-on.

MONDAYS NOT FRIDAYS

"I grew up in the lower middle class in Northeast Ohio, right outside of Akron," says Michael Morell about his humble beginnings. He shares, "My father was a blue-collar auto worker and my mother was a homemaker, and I was the first one in our family to go to college. While I knew that I wanted to go to college, I wasn't entirely sure what I wanted to do with my life. I thought about a career in law, and that sounded interesting to me, so I decided to major in political science. And interestingly enough, one of the required classes was economics, which I took in my very first semester. And I fell in love. So much so that I changed my major. I just thought that economics explained so much—not just about the economy, but pretty much everything else, including human behavior.

"Coming into my senior year, I began applying all over the private sector. But one of my professors from Taiwan encouraged me to apply to the CIA, and so I did, and got an interview request. Not really knowing much about the agency or even having been to Washington, DC, before, to me it was a chance to see the capital more than anything else. But in those two days of interviews, it really changed my life. The first thing that I was absolutely blown away by was the mission of the place—to protect the country by finding out what is going on in the world. And to, as objectively as possible, figure out and present that to decision makers. Even if your message is one that they do not want to hear. Even if your message is one that undermines the policy choices they have made, or makes life difficult for them politically. That really resonated with me, speaking truth to power. The second thing that blew me away was what they were able to share with me with in regard to the organization's capabilities. There's a lot they couldn't share with me, obviously, but what they could, kind of blew me away. And the thing that blew me away the most was the quality of the people I was talking to. These were incredibly smart and nice people. I felt a sense of family, a sense of commitment to the mission, and commitment to the nation.

"And so, I took the job," says Morell. He adds, "And since I said yes, I never looked back. I spent thirty-three years there. And I'll tell you. Honestly, there was not a single day I did not want to go to work. And through thirty-three years, because the work was so intellectually interesting and intellectually challenging, and not to mention critically important to the nation, I found myself looking forward to Mondays, not Fridays. It's been eight years since I left and I still miss it."

While Morell is a shining example of finding purpose in the government's mission by actually going to work for the government, you don't necessarily have to remain in public service to find purpose in mission and support it.

Chris Lynch, the CEO and cofounder of Rebellion Defense, has found purpose in working for the government's mission. Lynch, a serial entrepreneur from Seattle, began his career as a development manager at Microsoft before launching venture-backed startups such as Thoughtful.co, Flypaper, and KCBMedia. Ultimately, Lynch entered the government, working for both the United States Digital Service (USDS) and the Defense Digital Service, and went on to find public-sector inspiration for his private-sector entrepreneurial skill set.

"Growing up on the West Coast, and being an entrepreneur, I was never really exposed much to the government. I did not ever think that I would work for the government—it seemed slow and static. But when the opportunity arose, and I really got to know about the USDS and what it was trying to do, I was intrigued. The agency was essentially trying to make the federal government more technology-friendly while transforming the digital services they provide. This was right up my alley. And I saw this as a chance to apply my skill set to something larger, to do a tour of civic service. And what I learned out of it was that the government is a group of people trying to provide essential services to families. The government had a critical mission. And working toward that mission, I felt like I was doing something bigger than I had ever done before. I felt like I was trying to do the greatest good for the greatest number of people in the greatest need," Lynch says. He goes on to describe the rest of his time in government. "And then I became founding director at Defense Digital Service, where I really began to see how transformative the government's mission could be. We began launching these high-impact programs, including the Joint Enterprise Defense Infrastructure Cloud and Hack the Pentagon. And we took on some of the Department of Defense's most critical technology challenges for the warfighter. It was an amazing experience."

After working for the federal government for seven years, Lynch decided to go back into the private sector as an entrepreneur. This time, Lynch was armed with purpose, and that purpose was the mission of government. He recalls, "I got together with Nicole [Camarillo] and Oliver [Lewis] and we began to discuss this idea of how we can support the government's mission in a commercial manner that drew more technologists into the mission. And we arrived at this idea of Rebellion Defense." Lynch's journey is special in that it shows how a stint in government gave him the purpose and meaning to pursue the government's mission in the private sector. When pressed for advice for people thinking about how to find purpose in their work, Lynch says, "I never thought I would end up taking the path I did. But I am glad that I did. And I hope that people can see my story and decide to also get involved. Without more people buying into this mission, we are heading down a dangerous path. Get involved. Make the world you want to see."

Michael Morell and Chris Lynch show us how purpose, passion, and proficiency work together in building a successful career in the Venture Meets Mission ecosystem. There are important takeaways from their experiences. First is —about finding meaning in pursuing the mission of the government. Second is the passion to make a difference. Both Morell and Lynch have an excitement in their careers that turns work into pleasure. Third is technical expertise and bringing skills and experiences from one domain to the other. The perceived dichotomy between government work and entrepreneurial undertakings has proved to be false. Morell and Lynch built careers that chased a passion and not a salary. And it is this passion for mission that will help rebuild trust in society.

Their advice also mirrors the Japanese concept *Ikigai*, which refers to something that gives a person a sense of purpose or a reason for living. Search for a career that combines your skill set, your personal desires, society's well-being, and your financial drive.[10] For an example of how this unfolds for professionals, think of Jiro Ono, a famous Japanese chef who has spent seventy years perfecting sushi while becoming a strong vocal advocate for reducing the adverse effects of overfishing and for regenerating the environment.[11] So, what steps can you take to help find your *Ikigai*? Ask yourself these questions:

- What am I good at doing? **(SKILL)**

- What do I love doing? **(PASSION)**

- What will others pay me to do? **(PROFIT)**

- What will benefit the world? **(MEANING)**

The *Ikigai* framework is ideal for constructing mission-driven entrepreneurial ventures, which combine passion, purpose, and profit in partnership with organizations that are in pursuit of a mission.

The expert accounts in this chapter highlight the resolve to act in the Venture Meets Mission ecosystem. Each professional experience aided in these individuals' ability to navigate and succeed. Throughout this book, we remarked upon the need to break down the silos that alienate the various actors in the ecosystem. What does this mean? First, this means leading at the intersection like Nate Fick, and understanding that all players in this ecosystem have a similar purpose—a larger mission. Also, we need to create a revolving door in academic institutions that introduces students and academics to the different roles in the ecosystem. Second, we need to go against the social forces of conformance. We observe how students confront these forces with intentionality and make their way into ventures, investing, and government. Third, we need to break down the structural funneling forces and build institutional permeability. We encourage institutions to experiment with finding ways to guide students into the Venture Meets Mission ecosystem. Fourth, we need to reimagine our careers along the diagonal. Toni Townes-Whitley and Don Gips are perfect examples of those who constructed both depth and breadth in their careers, and of developing skills to thrive in an array of settings and contexts. Finally, the individual stories discussed the importance of mission, but to make a change, we must follow in the footsteps of those who found happiness in their work. Mission, more than any other factor, will be the driving force of positive societal change. Ultimately, it is when talent rises to meet this mission that we will begin to rebuild trust and forge a better world.

Seven

THE VIRTUOUS CYCLE

Aligning People, Purpose, and Profit
to Create the Future We Want

"My basic optimism about climate change comes from my belief in innovation....It's our power to invent that makes me hopeful....More than anything, we will succeed because of the network of partners we bring to this effort. The investors, philanthropists, corporate and policy leaders who are a part of the ecosystem. It will take all of us to compel the major market changes we need to create the future we want for the world."

—BILL GATES[1]

Trust is the bedrock of all collaboration. We have a generational opportunity to create the future we want by rebuilding that trust between government, venture, and civil society. Civil society has bounced back from the pandemic with an appetite for mission-driven work but is confronting barriers to action. Ventures have emerged as a willing, yet unguided and uncoordinated force for societal impact. Governments remain politically polarized and limited in their ability to solve society's most pressing challenges. For these groups to work together to solve societal problems, trust becomes the bedrock of their collaboration and the enabler of impact. Trust in the government can rally these groups behind a guiding mission; trust in business can facilitate more effective trisectoral collaborations; and trust in civil society can bring talented changemakers into mission-driven work. We need trust to bring us together to meet society's most pressing problems head-on.

Each chapter in the book has followed this path to rebuilding trust, noting the key hurdles and opportunities in it, and the actions we can take to remedy the fraying societal fabric. Chapter 2 emphasized the importance of elevating common (mission) objectives and harmonizing the values of entrepreneurs and the government. Chapter 3 identified the design challenges of government-venture arrangements, which are markedly different from traditional conceptualizations of public-private partnerships. The ensuing chapters then built from these design challenges as ways that government, venture, and civil society can bridge their differences and rebuild trust. Chapter 4 highlighted actions that entrepreneurs can take to address complexities of working with government. The discussion focused on the importance of being able to create public value, a signal of ventures' commitment to mission. Then, Chapter 5 reviewed the bridging actions that the government can take to rebuild much needed trust in this institution. Through various methods of engagement with ventures, the government can enable, orchestrate, and mobilize the Venture Meets Mission ecosystem. In Chapter 6 the focus shifted to civil society. A return to discussions on the intention-action barriers and on the design challenges of government-venture arrangements highlighted the importance of intersectionality, intentionality, and nonlinearity in careers. Exemplar careers reveal how individual citizens can embrace the Venture Meets Mission ecosystem. The strategies and practices of each participant in the ecosystem are visually summarized in Figure 7.1.

We must also acknowledge how the roles of ventures and the government have adapted over time. No longer are governments acting as a vertically integrated unit behind innovation as we saw during the 1960s space race, when the U.S. government brought the vision, the capital, and the workforce together for "moonshot" programs like the Mercury, Gemini, and Apollo space programs. Today, innovation occurs horizontally. While the government's role is still to provide that same vision and capital—it needs to use its scale and influence to align and incentivize a more developed private capital and talent ecosystem for solving current "moonshots." Innovative work around mission is truly becoming an ecosystem (Figure 7.2).

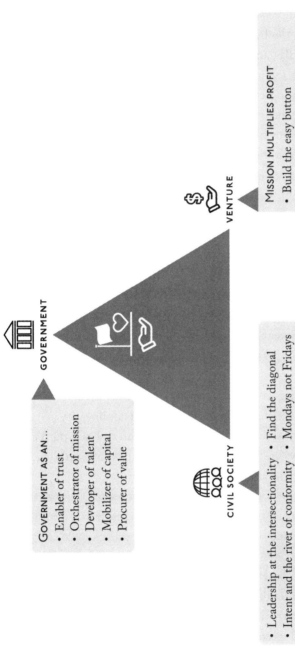

GOVERNMENT

GOVERNMENT AS AN...
- Enabler of trust
- Orchestrator of mission
- Developer of talent
- Mobilizer of capital
- Procurer of value

VENTURE

MISSION MULTIPLIES PROFIT
- Build the easy button
- Customize for the unknown
- Learn the language of government
- Build for the long haul

CIVIL SOCIETY

- Leadership at the intersectionality
- Intent and the river of conformity
- Funneling
- Find the diagonal
- Mondays not Fridays

FIGURE 7.1. Rebuilding Trust in the Venture Meets Mission Ecosystem. Source: Authors.

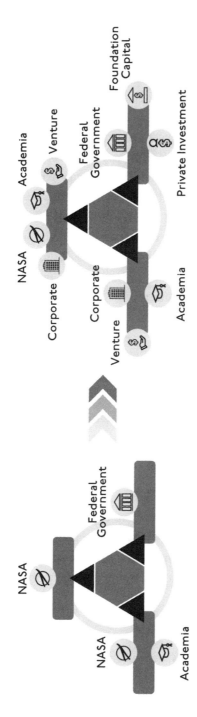

FIGURE 7.2. United States Government Innovation Ecosystem—Space. Source: Authors.

Liberal democracies provide the ideal foundation for this ecosystem to thrive. The "superpower" of liberal democracies has historically been the ability to foster an environment of creative innovation—educating the best minds and directing creative energy to develop new industries for fueling economic growth and higher quality of life. Using this power of innovation, humankind has made transformative progress. Life expectancy in the United States is now 78.8 years, as compared to 47.3 years in 1900.[2] Cancer death rates have fallen 32 percent from 1991.[3] Globally, we have seen undernourishment in developing countries decrease by 22 percent from 1970.[4] Child mortality worldwide fell from 19 percent in 1960 to just below 4 percent in 2017.[5]

More important, the ecosystem approach will help promote liberal democracy. As stated by the U.S. White House Office of Science and Technology in their International Grand Challenges on Democracy-Affirming Technologies for the Summit for Democracy,[6] innovation and technological breakthrough are deeply tied to democratic values, including privacy, freedom of expression, access to information, transparency, fairness, inclusion, and equity. It is our responsibility and obligation as innovators to ensure that the ideals of liberal democracy are not being taken for granted when pursuing mission through venture. We must ensure that democratic values are preserved and advanced through these breakthroughs.

However, using the ideals of a liberal democracy and the power of ventures to solve society's biggest problems can only happen if we construct an aligned and intentioned vision for the future around the three Ps: People, Purpose, and Profit. We can capitalize on the diversity of our strengths and the unity of our mission to create for-profit ventures that focus on developing sustainable and scalable solutions. What does a thriving Venture Meets Mission ecosystem, which embraces the ideals of a liberal democracy, look like?

Our collective actions, built upon shared mission and values, are critical for rebuilding trust to create the future we want. In the Venture Meets Mission ecosystem, ventures become the driver of mission through meaningful innovation and change. The private sector becomes an ally in public value creation while debunking the dichotomy myth

FIGURE 7.3. The Virtuous Cycle of the Venture Meets Mission Ecosystem. Source: Authors.

between profit and purpose. The government becomes an enabler, orchestrator, and mobilizer of mission-driven groups around collective sustainability. With its vast resources and regulatory levers, the government offers a platform by which ventures can scale their societal and commercial impact. People express their passion for mission while serving as bridges of trust among the participants in the ecosystem. As a result, the walls that divide us slowly crumble as we are able to bridge the distance between us with trust. An ecosystem implies that all actors—public, private, academic, nonprofits and individual citizens—are working together and using their unique skills and strengths to drive positive change. And, as momentum builds around the Venture Meets Mission ecosystem, it results in a self-reinforcing, virtuous cycle (Figure 7.3). The following sections explore each of these self-reinforcing elements of a virtuous ecosystem.

EMERGING SECTORS, NEW OPPORTUNITIES

Just as problems abound, opportunities exist within to create a desirable future state of the world. Much of the global discourse on societal problems has adopted the language of "grand challenges" or "sustainable development goals." For citizens, communities, and environment, these societal challenges frame the monumental task ahead. But for the innovative, they also present a massive market opportunity. We see sizeable markets, attractive growth rates, and enabling conditions for ventures to enter markets and develop sizable businesses across mission-focused sectors, ranging from space to cybersecurity, and energy to education, and climate to health care. Each of these sectors ranges from $20 billion to $200 billion in market size, with expected growth rates as 10 to 20 percent over the next ten years.

In biomanufacturing, for example, an industry estimated at nearly $20 billion in market size, with an expected annual growth of 10 percent over the next ten years, recently founded companies such as EQRx and Antios Therapeutics have received billions in funding and are making meaningful strides in promoting a mission to make biotechnologies safer, more efficient, and more effective.[7] Similarly, entrants such as Impossible Foods, Good Catch, and Mosa Meat are tackling issues of food sustainability and environmental impact by creating alternatives to traditional meat and seafood.[8] Despite challenges, mission-driven ventures are identifying valuable market opportunities, sprouting and growing.

Climate and food industries are greater than $400 billion in market size and projected to have a 10 percent annual growth rate over the next ten years. Companies such as Commonwealth Fusion Systems have reached billion-dollar valuations by working toward making energy cleaner and safer to store,[9] with the company recently raising $1.8 billion in a 2021 Series B round of funding.[10] What is fascinating is how this venture grew—beginning as a government-funded research project in the MIT Plasma Science and Fusion Center. After eventually running out of government funding, the group, which was aiming to build a compact fusion reactor based on the ARC tokamak power plant concept, decided to pursue philanthropic capital to keep afloat. However, they quickly realized philanthropic funds would not enable them to scale and that they would need to raise for-profit funds in order to be successful, garnering investments from Bill Gates's Breakthrough Energy Ventures, Singapore's Temasek Holdings, Norway's Equinor, and Devonshire Investors.[11]

Biotechnology is another area budding with innovation and breakthroughs. One biotech company, founded in 2009 by scientists from Massachusetts Institute of Technology, is Ginkgo Bioworks.[12] Using grants from the National Science Foundation, DARPA, and the Department of Health and Human Services, Ginkgo Bioworks invested in a long-term vision for synthetic biology by developing a specialized capacity of using genetic engineering to produce bacteria with industrial applications.[13] It did so by innovating the traditional method of engaging in organism engineering. Traditionally, companies searched for genetic DNA sequences from nature to perform particular functions and worked to scale manufacturing when they had the right sequencing of strains. In contrast, Ginkgo Bioworks developed organisms specific to the agriculture, food, health care, and energy sectors, and built specialized foundries to optimize these strains. Their codebase of engineered strains was able to create network effects, as they did not need to code new applications from scratch and could start from their knowledge and relationships among the different strains. In 2021, Ginkgo Bioworks' innovative model led the company to go public at a $17.5 billion valuation.[14]

Digitization also opens the door to more opportunities in public-purpose technologies. StateUp 21, an advisory firm that aggregates and disseminates knowledge and ideas about public-purpose technologies through research, data, and upskilling, defined public-purpose technology as "a technology that addresses big public needs, and the public policies, organizations, cultures, investments and business models around it."[15] It also highlights core areas in which technology can be used to address public problems, as displayed in Figure 7.4.

Waves of digital innovations are opening new doors. We are seeing examples of how data enables innovation and breakthroughs in the public sector. For example, the education sector is ripe for data-driven innovation. Online learning, or blended learning environments of tra-

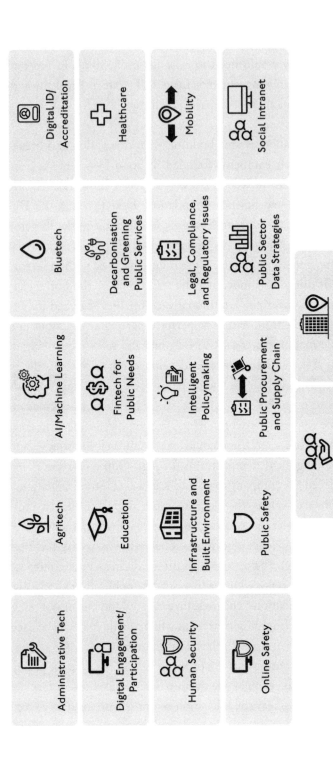

FIGURE 7.4. StateUp 21's Twenty-Two Core Problem Areas. Source: StateUp 21—Data Driven Insights into Global Purpose Tech.

ditional and digital instruction, has been identified as an area in which disruptive innovation can not only break the cycle of traditional learning models but also open up education to be more accessible, inclusive, and customizable. Coursera, a massive open online course provider founded in 2012 by Stanford University professors, works with organizations to offer online classes, certifications, and degrees. Coursera has partnered with businesses through corporate e-learning, and governments, and earns revenue through selling certificates that verify successful completion of courses. However, the company subsidizes paid programs if the learner has a financial need, and its courses can also be accessed online for free without the paid certificate. Coursera, offering over five thousand courses and working with over two hundred universities and companies, went public in 2021 with a valuation of over $4 billion. Coursera is not alone. The education and skills learning sector now has several worthy competitors, including EdX, PluralSight, Linkedin Learning, Udacity, Cloud Academy, Udemy, and SmartUp, that offer compelling alternatives to traditional classroom learning models.

And these opportunities are particularly present in emerging markets. Digitization, for example, opened the door for entrepreneur David Vélez to target inefficiencies in the Brazilian banking system. Looking at Brazil's banks, Vélez observed notoriously high fees and poor service, and a general obliviousness to new technologies. With the introduction of broadband internet and smartphones, Vélez started Nubank, with the goal of disrupting existing models of banking with digital services. With the support of both early stage and growth-stage venture investors such as U.S. private tech investor Sequoia Capital and fintech investor QED, in just eight years Nubank was able to grow to have nearly $1 billion in revenue.[16]

In the coming years, emerging technologies such as artificial intelligence, cloud computing, the internet of things, cyberwarfare, and "big data" will present new opportunities and magnify each other's impact. For example, digital sustainability offers a new technological framework for ventures to mitigate climate change and work alongside government and local communities.[17] For ventures, the public sector will be a critical market in which their innovations can lower the costs of government operations while providing more profitable, efficient, and effective solutions.

The geographic diversification of mission-driven ventures is something that cannot be taken lightly. No longer are the new ventures concentrating only in Silicon Valley, New York City, and Boston, the traditional entrepreneurial hubs in the United States. Instead, mission focus is leading to geographic diversity, and that is because diversity is a key feature in the pursuit of mission outcomes. With the backdrop of liberal democracy, a general partner of a leading venture capital firm argues, "We are seeing incredible diversity at all levels where mission is being pursued because of how applied technologies are being developed. Many ventures are being founded in locations where the problems are most central and the workforce is the most specialized. Ventures in the same sector are rising in different places across the country. And this is because there's diversity in the use of these products that targets particularities in problems."

Geographic diversity of mission-driven ventures can tap into a digital workforce that may otherwise feel left behind in the broader digital revolution. This workforce brings the necessary domain expertise (related to food, energy, manufacturing, and so on), which can then be augmented with a digital workforce that is upskilled and trained locally or connected remotely. These ventures have the potential to change the economic trajectory of their local community with employment opportunities. These emerging sectors can reenergize the local economies in noncoastal urban centers of the United States.

Examples include Flock Safety, described in Chapter 4, which has built a public safety operating system for businesses, neighborhoods, and law enforcement agencies located in Atlanta. Having started by offering solutions to local neighborhood safety problems, Flock was eventually able to show product value to the public sector, and expand into new markets and products. Footprint is another venture, founded in Gilbert, Arizona, which designs, develops, and manufactures plant-based fiber solutions to plastic-based consumer packaged goods. One notable example of the value of their product can be seen in their partnership work with Gillette Labs (owned by Proctor & Gamble), where they were able to create 100 percent plastic-free and recyclable packaging. Venture funds, such as Revolution's Rise of the Rest Seed Fund, see this as an opportunity and invest catalytic capital in early stage companies by recognizing that compelling investment propositions will emerge from startups in cities all across the United States. The fund is backed by iconic entrepreneurs and investors including Steve Case, cofounder of America Online, who serves as chairman and CEO of Revolution, and Ted Leonsis, chairman and CEO of Monumental Sports and cofounder of Revolution Growth.[18]

Finally, new opportunities are emerging as some traditional nonprofit founders are realizing that to have scalable impact, they must redefine themselves as for-profit ventures to attract the requisite capital and talent, and go from "doing good work" to "transforming industries." One such example is Iora Health, a health care company that redesigned primary care to allow patients to better manage their health and navigate the health care system.[19] With an idea to tackle the existing barriers and excuses that linger in the health care system, Dr. Rushika Fernandopulle cofounded Iora Health in the Boston Area in 2010.[20]

"When I set out to build an organization to transform primary care, I initially thought that as a mission-driven organization, we needed to be a nonprofit," says Fernandopulle. "So I went to all the usual nonprofit funders and I learned quickly that they were willing to fund studying the problem, but not actually building solutions. I realized that it would take a lot of work to raise tens of thousands of dollars, and I needed a lot more (it turned out we raised over $350 million), and that I needed sustained funding over a decade (really took over eighteen years), and nonprofit funders unfortunately would move on to the next priority too soon even if Iora was successful. So, eventually, I decided it was best to harness capitalism to fund social change by being a for-profit...and it worked." Iora focused on patients over the age of sixty-five years who do not have easy access to the health care system, and linked each patient with a personal physician and/or health coach. The company used technology to keep the patient and provider in close contact, whether by email, text, or video, in addition to the traditional in-office visits. To keep patients on track with their health goals, it also provided educational offerings and group sessions.[21] Iora was able to use their private-sector capabilities to solve a key public-sector problem. The company's market success led One Medical to acquire it for $2.1 billion in 2021.[22]

Attractive markets and societal needs are increasingly leading to the creation of mission-driven ventures, where a tighter coupling between purpose and profit is a winning proposition.

SUCCESS INSPIRES MORE VENTURES

Everyone loves a success story, whether it be the scrappy underdog boxer from south Philadelphia, the rejected British novelist who authored one of the best-selling book series of all time about a wizard and his friends, or the entrepreneur who turned a garage office into a multibillion-dollar software enterprise. Success stories are timeless representations of an individual's perilous climb to the top, and they inspire and encourage us to follow previously uncharted paths. As humans we are wired to pay attention to stories. In the Venture Meets Mission ecosystem, success stories are catalysts. They provide broader visibility to the attractiveness of the market and help in developing a diaspora of entrepreneurs who know the playbook for creating new ventures, recruiting top talent, and attracting institutional capital.

Many of today's leading tech corporations were in some way, shape, or form molded by mission-focused federal government dollars. But far too often these enterprises' government roots are overshadowed by a charismatic leader or the performance of their ticker on Wall Street. As a result, what was once a small venture aided by the government is now a championed success story of a relentless and individualistic entrepreneur. But the Venture Meets Mission success stories will not be like those. As the policy pendulum swings back toward creating and innovating markets in light of the grand challenges of society, entrepreneurs and their new ventures are a driving force behind this change. And they must be championed as the partners of government that they are.

Palantir Technologies embodies one such example of a success story in the Venture Meets Mission ecosystem. This public software company founded in 2003 and headquartered in Denver, Colorado, has become one of the biggest names in the Intelligence Community. Peter Thiel, one of the cofounders of Palantir and a former cofounder of PayPal, created it as a "mission-oriented company" that would apply software similar to PayPal's fraud recognition systems to "reduce terrorism while preserving civil liberties."[23] After an initial struggle, the company received $2 million from In-Q-Tel and $30 million from Founders Fund, a VC firm which has invested in companies such as Airbnb, Facebook, and SpaceX. Palantir developed technology by recruiting analysts from intelligence agencies through pilot programs that were facilitated by In-Q-Tel. In contrast to using artificial intelligence alone, Palantir constructed a business model that used human analysts to explore data from an array of sources, called human-computer symbiosis.

Palantir experienced unprecedented growth as it launched projects such as Gotham, a data integration and network visualization platform that has been used by counterterrorism analysts in the Intelligence Community and DoD, and Foundry, a platform for data-driven decision making and situational intelligence that has been used by Pacific Gas and Electric, a major utility company that services over sixteen million people in California, to better inform decisions about wildfires and power grid resiliency. Their ability to create products that satisfy both the public- and private-sector needs has made the company's valuation skyrocket from $9 billion in 2014 to $41 billion in 2019.[24] In a market ruled by major defense contractors such as Raytheon and Lockheed Martin, Palantir was able to successfully develop government-facing technologies and penetrate this market. Even more impressive was their concurrent achievement of commercializing their products successfully. Palantir's mission led not only to the development of technological wizardry that supports the initiatives of the U.S. government in regard to national security, but also the creation of one of Silicon Valley's biggest unicorns.

Palantir's story has inspired many others. Trae Stephens is one such example of someone who learned from Palantir's success to pursue a mission-driven venture. Stephens, as mentioned earlier a partner at Founders Fund, as well as a former early employee at Palantir Technologies and a Georgetown University alumnus, cofounded Anduril Industries, a defense company focused on autonomous systems. This mission-driven spinoff has seen tremendous success, with an estimated valuation of around $7 billion.[25] There are also other companies founded by Palantir alumni that have seen early success in pursuing mission-driven work. They include Israeli biotech startup Immunai, a multidisciplinary team of immunologists, engineers, drug developers, computer scientists, and entrepreneurs focused on bringing breakthrough medicines to patients, which has raised nearly $300 million at a valuation of just over $1 billion.[26] Another one is Bravo Sierra, a unique care company built for active military personnel that has raised nearly $20 million in funding.[27] Palantir's success in building a company pursuing mission has clearly inspired their employees to follow a similar pattern of venturing.

Bonnie Tom, senior executive at Palantir, sees how Palantir experience has transformed alumni's future careers trajectories, with many wanting to remain in the mission space. What has she seen people do post-Palantir? "We have seen a number of former employees start mission-oriented companies, like Sage, a company tackling the problems of modern aging in the Medicare system, and Nira, a company focused on energy prospecting and transmission capacity. Many others join mission-oriented companies because they believe that former Palantir-founded companies have pieces of the culture that they enjoy. Quite a few go into mission-focused venture investing and index ventures. A good number of people go back to school in public policy or to law school. But perhaps most interesting is the number of people who go into government work. We even had a former engineer run for political office and win a New York Assembly seat." Clearly, Palantir's success is fueling more people to pursue mission-driven careers.

You may have heard of the largest private mission-driven company, Space Exploration Technologies (SpaceX), a commercial space company founded in 2002 in El Segundo, California. The company started with an objective to decrease the cost and improve the reliability of access to space. But this wasn't always possible. While NASA had a long history of working with contractors, the federal government had exclusive rights to launch spacecraft and satellites through their civilian space arm until the mid-1980s. With the winding down of the Cold War and the highs of the space race, President Reagan signed the Commercial Space Launch Act of 1984 to facilitate the private enterprise of the commercialization of space and space technology.[28] No longer were the commercial satellite launches in the United States restricted by federal regulation to NASA's space shuttle. But we did not see a dominant commercial participant emerge in the commercial launch market until SpaceX in the late 2010s. SpaceX achieved significant cost savings through rocket reusability, launch vehicle reliability and simplicity, and vertical integration, besides using economies of scale. By 2018, it had captured over 60 percent of the global launch market share. Their Dragon, Falcon, and Starship rockets are capable of launching commercial payloads and astronauts into near earth orbit and beyond, and the company has stated its next major objective is to send a crewed spacecraft to Mars.

Through twenty years of operation, SpaceX has over twelve thousand employees and has become the most valuable startup in the United States at a $125 billion valuation. While the success of SpaceX can certainly be attributed to business-savvy founder Elon Musk and the rest of the leadership team, it would be ignorant to overlook the role of the mission focus of the company. SpaceX showed not only a commitment to the government's mission of space exploration, but also the ability to create public value with their operations by lowering the costs of reaching space. For example, when NASA investigated SpaceX's estimate of $300 million as the cost of developing the Falcon 9, they found that their own attempts to develop the spacecraft would cost $4 billion.[29] This was largely due to SpaceX's ability to disrupt the processes of legacy players' relationship with the government. SpaceX took advantage of the 2006 Commercial Orbital Transportation System (COTS) program, which subsidized the development of private launch vehicles for resupply missions to the International Space Station (ISS). Legacy players such as Boeing and Lockheed Martin had long argued in favor of the cost-plus contracts in the industry, as companies were required to make heavy up-front R&D expenditures on products that had limited and uncertain commercial viability. SpaceX, like other nascent launch companies, took advantage of the COTS as a cost-sharing program that paid fixed amounts for achieving certain milestones. Over 2006 to 2018, SpaceX conducted sixty-eight successful launches and received over $5.2 billion from NASA.[30] Moreover, most of this was on the back of success-contingent financing.

SpaceX continues to demonstrate how to blend commercial products and services with public-purpose technologies. Building from their capabilities developed in launch services, SpaceX has been identifying a number of commercial markets. In May 2019, SpaceX launched sixty satellites into low earth orbit, the first of a twelve-thousand to forty-two-thousand satellite internet constellation, Starlink, to provide commercial internet service to rural communities and populations with low connectivity. The next commercial market it is targeting is space tourism. By 2030, it is estimated that space tourism could be worth $3 billion, and could eventually reach an annual market of $20 billion.[31] Finally, SpaceX continues to grow their small satellite launch market for both the public and private sectors. For example, in June 2022, SpaceX launched Germany's SARah 1 radar reconnaissance satellite into polar orbit as well as the Globalstar FM15 satellite, which provides voice and data services to phone users around the world.[32] As the company further develops its launch capabilities and achieves even greater economies of scale, the prices for its commercial and public services will continue to decrease. Each of these products and services support the company's goal of developing its capabilities to put humans in Mars.

And the success of SpaceX in the commercial space market has spawned a number of unicorns, including Axiom Space. In 2022, the company reached over $2 billion in customer contracts, launched four astronauts to the ISS this year—the only time in history that a private company has sent a crew to the ISS— and installed the first Amazon web services cloud server on the ISS.[33] Most recently, Axiom won a $3.5 billion space suit development contract from NASA to create the space suits that will be used in the Artemis missions to the moon. Clearly, the success of SpaceX has inspired new entrepreneurs to enter the commercial space market.

These are just a few examples of breakout companies that have emerged in the Venture Meets Mission ecosystem. These companies demonstrate the tight coupling between the mission driving the company, their ability to create substantial profits, and the positive societal impact of their scaled operations. Their success also serves as a flywheel for their alumni to go start their own mission-driven ventures. This diaspora of successful entrepreneurs have a playbook on how to combine profit and purpose and attract top people in partnership with government.

But success stories aren't just limited to ventures. Such stories that inspire impact are also seen in both nonprofits and government work. José Andrés' World Central Kitchen saw firsthand the power of a story on the border of Poland and Ukraine. As millions of Ukrainian citizens fled west to escape the missile attacks in the central and eastern parts of the country, José and Nate Mook began mobilizing World Central Kitchen's game plan to respond to the impending food crisis. "Our time in Ukraine has only underscored what we already knew following what we did in Puerto Rico and dozens of disasters since, and that is that the importance of what we do lies in our ability to tell stories," says Mook. "Storytelling creates a groundswell of interest and a groundswell of caring, from the public, from governments, from businesses. When World Central Kitchen are able to get our narrative out there, of what we are trying to do, what we are doing, we are able to really make a difference. We can become the promoter of change in policy, we can mobilize resources in ways unimaginable, and we can inspire other people to fulfill their sense of mission. Our stories are genuine, they're real."

In the Venture Meets Mission ecosystem, success exists. And it is a duty to promote it, especially in academic institutions so that students are made aware of the opportunities that exist across the ecosystem. As students, parents, and professionals get exposed to these successes, they become catalysts for more engagement with work around mission. Success in ventures supporting mission show uncertain entrepreneurs and risk-averse private-sector employees that mission-driven ventures are possible and rewarding. These stories communicate and perpetuate the importance of pursuing work in the Venture Meets Mission ecosystem. The companies that served the government twenty-five years ago (the "last supper" defense companies), look a lot different than the companies serving the government today (the hybrid tech companies), many of whom did not exist twenty-five years ago—such as Amazon Web Services, Google, Palantir, and SpaceX. And twenty-five years from now, there will be new giants serving this space.

CAPITAL FOLLOWS SUCCESS

Success stories don't just inspire, they also attract capital. They create much-needed momentum, which means a swell of capital from a number of sources such as the government, private investors, and family offices.

The government's recent commitment to innovation spells well for mission-driven ventures. In 2021 and 2022, the U.S. House and Senate worked together, with bipartisan support, to pass the America COMPETES Act, which has important implications for the Venture Meets Mission ecosystem. This bill was passed to fund domestic semiconductor chip manufacturing, strengthen the supply chain to make more goods in America, increase scientific research and development funding, revive expired trade programs, and reorient the international posture of the United States toward competition with China.[34] The CHIPS and Science Act of 2022 will transform and revitalize America's domestic manufacturing base while tackling uneven distributions of economic benefits. In addition, the bill contains the Rebuilding Economies and Creating Opportunities for More People to Excel pilot grant program to form and implement economic development strategies in distressed labor markets and communities to boost long-term economic growth and create lasting, quality jobs. This is underpinned by a larger push in the bill to promote pathways to equitable and sustainable career pathways in STEM, while making training and education more accessible and affordable.[35]

The 2023 budget also created headlines for having the most substantial investment in science and technology in history, with spending levels for basic and applied research topping $100 billion and spending for total federal research and development topping $200 billion.[36] This budget has a clearly stated purpose of driving breakthroughs through transformative and high-risk research approaches to tackling societal challenges. Some of the "priority areas" in which government funding will be invested include energy infrastructure, STEM workforce development, climate tech, deep tech, and national security. In addition, a substantial amount of capital is earmarked for energy security and climate change in the Inflation Reduction Act. This budget reconciliation bill will put the United States on a path to roughly 40 percent emissions reduction by 2030, representing the single biggest climate investment in U.S. history.[37]

We are also seeing global governmental initiatives aimed at stimulating innovations toward grand challenges. For instance, in 2021, the NIH's National Cancer Institute and Cancer Research in UK launched the Cancer Grand Challenges, which provides multiple rounds of funding for teams whose novel ideas offer the greatest potential to improve outcomes for people affected by cancer. Grand Challenges Canada has supported a pipeline of over fourteen hundred innovations in ninety-four countries. The group estimates that these innovations have the potential to save up to two million lives and improve up to sixty-four million lives by 2030. Singapore's Temasek Holdings committed $3.6 billion to launch its GenZero investment platform aimed at accelerating decarbonization, the largest such investment in the technology by any state actor.[38]

Multilateral alliances such as NATO have joined in supporting mission-driven ventures, launching an innovation fund and defense innovation accelerator initiative to remain technologically ahead of Russia and China. In June 2022, NATO announced that the alliance would invest $1 billion dollars in startups across twenty-two nations over fifteen years. This fund complements the recent initiative of NATO, the Defense Innovation Accelerator for the North Atlantic (DIANA). NATO Secretary General Jens Stoltenberg says, "DIANA will bring defense personnel together with the Alliance's best and brightest startups, scientific researchers, and technology companies to solve critical defense and security challenges." He adds, "Working with the private sector and academia, Allies will ensure that we can harness the best of new technology for transatlantic security."[39] Coupled with the NATO

Innovation Fund, it is quite clear that venture innovations sit at the core of the DIANA ecosystem.

While federal investments are a great signal for aligning technology efforts around areas of national importance, they must connect the research technology with talent and capital that is more accustomed to bringing breakthrough technologies to market. For instance, programs such as NobleReach Emerge have a unique opportunity to create a vibrant ecosystem of partners, one that can accelerate entrepreneurial technology and talent mapping needed to seed an aligned national innovation pipeline by attracting private risk-taking capital. While returns are privatized, it is fair to ask whether the agency should be taking a minority ownership for its grant so that it can participate in the upside as well.

And as these public investments clearly spur early stage research innovation, the government can use its role as a market-shaping purchaser for later-stage technology to incentivize risk capital of the venture ecosystem. As discussed in Chapter 5, the federal government uses the U.S. International Development Finance Corporation (DFC) internationally to mobilize private capital in regions where it is difficult to attract capital, while reducing risk with first loss provisions. Similarly, the United States could benefit from a domestic-focused DFC equivalent that mobilizes private-capital investments in sectors that need more capital inflow. With government financing contingent on successes, such as that of SpaceX with the creation of the commercial space market and that of Moderna and Pfizer with the COVID-19 vaccine, private-sector participation can promote more efficient capital mobilization.

In the government's role as a purchaser, it can use its unique purchasing power to drive demand for next-generation technologies, and hence incentivize private capital to invest in the space. For example, to grow the domestic semiconductor industry market, if the government took a first 10 to 20 percent loss on chip investments or provided purchase orders for contracts, it would get a force multiplier on its initial funding by attracting private capital—not to mention the top talent that will likely flow in with this investment. In the Venture Meets Mission ecosystem, the government's role should be to establish the ambition of the goal and mobilize capital behind today's "moonshots."

But government agencies aren't the only groups catalyzing the Venture Meets Mission ecosystem with capital. In fact, for the larger part of the last seventy years, the majority of investment in research and development has come from business and the private sector. In 2019, around 71 percent of all research and development was provided by the private sector.[40] And it appears that the pandemic is accelerating investments in mission-driven ventures. Advisory firm StateUp found that annual venture capital funding for government technologies reached $1 billion during the pandemic. With the financial success of mission ventures in areas such as food, energy, and health care, there is a heightened interest to invest in emerging mission-driven ventures.

Increasingly, traditional blue-chip venture funds are creating investment practice groups and even separate funds to invest in opportunities at the intersection of mission, tech, and entrepreneurship. There is substantial investment interest from established venture funds, such as Insight Partners (Rebellion Defense), Khosla Ventures (Commonwealth Fusion), Bessemer Venture Partners (Rocket Labs), and Sequoia Capital (Nubank), who have investment professionals focusing on mission sectors. Some established tech venture funds such as Andreesen Horowitz, TPG Capital, and Cerberus are even creating new dedicated mission-focused funds, like the Andreesen Horowitz Dynamism Fund (Anduril, OpenGov, Shield AI); TPG Rise Fund (EverFi, Airtel Africa, C3.AI); and Cerberus Supply Chain and Strategic Opportunities Fund. And there are a number of existing players that are continuing to raise new funds focused on mission, health, and climate, such as Lux Capital, Arch Ventures, and Energy Impact Partners.

In addition, a number of new mission-focused funds are being formed, highlighting investment interest from limited partners. America's Frontier Fund was recently created to build and scale deep-tech companies and reinvigorate the innovation prowess of the United States in critical frontier technology sectors. Ballistic Ventures was created by experienced valley venture capitalists and tech executives to create a fund to incubate innovations in cybersecurity. The US Innovative Technology Fund, founded by Hollywood producer Thomas Tull, targets the defense, AI, biotech, cyber, and space industries, specifically with the goal of enhancing the United States's strategic advantage over China.[41]

International funds too have begun to mobilize capital for mission-driven investing, with Pale Blue Dot (Sweden), Softbank Vision Fund (Japan), Team8 (Israel), and Helios (Africa) investing billions of dollars across mission-focused sectors. Teachers' Venture Growth of Ontario Teachers' Pension Plan is another fund investing internationally in companies looking to build a better future, addressing issues of climate and inequality.[42]

Look at the amount of capital that has moved into the climate technology space, for another example. It would not have been surprising if venture capital firms were to remain skeptical about investments in climate technology, given early losses in the sector over 2005–2015. As public awareness and concern over climate change grew, and successful market participants began to emerge, the clean-tech ventures started turning out to be incredibly successful despite the failure of earlier companies. This is a major reason why venture capital firms are paying attention to and investing in climate technology. With companies such as Tesla and Beyond Meat delivering strong returns for their investors, venture capital has returned to the space, with investments growing steadily since 2016 and now exceeding $20 billion annually. In 2022, for example, TPG Capital, a leading global alternative asset management firm, announced the $7.3 billion close of TPG Rise Climate, the dedicated climate investing strategy of its global impact investing platform TPG Rise.[43] Saudi Arabia's Public Investment Fund, currently with $620 billion in assets, has recently pledged to reach net-zero by 2050, financing projects that will support this "green" transition.[44] And the European Investment Fund provides specific equity investments to ventures working on clean energy transition and sustainable transport, among other thematic strategies.[45] In fact, recent reports observe that climate technology VC funding totaled $70.1 billion in 2022, nearly double 2021's record.[46] Behind this trend are leading venture firms such as LowerCarbon (Commonwealth Fusion, Remora), Energy Impact Partners (Mosaic), and Activate Capital.

It is quite clear that this trend needs to continue. Climate technology is a critical next wave of innovation and growth that will not only solve a critical societal problem, but also generate substantial economic returns. This is a key reason for the United States to continue to be the location of more innovative and well-capitalized climate tech companies than any other country. However, while the U.S. is the headquarters for a number of climate tech unicorns, China is increasingly investing in climate technology, a sector listed by the nation as one of its top priorities for the next decade.

And success is bringing more than just venture capital. It perpetuates a virtuous cycle. Entrepreneurs who benefitted the most over the past thirty years from tech growth and innovation are now creating large family offices with dedicated mission-focused capital—in many cases larger than traditional funds. There are some twenty thousand family offices worldwide managing over $25 trillion of assets, far exceeding the assets under management of private equity ($11.12 trillion), venture capital ($1.68 trillion), and hedge funds ($4 trillion).[47] There is momentum of this money chasing mission-ventures, with a recent study of family offices showing a significant increase in portfolio allocations into sustainable investing—from 20 percent in 2019 to 36 percent in 2020, and predicted to rise up to 54 percent by 2027.[48]

Notable large active family offices include the Gates Foundation with $50 billion[49] (Bill and Melinda Gates),[50] Bezos Earth Fund with $10 billion (Jeff Bezos),[51] Declaration Partners with $2 billion (David Rubenstein), Emerson Collective with $1.8 billion (Laurene Powell Jobs),[52] and Schmidt Futures with $1 billion (Eric and Wendy Schmidt). Ken Griffin and Eric Schmidt pledged $50 million to support small, nonprofit research groups, which "support an ecosystem of small-to-mid-scale projects that fall between the cracks of what startups, academia and other organizations do."[53] Another interesting fund is Breakthrough Energy, a coalition of private investors concerned about the impacts of accelerating climate change. The collective has invested in a variety of startup companies across North America and Europe, provided capital to researchers and scientists, and assembled a group of experts and advocates to advance public policy that encourages innovation to tackle carbon-ization.[54] You may recognize some of the investors and board members: Richard Branson, Jack Ma, and Michael Bloomberg, among others.

In the Venture Meets Mission ecosystem, success draws capital. The government uses success-contingent financing to benchmark its "moonshots," and is also the purchaser of outcomes. Ventures, stimulated by private investments and family offices, set big goals with success-contingent financing, and entrepreneurial teams and investors figure out the most effective and efficient processes to reach these outcomes. Ultimately, as discussed by Tom Kalil of Schmidt Futures, the ecosystem evolves into a "marketplace of outcomes" that includes four key participants: government as purchaser of successful outcomes for well-defined "moonshots"; venture teams that believe they can uniquely solve the problem; investors, including institutional capital and family offices, who invest in ventures; and subject matter experts who develop actionable performance-based contracts in which the government articulates well-defined interim success-based milestones.

The Venture Meets Mission ecosystem will continue to thrive so long as the public and private sectors collaborate to rally investments behind ventures that are pursuing innovation to address grand challenges. But for greatest success, this must follow a coordinated approach. While many have written about the government being the platform to scale technology from within, we assert that government at the end is a federation of agencies. Therefore, while in concept, the size of government can help scale up innovation, we believe the platform may not be inside of government but outside of it. As the model of government innovation becomes less vertically integrated and assumes a horizontal archetype, coordinating the funding of mission becomes a priority. Thus the platform behind the Venture Meets Mission ecosystem may be best suited to sit outside of the government, to mobilize and coordinate the government's capital in the private sector.

TALENT MOVES FROM "WHY?" TO "WOW!"

Global youth are tech savvy, a promising sign for the Venture Meets Mission ecosystem. With both success stories and capital pushing mission-driven initiatives, there is a strong momentum behind attracting talent into the ecosystem—either to work in government or collaborate with the government while working in ventures and nonprofits. To develop the ecosystem, it is critical to attract the best and the brightest. So, where lie the opportunities to bring in the best talent into the ecosystem?

First, we need to tear down perceptions of the dichotomy between purpose and profit. Research by Professor Murat Tarakci at Erasmus University finds that professionals are more likely to seek higher salaries in for-profit social ventures because they perceive less career growth opportunities due to the social focus of the organization.[55] And while this may sound an alarm for how much we can mobilize talent around such ventures, it is worth digging deeper into the opportunities which truly exist in the Venture Meets Mission ecosystem. Increasingly, we see that there is not a binary choice between "doing good" and "making money." Successes like Palantir and emerging unicorns like National Resilience highlight that there is significant money in mission. As put by Jack Kerrigan at Razor's Edge VC, "If your focus is on the mission and not just the money, you'll end up making money, way more than if your only focus is on the money." It is quite clear to see how mission-driven opportunities differ from market opportunities. A common shortcoming of entrepreneurs is trying to create market demand or solve consumer pains for problems that they don't have. In contrast, a mission focuses on real and pressing problems. The demand is there, the need is there, and the money naturally follows.

In addition, we need to foster a culture of being intentionally non-linear in careers. A key feature of mission is empathy for the concerns of others. Empathy is a capacity to place oneself in another's position to understand and share the feelings of their experiences from their frame of reference. To inculcate empathy in mission-driven talent, diversity in experience is a valuable tool as it enables a deeper engagement of our shared values. Amidst a backdrop of political polarization and social inequities, it is easy to incorrectly conclude that we all hold different values, different beliefs, and different ideals. This threatens our sense of shared responsibility to the biggest societal problems. A culture of career nonlinearity will promote an empathy to stimulate mission-driven talent and reduce the barriers to action.

Second, we need to better promote the prestigious opportunities for students and professionals to consider being part of the Venture Meets Mission ecosystem. Unfortunately, a multidecade narrative of government has reduced the desire of much of the top talent to go into government, especially technology talent. The social feedback on college campus pushes students to positions that are perceived as more prestigious: banking, consulting, and big tech jobs. As a former student shared, when she mentioned wanting to put her computer science degree to work at Kessel Run (U.S. Air Force), her peers asked, "Why do that? What will you do after?" Conversely, her classmate's decision to teach third-grade mathematics for Teach for America was met with "Wow," on the basis of peers' perception of civic service while also enhancing future career opportunities in the private and public sectors. While both are public service roles, the response from their peers could not have been more different. We need to reenergize the desire for service at the intersection of mission, tech, and entrepreneurship. When students or young professionals pursue experiences in this sector they should not be met with "Why?" but rather with "Wow!" It is incumbent on us to restore prestige in solving big societal problems by not framing this as an "either-or" choice but as an "and" option—to do good *and* do well.

Perhaps the military services provide a model for such engagement, as Dave Wennergren of ACT-IAC suggests. "Issues like lack of financial support still exist in some form for students and young professionals who decide to join the military. But people can do their service and leave for graduate school or other careers, and in all instances, the training they receive while in the military is looked upon favorably by employers. In many ways there is social prestige associated with having a military background. It begs the question: can the civil service be reformed to become a more prestigious service where the best and the brightest go to serve their country? Can the military model be extended to the civil service?"

Think about the youth and tech deficit in the U.S. federal government, with just over 6 percent of all permanent, full-time federal employees under the age of thirty, compared to more than 21 percent of all private-sector employees. In the U.S. federal IT workforce, there are nineteen times more employees over the age of fifty years than those under thirty years.[56] There remains a strong perception that doing technology work around mission is not as prestigious or rewarding as a career in some private-sector organizations. Promoting prestigious opportunities in mission-driven organizations will aid in inspiring young people to pursue mission.

Government fellowships represent one entry point into the public sector for college students and mid- to late-career professionals. Prestigious fellowships for consideration by professionals at all stages include the Civic Digital Fellowship, Franklin Fellows Program, Presidential Innovation Fellowship, and Presidential Management Fellows, among others. There are also a number of nonprofit fellowships for students and professionals at all stages including the Fulbright Grant, Hertz Fellowship, Teach for America, and Truman-Albright Fellowship. Raising the visibility and prestige of such opportunities is critical to changing perceptions of working with the government or in mission-driven roles from "Why?" to "Wow!"

And while many programs already exist inside government, their prestige has been diminished over the years by the polarization of American politics. We may benefit from an outside-government platform to rebuild this aspirational narrative for the next generation, which shares stories, creates firsthand personal interaction with leaders, and highlights the great work done by many that can be sustained visibly and apolitically across administrations in partnership with private partners; in other words, a nonprofit platform that can do for government service what Teach for America did for public education. This platform can fill the need of government on campus, as the government is not showing up on campus and recruiting like banks, big tech, and consulting firms. This platform can tap into that sense of mission among students, structuring fellowships that promote a "tour of duty" model that is viewed as a career enhancer when students complete the program. In Israel, government experience is seen as a career enhancer, not a career limiter. In India, getting an appointment in the Indian Administrative Service (the civil service) is seen as the ultimate ticket to upward social mobility. The best and the brightest join the civil service in Singapore because of its fellowship system that fully pays for higher education. The challenge there is not in joining the government itself but rather attracting the best tech talent to create a vibrant Venture Meets Mission ecosystem.

It is important to consider how to attract mission-driven talent into venture. For one, the momentum of success stories will drive larger awareness. The opportunity to work in a venture that offers challenging and fulfilling work for a "rising" brand will attract a substantial amount of qualified talent. In parallel, the investment into mission-driven enterprises signals a change in tide for how potential employees perceive these ventures' ability to compensate them. While pay certainly may not be the most important factor for those seeking to work for mission, employees do want to feel that they are being paid fairly, which the substantial investment will allow. Just look at some of the examples provided in this book. Former executives at Palantir left the company to start new companies in the space. Trae Stephens, one such former Palantir employee, starts Anduril and turns it into a massive enterprise, hiring more top talent, which is then inspired to pursue other opportunities, pushing the ecosystem forward. Just like what developed Silicon Valley, one success story can spawn dozens of new opportunities.

It would be prudent to also expand upon how to attract more senior executives and technologists into government. Much like how prominent business leaders were drawn to support the government on the eve of World War II, these private-sector experts can rally behind the mission of government. For those considering a "second career," a new challenge, or a more fulfilling job, public service is a great option. Examples include Kurt DelBene, who brought his skills from Microsoft to the Veterans Administration, and Michael Brown, former CEO of Symantec and CEO of Quantum who engaged his executive talents as the director of the Defense Innovation Unit. Nand Mulchandani, the CIA's first CTO, is another aspirational example of successful entrepreneurs beginning to include government service in their career mosaic. As his

LinkedIn page describes, "I am a serial entrepreneur with a passion for public service. I love small, fast-moving teams focused on disrupting big markets." Nand cofounded and was CEO of multiple startups in Silicon Valley before pivoting to joining the Department of Defense and then the CIA.

The NobleReach Foundation brings in first- and second-career professionals to contribute to public service by offering their subject areas expertise to the government. One such example is Kirt Poss, a senior commercialization advisor and fellow at the NobleReach Foundation, who joined the organization after twenty-five years of founding, running, and exiting two different life-science companies. Kirt recalls his interest in the organization's message. "Following my early work in biomedical research and then running my own companies, I was really interested in seeing new scientific and business ideas from a different perspective, and also getting exposed to different avenues where I could get involved and help advance the space more broadly. I'd spent time in Washington, DC, during college, and always loved the sense of political thinking, mission, and service there as well." Kirt goes on to recognize the opportunity the NobleReach Foundation provided for him to take on a second career. "Being introduced to NobleReach Emerge, I was particularly excited to be in a position where I could see the truly impressive innovation in key strategic areas funded by the U.S. government. I've been very excited and energized at this stage in my 'second career' to be combining my experience in business growth, with key high-impact and mission-driven areas directly underlying our next-gen economy and national security. At this stage in my second career, NobleReach is really a remarkable platform by which I can deeply engage with amazing and talented people in academia, industry, and government around cutting-edge and key advanced technology areas." Systems and platforms that empower these professionals to use their expertise to make important decisions when they join government are a critical requirement to unlocking their potential for impact. Such executives can hold a critical role in transforming the Venture Meets Mission ecosystem.

Entrepreneurship can be the sandbox to attract intersectional talent—technologists, government officials, public servants, and young professionals across disciplines. We need to change the marketing narrative on college campuses and create more prestigious "tour of duty" fellowships in collaboration with the private sector to entice our top students in wanting to serve in government, especially in a tech capacity. By collaborating with leading private-sector firms that recruit aggressively on college campuses, students can rest assured that they have an offramp if they desire to go back to the private sector. While some may argue that there is no point in training top talent that is not committed to government, we contend that lack of exposure has contributed to our polarized society. With more citizens spending even two years working on mission, the more we can restore the "capacious sense of we," while maintaining their professional and personal goals.

PROMOTING INTERSECTORAL COLLABORATION

Chapter 2 highlighted the perils of a world defined and dominated by silos—whether they be political, social, or institutional. And this rings even more true in the case of government-venture arrangements. Yet despite the polarization of contemporary society, we are starting to see a proliferation of initiatives that are breaking down these silos. These initiatives are sorely needed. As we have seen in the recent geopolitical conflicts between the United States and China and the Russian invasion of Ukraine, there is increasing pressure on companies to work with democratic governments on geopolitical priorities.[57] And for the Venture Meets Mission ecosystem, trust is the currency of mission-driven collaboration.

Promising initiatives and models of collaboration exist across the ecosystem. In academia, for example, there is a resurgence of interdisciplinary collaboration for grand challenges. More interdisciplinary courses are being offered with applied opportunities in a societal context, and universities are creating fellowships, initiatives, and departments to support these partnerships. Georgetown University's Technology and Society Initiative is an interdisciplinary, university-wide collaboration among Georgetown's nine schools, with a shared goal to shape technology's promise for a better world by empowering practitioners and students to test, model, and scale cutting-edge projects.[58]

Stanford University's Emmett Interdisciplinary Program in Environment and Resources program brings together students and faculty from different academic disciplines —the physical and natural sciences, engineering, social sciences and humanities, law and policy, medicine, and business—to foster new insights and novel solutions for urgent global problems.[59] Harvard University's Institute for Applied Computational Science serves as the hub for interdisciplinary collaborations in computational and data science at Harvard and the Boston area, conducting research to solve real-world problems through mathematical models, systems innovations, and statistical tools.[60]

It is also important to consider how universities provide and inspire talent to enter the Venture Meets Mission ecosystem. Initiatives that would support this goal include making people "T-shaped"—so that they have depth in one area as well as enough multidisciplinary breadth to participate effectively in multifunctional teams and draw connections between disparate fields—a callback to Toni Townes-Whitley's advice of having horizontal and vertical experiences. For example, an engineering student interested in the problem of access to safe drinking water in developing countries might also understand public health, and the business context. Another initiative to support this goal is to promote a specialization in universities for particular problem sets, based on localization of problems, interest and expertise of faculty, institutional commitments (such as UCLA's decision to pursue a grand challenge related to depression, or Stanford's commitments to climate tech), and regional challenges.

Examples of activities that serve as a building block for universities in tackling grand challenges include initiatives such as problem-centered research experiences for undergraduates, project-based courses like the "Hacking for Defense" course, and giving students credit for working on real-world societal problems. Other opportunities lie in having faculty working in service positions, which could expose the faculty to more applied research activities while providing for service-based instructions to inspire students. Academia can help this ecosystem thrive by conducting interdisciplinary and problem-focused research, instructing students with the objective of inspiring mission, and institutionalizing links to public service organizations.

It has become evident that to foster a thriving and collaborative ecosystem, coordination is key. While the government is critical in setting an agenda of "moonshots," there remains the need for a platform to coordinate the ecosystem across ventures and government. There also lie opportunities for the government to break down the silos that have come to define their relationship with the private sectors. And some examples of successful models of government-business collaborations already exist. Take NASA's Center of Excellence for Collaborative Innovation, which built the concept of small bets into its procurement process. Here, the agency runs challenges and prize-oriented competitions, harnessing the power of the crowd to solicit solutions to real-world operational problems. The process allows the center to obtain engineering concepts, designs, and prototypes for existing NASA challenges, offering solutions in a faster time frame and at a lower cost than more traditional acquisition methods. Another NASA project, the Frontier Development Lab, convenes data scientists, computer scientists, subject-matter experts, and private-sector stakeholders from different industries for short periods of time—usually eight weeks—to identify and quickly prototype possible solutions to their research questions. These partnerships provide NASA access to the latest technologies and ideas from the private sector and increase its ability to address mission-critical problems through collaboration. These are just a few of the ways that government is working to break down knowledge silos.

It is also imperative that the government enact initiatives to break down the professional barriers that exist between the public and private sectors. As reviewed in Chapter 6, intersectionality and leadership in the middle spaces is critical to developing the Venture Meets Mission ecosystem. In a recent op-ed in the *Washington Post*, Max Stier and Anthony Fauci, former chief medical advisor to the president of the United States, laid out steps for the government to break down the intersectoral professional barriers, particularly for young Americans.[61] They mention the need for more student programs, like internships, to assess talent and help those who excel to navigate the arduous government hiring process. Also critical is the ability to expand expedited hiring for students and college graduates, as few prospective civil servants will wait months to land a government job when other enticing opportunities are available immediately in the private sector. Another key initiative they discuss is the need to develop contemporary messages that resonate with young people. A key theme in this book has been the need to tear down the incorrect biases and perceptions of the government, particularly among the younger generation.

In addition, there are other initiatives meant to bring career professionals in and out of the government. Talks have emerged, for example, around creating a national digital reserve corps program that would help with student loans.[62] In this program, some or all of student debt would be forgiven if a student goes into government for two years after college graduation and continues their service through training for two weeks each year and in times of national crisis. This stems from a need to "establish, manage, and assign a reserve of individuals with relevant skills and credentials to help address the digital and cybersecurity needs of executive agencies."[63]

From these discussions on the need for better intersectoral collaboration, we can clearly see the value of coordinated action by ventures, academic institutions, and governments. So what should be the best way in which to organize this collaboration? Earlier, we discussed how technology is leading to the creation of platform-based business models in the private sector, and horizontally integrated models of innovation in the government. And a platform model may actually be the optimal way to organize collaboration within the Venture Meets Mission ecosystem. Mitch Weiss, professor of management practice at Harvard Business School, created a course around public entrepreneurship, which notes the critical role of a platform in this context.[64] Weiss argues that platform thinking can be leveraged for both government and ventures by making known public needs, private-sector capabilities, and their intersectional role. This highlights the value of companies that have developed a network of government and industry experts, in addition to communicating the government agencies' various needs and capabilities. Ventures and people that pursue and provide societal value need to be able to find their way successfully into the government. Government initiatives that facilitate more effective interactions can help deepen the ecosystem, and also build trust in the government.

The NobleReach Foundation was recently created to build this value. By sitting as the platform outside of the U.S. government, NobleReach is catalyzing the government's technology and talent initiatives. NobleReach aims to mobilize and connect top talent with innovation across government, industry, and academia to drive high-impact mission outcomes for national and economic security in the next-gen economy.[65] This nonprofit is ideally seated to help the government address its talent gap. The organization has plans to launch a number of different talent programs which help promising students, early career professionals, and leading experts develop mission-driven careers. By offering a platform by which top talent can mobilize around key strategic tech areas for the U.S. government, NobleReach is creating the forum by which expert academics and industry professionals can contribute to and work toward the government's mission. Positioned at the center of academia, industry, and government, NobleReach is working to promote intersectoral collaboration and organize emerging technologies and the brightest minds around government's mission.

THE FUTURE WE WANT

Weeks and months of quarantine led us to reflect about our core beliefs, values, and ideals. As neighbors and communities rallied together to prevent the spread of the pandemic, a clear mission focus emerged. This focus was reinforced following the Russian invasion of Ukraine, with people all around the world stepping forward to preserve the ideals of liberal democracy. While we observe a global recession of democracy, with countries continuing to restrict individual expressions and freedoms, we are reminded of the superpower of democratic systems as creating an environment for innovation and progress. Freedom of thought and empathy for compatriots continues to propel democratic nations forward in the face of emerging challenges.

There are a number of sobering facts to which the pessimists will point to support the belief that the United States and liberal democracies are in decline. But we must not subscribe to or promote this false and dangerous narrative. Despite our divisions, history has continuously shown the innovativeness and resilience of liberal democracies to prevail. History shows that both in the U.S. and globally, the standards of living and quality of life have continued to advance and progress.

So it is here that we must acknowledge this generational opportunity to harness the power of collective purpose and liberal democracy. In the Venture Meets Mission ecosystem, we capitalize on both this purpose and the ability to innovate forward. The government, as an orchestrator of mission, sets societal ambitions and rewards the private sector's ability to meet those ambitions. The pool of talent is broadened to be more inclusive of those able to play in mission-driven work. Academic institutions create more intersectional changemakers who play at the intersection of the private sector and public service by encouraging and embracing nonlinear career paths. And ventures show strategic empathy for the government by trying to solve big problems and building intersectional teams.

We are at an inflection point to create the future we want. Either we can continue down the path of problem creation and too-late mitigation, or we can begin to shift toward solution formation and societal regeneration. All of the tools to tackle society's biggest problems exist. The Venture Meets Mission ecosystem's role is to bring together these tools: power of people seeking mission, the innovativeness of venture, and the scaling capacity of government. We have the capacity to make significant strides toward solving these problems and leaving the world a better place for future generations through people, purpose, and profit. We must now rebuild trust across people, venture, and government for the future we want around a common vision for...

A safer society.
A healthier society.
A more equitable society.
A more sustainable society.
A better society.

ACKNOWLEDGMENTS

We would like to express our heartfelt gratitude to all who helped make this project happen. We are grateful to all of those who provided feedback and valuable input into this project, including Adam Palmer, Adriana Bendaña-Fewer, Adrienne Jamieson, Akash Gupta, Akshay Gupta, Amy Zegart, Anand Shah, André Pienaar, Andrew Miller, Aneesh Chopra, Angela Chen, Anjali Mehta Gupta, Ann Dunwoody, Bonnie Tom, Chris Darby, Chris Kuang, Chris Lynch, Costa Saab, Dr. Dali Ma, Daniel Brunner, Daniel Sabzehzar, Daniel Tangherlini, Daniel Van Warner, Dave McCurdy, Deborah Spar, Deepak Hathiramani, Dimitrios Dionysopoulos, Don Gips, Doug Wagoner, Edlyn Levine, Francis Fukuyama, Gene Riechers, Geo Saba, H. R. McMaster, Isa Foster, J. D. Englehart, Jack Fewer, Jack Kerrigan, Jason Matheny, Jay Emmanuel, Jeanie Pembroke, Jeanne Tisinger, Joe Felter, Jonathan Silver, Jordan Blashek, Joshua Wilson, Katherine Boyle, Ken Krieg, Kirt Poss, Leslie Smith, Dr. Linda Bixby, Linda Zecher, Lisa Disbrow, Lysandra Weston, Marissa Gerchick, Mathew Lira, Matt Turpin, Max Stier, Michael Kratsios, Michael McFaul, Mika Gupta, Mike Morell, Mitch Weiss, Dr. Murat Tarakci, Nancy Fewer, Nand Mulchandani, Nate Fick, Nate Mook, Nick Sinai, Nicole Camarillo, Niloofar Razi Howe, Patricia Constantine, Peggy Styer, Phaedra Chrousos, Pritha Mehta, Rafi Martina, Rahul Singhvi, Raquel Bono, Reggie Aggarwal, Rob Meyerson, Robert Dail, Roy Kapani, Dr. Rushika Fernandopulle, Samsara Durvasula, Sanju Bansal, Scott Frederick, Shiro Wachira, Simon Davidson, Sonal Shah, Sonu Singh, Sree Ramaswamy, Steve Blank, Steve Bowsher, Steve Demetriou, Sumeet Shrivastava, Ted Davies, Teresa Carlson, Thomas Kalil, Tiffany Saade, Dr. Timothy Salkowski, Todd Stottlemyer, Tom Davidson, Toni Townes-Whitley, Trae Stephens, Val Singer, Vivek Kundra, Will Porteous, Will Wu, William Constantine, and others.

We are also thankful to the Georgetown Entrepreneurship Initiative, Georgetown University McDonough School of Business, and Tamsen and Michael Brown for the support and resources needed to complete this project. Our research assistant team, Kelly Grace Richardson, Kevin Jennings, Chris Forst, and Allison Tem, were instrumental for their tireless efforts as project RAs on this book. Their invaluable efforts were instrumental in bringing this project to fruition. The Freeman-Spogli Institute for International Studies and Hoover Institution at Stanford University were both incredibly helpful as we collected information for this manuscript.

Special thanks to Richard Narramore, Cindy Lim, and Kate Wahl of Stanford University Press, for their guidance and support through the publishing process, as well as to the reviewers for their constructive feedback that improved the quality of this book. We are also grateful to production editor Tim Roberts and copyeditor David Horne for their careful attention to this manuscript.

Most important, we want to thank our families—spouses, children, parents, siblings, and in-laws—for their unwavering support and encouragement through the ideation, writing, revision, more writing, more revision, and then ultimately the publishing process.

NOTES

CHAPTER 1

1. "Address before the 18th General Assembly of the United Nations on September 20, 1963," John F. Kennedy Presidential Library and Museum, accessed August 17, 2022, https://www.jfklibrary.org/learn/about-jfk/life-of-john-f-kennedy/john-f-kennedy-quotations.

2. The National, "100 Days of Coronavirus: The Most Heartwarming Stories to Be Shared Since Pandemic Started," Lifestyle, April 8, 2020, https://www.thenationalnews.com/lifestyle/100-days-of-coronavirus-the-most-heartwarming-stories-to-be-shared-since-pandemic-started-1.1002987.

3. "Kids Who Changed the World! Extraordinary Young People—Past & Present," iDTech, March 31, 2021, https://www.idtech.com/blog/kids-who-changed-the-world.

4. James Guerrier, "The Pandemic Has Inspired Young People to Trust Their Families and Their Doctors More," Paramount Insights, March 17, 2021, https://insights.paramount.com/post/the-pandemic-has-inspired-young-people-to-trust-their-families-and-their-doctors-more/.

5. Direct quotes in text that are not cited to specific sources are taken from interviews conducted by the authors.

6. Rebecca Henderson and Eric Van den Steen, "Why Do Firms Have 'Purpose'? The Firm's Role as a Carrier of Identity and Reputation," *American Economic Review* 105, no. 5 (2015): 326–30, https://doi.org/10.1257/aer.p20151072.

7. Gerard George, Martine R. Haas, Anita M. McGahan, Simon J. D. Schillebeeckx, and Paul Tracey, "Purpose in the For-Profit Firm: A Review and Framework for Management Research," *Journal of Management* (2023), https://doi.org/10.1177/01492063211006450.

8. "Vision, Mission and Purpose Statements—What Is the Difference?" Effective Governance—Part of the HopgoodGanim Advisory Group, accessed August 17, 2022, https://www.effectivegovernance.com.au/page/knowledge-centre/news-articles/vision-mission-and-purpose-statements-%E2%80%93-what-is-the-difference#:~:text=A%20purpose%20statement%20provides%20the,you%20do%20and%20for%20whom.

9. "What Is the Paris Agreement?" United Nations Climate Change, accessed August 17, 2022, https://unfccc.int/process-and-meetings/the-paris-agreement/the-paris-agreement.

10. Ferid Belhaj, "Fixing the Education Crisis in the Middle East and North Africa," The World Bank, November 13, 2018, https://www.worldbank.org/en/news/opinion/2018/11/13/fixing-the-education-crisis-in-the-middle-east-and-north-africa.

11. "GloLitter Partnerships Project," International Maritime Organization, accessed August 17, 2022, https://www.imo.org/en/OurWork/PartnershipsProjects/Pages/GloLitter-Partnerships-Project-.aspx.

12. Courtney Buble, "The Aging Federal Workforce Needs 'New Blood,' Experts Say," Government Executive, August 30, 2019, https://www.govexec.com/workforce/2019/08/aging-federal-workforce-needs-new-blood-experts-say/159585/; "Future of the Federal IT Workforce Update," CIO Council, May 2020, https://www.cio.gov/assets/resources/Future_of_Federal_IT_Workforce_Update_Public_Version.pdf.

13. William R. Kerr, "The Gift of Global Talent: Innovation Policy and the Economy," *Innovation Policy and Economy* 20, no. 1 (2020): 1–37, https://doi.org/10.1086/705637.

14. Carsten Fink and Ernest Miguelez, "Measuring the International Mobility of Inventors: A New Database," World Intellectual Property Organization 8, 2013, https://www.wipo.int/publications/en/details.jsp?id=3952.

15. According to the U.S. Department of State, "The Organization for Economic Co-operation and Development (OECD) is a unique forum where the governments of 37 democracies with market-based economies collaborate to develop policy standards to promote sustainable economic growth" ("The Organization for Economic Cooperation and Development (OECD)," U.S.

Department of State, accessed August 17, 2022, https://www.state.gov/the-organization-for-economic-co-operation-and-development-oecd/).

16. "Value of Venture Capital Investment in the United States from 1995 to 2020," Statista, November 10, 2022, https://www.statista.com/statistics/277501/venture-capital-amount-invested-in-the-united-states-since-1995/.

17. Josh Lerner and Ramana Nanda, "Venture Capital's Role in Financing Innovation: What We Know and How Much We Still Need to Learn," *Journal of Economic Perspectives* 34, no. 3 (2020): 237–61, https://doi.org/10.1257/jep.34.3.237.

18. Shane Harris and Dan Lamothe, "Intelligence-Sharing with Ukraine Designed to Prevent Wider War," *The Washington Post*, May 11, 2022, https://www.washingtonpost.com/national-security/2022/05/11/ukraine-us-intelligence-sharing-war/.

19. Andrew Chatzky and James McBride, "China's Massive Belt and Road Initiative," Council on Foreign Relations, last updated January 28, 2020, https://www.cfr.org/backgrounder/chinas-massive-belt-and-road-initiative.

20. Behrouz Shademan, Alireza Nourazarian, Saba Hajazimian, Alireza Isazadeh, Cigir Biray Avci, and Mahin Ahangar Oskouee, "CRISPR Technology in Gene-Editing-Based Detection and Treatment of SARS-CoV-2," *Frontiers in Molecular Diagnostics and Therapeutics* 8, (2021), https://doi.org/10.3389/fmolb.2021.772788.

21. Juliana Menasce Horowitz, Ruth Igielnik, and Rakesh Kochhar, "Trends in Income and Wealth Inequality," Pew Research Center, January 9, 2020, https://www.pewresearch.org/social-trends/2020/01/09/trends-in-income-and-wealth-inequality/.

22. Amy Roeder, "Zip Code Better Predictor of Health Than Genetic Code," Harvard T. H. Chan School of Public Health, August 4, 2014, https://www.hsph.harvard.edu/news/features/zip-code-better-predictor-of-health-than-genetic-code/.

23. Chatzky and McBride, "China's Massive Belt and Road Initiative."

24. Celia Hatton, "China: Big Spender or Loan Shark?" BBC News, September 29, 2021, https://www.bbc.com/news/world-asia-china-58679039.

25. "Gordon Moore: Raising the Bar for Silicon Technology and Innovation," Intel Corporation, accessed August 17, 2022, https://www.intel.com/content/www/us/en/history/museum-gordon-moore-law.html.

26. Gerard George, Jennifer Howard-Grenville, Aparna Joshi, and Laszlo Tihanyi, "Understanding and Tackling Societal Grand Challenges Through

Management Research," *Academy of Management Journal* 59, no. 6 (2016): 1880–1895, https://doi.org/10.5465/amj.2016.4007.

27. Elaine Hollensbe, Charles Wookey, Loughlin Hickey, Gerard George, and Cardinal Vincent Nichols, "Organizations with Purpose," *Academy of Management Journal* 57, no. 5 (2014): 1227–34, https://doi.org/10.5465/amj.2014.4005/.

28. See George et al., "Purpose in the For-Profit Firm."

29. "Business Roundtable Redefines the Purpose of a Corporation to Promote 'An Economy That Serves All Americans'," Business Roundtable, August 19, 2019, https://www.businessroundtable.org/business-roundtable-redefines-the-purpose-of-a-corporation-to-promote-an-economy-that-serves-all-americans.

30. "BRT Welcomes President Obama's Meeting with CEOs," Business Roundtable, accessed November 17, 2022, https://www.businessroundtable.org/archive/media/news-releases/brt-welcomes-president-obamas-meeting-with-ceos.

31. "Stakeholder Capitalism: The Time to Build a Better Future Is Now," Salesforce, accessed August 17, 2022, https://www.salesforce.com/company/stakeholder-capitalism/.

32. A venture is "a business enterprise or speculation in which something is risked in the hope of profit; a commercial or other speculation." This typically includes a high degree of growth opportunity. Dictionary.com, accessed December 14, 2022, https://www.dictionary.com/browse/venture.

33. A B Corp certification is a designation that a business is meeting high standards of verified performance, accountability, and transparency on factors from employee benefits and charitable giving to supply chain practices and input materials. "Measuring a Company's Entire Social and Environmental Impact," BCorporation.net, accessed November 17, 2022, https://www.bcorporation.net/en-us/certification.

34. Shelley E. Kohan, "Customers Seek Purpose Driven Companies Creating a Rise in B Corps," Forbes, March 28, 2021, https://www.forbes.com/sites/shelleykohan/2021/03/28/customers-seek-purpose-driven-companies-creating-a-rise-in-b-corps/?sh=47c472d86dd2.

35. Jerome H. Kim, Peter Hotez, Carolina Batista, Onder Ergonul, J. Peter Figueroa, Sarah Gilbert, Mayda Gursel, Mazen Hassanain, Gagandeep Kang, Bhavna Lall, Heidi Larson, Denise Naniche, Timothy Sheahan, Shmuel Shoham, Annelies Wilder-Smith, Nathalie Strub-Wourgaft, Prashant Yadav, and Maria Elena Bottazzi, "Operation Warp Speed: Impli-

cations for Global Vaccine Security," *The Lancet Global Health* 9, no. 7 (2021): e1017–e1021, https://doi.org/10.1016/S2214-109X(21)00140-6.

36. The Constitution of the United States. 1787. The National Archives, accessed December 15, 2022. https://www.archives.gov/founding-docs/constitution.

37. "2022 Edelman Trust Barometer: The Cycle of Distrust," Edelman, accessed December 14, 2022, https://www.edelman.com/trust/2022-trust-barometer.

38. Dylan Matthews, "Graph of the Day: Congress Is Less Popular Than Lice, Colonoscopies, and Nickelback," *Washington Post*, January 10, 2013, https://www.washingtonpost.com/news/wonk/wp/2013/01/10/graph-of-the-day-congress-is-less-popular-than-lice-colonoscopies-and-nickelback/.

39. Francis Fukuyama, *Liberalism and Its Discontents* (New York: Farrar, Straus and Giroux, 2022).

40. "Francis Fukuyama on Why Liberal Democracy Is in Trouble," NPR Morning Edition, April 4, 2017, https://www.npr.org/2017/04/04/522554630/francis-fukuyama-on-why-liberal-democracy-is-in-trouble.

41. "2022 Edelman Trust Barometer."

42. "Most Trusted Universities: August 2022," Morning Consult, accessed December 14, 2022, https://go.morningconsult.com/2022-Q3-pg8260a1-most-trusted-universities-2022-download.html.

43. Francis Fukuyama, *Trust: The Social Virtues and the Creation of Prosperity* (New York: Free Press, 1995).

44. Jason Matheny, "'The Future Could Be Brilliant': RAND's CEO Is an 'Apocaloptimist'," *RAND Review*, August 4, 2022, https://www.rand.org/blog/rand-review/2022/08/the-future-could-be-brilliant-rands-ceo-is-an-apocaloptimist.html.

45. Brian Bradley, "Global Spending on Virtual Reality, AI in Education Poised to Skyrocket, Report Says," EDWeek Market Brief, February 17, 2021, https://marketbrief.edweek.org/marketplace-k-12/global-spending-virtual-reality-ai-education-poised-skyrocket-report-says/.

46. "Developments in the Global Water Sector: Trends, Technologies and Financing," Apricum, November 24, 2021, https://apricum-group.com/developments-in-the-global-water-sector-trends-technologies-and-financing/?cn-reloaded=1.

47. "The Future of Insights: Intelligence in an Age of Data-Driven Competition," Special Competitive Studies Project Intelligence Interim Panel

Report, October 25, 2022, https://scsp222.substack.com/p/the-future-of-insights-intelligence.

48. Simon Commander, Saul Estrin, and Thamashi De Silva, "Political Systems Affect Innovation," April 5, 2022, https://blogs.ise.ac.uk/businessre-view/2022/04/05/political-systems-affect-innovation.

49. Amy Shira Teitel, "Nasa's Spinoff Showcases Decades of Trick-le-Down Space Tech," VICE, February 13, 2012, https://www.vice.com/en/article/mggxqa/nasa-s-spinoff-showcase; Slava Gerovitch, *Voices of the Soviet Space Program: Cosmonauts, Soldiers, and Engineers Who Took the USSR into Space* (London: Palgrave Macmillan, 2014).

50. Gina M. Raimondo, "Remarks by U.S. Secretary of Commerce Gina Raimondo on the U.S. Competitiveness and the China Challenge," U.S. Department of Commerce, November 30, 2022, https://www.commerce.gov/news/speeches/2022/11/remarks-us-secretary-commerce-gina-raimon-do-us-competitiveness-and-china#:~:text=we%20need%20the%20private%20sector, economic%20strategy%20begins%20at%20home.

51. Anthony F. Pipa and Zoe Swarzenski, "The Potential of the CHIPS and Science Act for Rural America," Brookings Institution, September 29, 2022, https://www.brookings.edu/research/the-potential-of-the-chips-and-science-act-for-rural-america.

52. "Restoring U.S. Manufacturing: Skills and Value Chains," Center for Strategic and International Studies, accessed December 18, 2022, https://www.csis.org/programs/renewing-american-innovation-project/restoring-us-manufacturing-skills-and-value-chains.

53. Raimondo, "Remarks by U.S. Secretary of Commerce."

54. Gerard George, Ryan K. Merrill, and Simon J. D. Schillebeeckx, "Digital Sustainability and Entrepreneurship: How Digital Innovations Are Helping Tackle Climate Change and Sustainable Development," *Entrepreneurship Theory and Practice* 45, no. 5 (2021): 999–1027, https://doi.org/10.1177/1042258719899425.

55. Matheny, "'The Future Could Be Brilliant'."

CHAPTER 2

1. Issie Lapowsky, "The Race to Pass Obama's Last Law and Save Tech in DC," WIRED, January 27, 2017, https://www.wired.com/2017/01/race-pass-obamas-last-law-save-tech-dc.

2. Thomas J. Fewer, "An Identity-Based View of Political Ideology in Modern Organizations," (PhD diss., Drexel University, 2021).

3. Reade Pickert, "U.S. Household Net Worth Hits Record on Home Values," September 23, 2021, Bloomberg, https://www.bloomberg.com/news/articles/2021-09-23/household-net-worth-in-u-s-hits-record-on-surging-home-values.

4. "Distribution of Household Wealth in the U.S. Since 1989," Board of Governors of the Federal Reserve System, accessed December 14, 2022, https://www.federalreserve.gov/releases/z1/dataviz/dfa/distribute/chart/#range:1999.2,2021.4;quarter:129;series:Net%20worth;demographic:net worth;population:all;units:levels.

5. Anna North, "The #McToo Generation Gap Is a Myth," Vox, March 20, 2018, https://www.vox.com/2018/3/20/17115620/me-too-sexual-harassment-sex-abuse-poll; Juliana Menasce Horowitz, "Support for Black Lives Matter Declined After George Floyd Protests, but Has Remained Unchanged Since," Pew Research Center, September 27, 2021, https://www.pewresearch.org/fact-tank/2021/09/27/support-for-black-lives-matter-declined-after-george-floyd-protests-but-has-remained-unchanged-since/.

6. Amber Hye-Yon Lee, "Social Trust in Polarized Times: How Perceptions of Political Polarization Affect Americans' Trust in Each Other," *Political Behavior* 44, (2022): 1533–54, https://doi.org/10.1007/s11109-022-09787-1.

7. "Political Polarization in the American Public: How Increasing Ideological Uniformity and Partisan Antipathy Affect Politics, Compromise and Everyday Life," Pew Research Center, June 12, 2014, https://www.pewresearch.org/politics/2014/06/12/political-polarization-in-the-american-public/.

8. Jean-Paul Sartre, *Being and Nothingness,* trans. Hazel R. Barnes (New York: Washington Square Press, 1993), 555.

9. "See How Your Community Moved Differently Due to COVID-19: Covid Community Mobility Reports," Google, accessed June 21, 2022, https://www.google.com/covid19/mobility/.

10. "COVID-19 Exposes American Philanthropy's Strengths and Weaknesses," *The Economist*, April 27, 2020, https://www.economist.com/united-states/2020/04/27/covid-19-exposes-american-philanthropys-strengths-and-weaknesses.

11. Patrick J. McDonnell, "U.S. Military Veterans Answer Zelensky's Call to Fight, but Not All Are Chosen," *Los Angeles Times*, March 31, 2022, https://www.latimes.com/world-nation/story/2022-03-31/u-s-military-veterans-answer-zelenskys-call-to-fight-but-not-all-are-chosen.

12. Mustafa Emirbayer and Ann Mische, "What Is Agency?" *American Journal of Sociology* 103, no. 4 (1998): 962–1023, https://doi.org/10.1086/231294.

13. Susan Michie, Michelle Richardson, Marie Johnston, Charles Abraham, Jill Francis, Wendy Hardeman, Martin P. Eccles, James Cane, and Caroline E. Wood, "The Behavior Change Technique Taxonomy (V1) of 93 Hierarchically Clustered Techniques: Building an International Consensus for the Reporting of Behavior Change Interventions," *Annals of Behavioral Medicine* 46, no. 1 (2013): 81–95, https://doi.org/10.1007/s12160-013-9486-6.

14. Falko F. Sniehotta, Urte Scholz, and Ralf Schwarzer, "Bridging the Intention–Behaviour Gap: Planning, Self-Efficacy, and Action Control in the Adoption and Maintenance of Physical Exercise," *Psychology & Health* 20, no. 2 (2005): 143–160, https://doi.org/10.1080/08870440512331317670.

15. Arne Gast, Pablo Illanes, Nina Probst, Bill Schaninger, and Bruce Simpson, "Purpose: Shifting from Why to How," McKinsey & Company, April 22, 2020, https://www.mckinsey.com/business-functions/people-and-organizational-performance/our-insights/purpose-shifting-from-why-to-how.

16. See Chapter 1, George et al., "Purpose in the For-Profit Firm"; Ranjay Gulati, *Deep Purpose: The Heart and Soul of High-Performance Companies* (New York: Harper Business, 2022).

17. Thomas J. Madden, Pamela Scholder Ellen, and Icek Ajzen, "A Comparison of the Theory of Planned Behavior and the Theory of Reasoned Action," *Personality and Social Psychology Bulletin* 18, no. 1 (1992): 3–9, https://doi.org/10.1177/0146167292181010.

18. "Where Americans Find Meaning in Life," Pew Research Center, November 20, 2018, https://www.pewforum.org/2018/11/20/where-americans-find-meaning-in-life/.

19. Brian Groom, "A Third of Start-Ups Aim for Social Good," *Financial*

Times, June 14, 2018, https://www.ft.com/content/d8b6d9fa-4eb8-11e8-ac41-759eee1efb74.

20. Brett M. Rhyne, "New Business Applications in the US Hit Historic Highs Last Year," World Economic Forum, September 12, 2021, https://www.weforum.org/agenda/2021/09/new-business-applications-in-the-us-hit-historic-highs-last-year/; Simeon Djankov and Eva (Yiwen) Zhang, "Startups Boom in the United States During COVID-19," PIIE, February 12, 2021, https://www.piie.com/blogs/realtime-economic-issues-watch/startups-boom-united-states-during-covid-19.

21. "COVID-19 Action Agenda Leaders on the Front Line: Why Social Entrepreneurs Are Needed Now More Than Ever," World Economic Forum, September 2020, https://www3.weforum.org/docs/COVID19_SocEnt_Alliance_Report_2020.pdf.

22. Paul C. Light, "Government's Most Visible Failures, 2001–2014," Brookings Institution, July 14, 2014, https://www.brookings.edu/interactives/governments-most-visible-failures-2001-2014/.

23. Brian Heater, "The Short, Strange Life of Quibi," TechCrunch, October 23, 2020, https://techcrunch.com/2020/10/23/the-short-strange-life-of-quibi/.

24. "Venture Capital Due Diligence: Guide to Performing Due Diligence in Venture Capital (VC)," Wall Street Prep, accessed August 17, 2022, https://www.wallstreetprep.com/knowledge/venture-capital-diligence/.

25. "In a Politically Polarized Era, Sharp Divides in Both Partisan Coalitions," Pew Research Center, December 17, 2019, https://www.pewresearch.org/politics/2019/12/17/views-of-government-and-the-nation/.

26. "Beyond Distrust: How Americans View Their Government," Pew Research Center, November 23, 2015, https://www.pewresearch.org/politics/2015/11/23/beyond-distrust-how-americans-view-their-government/.

27. Malin Malmstrom, Jeaneth Johansson, and Joakim Wincent, "We Recorded VCs' Conversations and Analyzed How Differently They Talk About Female Entrepreneurs," *Harvard Business Review*, May 17, 2017, https://hbr.org/2017/05/we-recorded-vcs-conversations-and-analyzed-how-differently-they-talk-about-female-entrepreneurs.

28. "Traditional Stereotypes of Entrepreneurs Out of Date and Preventing More Problem Solving," King's College London News Centre, November 15, 2020, https://www.kcl.ac.uk/news/

traditional-stereotypes-of-entrepreneurs-out-of-date-and-prevent-
ing-more-problem-solving.

29. Harley Finkelstein, "Our Image of an Entrepreneur Desperately
Needs an Update—Here's How We Change It," Fast Company, November 15,
2018,https://www.fastcompany.com/90267083/our-image-of-an-entrepreneur-desperately-
needs-an-update-heres-how-we-change-it.

30. "Culture: Entrepreneurial Perceptions and Attitudes," *Entrepreneurship
at a Glance* (2012), https://doi.org/10.1787/entrepreneur_aag-2012-26-en.

31. Kevin Briscoe, "Integrity in Business—A Priceless Essential for
Success," CFO Selections, August 20, 2019, https://www.cfoselections.com/
perspective/integrity-in-business-a-priceless-essential-for-success.

32. Timothy Carter, "How to Cultivate Humility as an Entrepreneur (And
Why You Should)," Entrepreneur, January 11, 2021, https://www.entrepreneur.
com/article/361351#: ~:text=In%20a%20practical%20context%2C%20this,-
seem%20to%20contradict%20this%20quality.

33. Michael D. Mumford, Erin Michelle Todd, Cory Higgs, and Tristan
McIntosh, "Cognitive Skills and Leadership Performance: The Nine Critical
Skills," *The Leadership Quarterly* 28, (2017): 24–39, https://doi.org/10.1016/j.
leaqua.2016.10.012; Heidi Mitchell, "Some Humility Can Really Help an
Entrepreneur Win Over Investors," *Wall Street Journal*, November 3, 2022,
https://www.wsj.com/articles/
humility-can-really-help-an-entrepreneur-win-over-investors-11635512755.

34. Matt Gavin, "5 Characteristics of a Courageous Leader," Harvard
Business School Online, March 3, 2020, https://online.hbs.edu/blog/post/
courageous-leadership.

35. Kristi Bockorny and Carolyn M. Youssef-Morgan, "Entrepreneurs'
Courage, Psychological Capital, and Life Satisfaction," *Frontiers in Psychology*
10, no. 789 (2019): 1–6, https://doi.org/10.3389/fpsyg.2019.00789.

36. Lowell W. Busenitz and Jay B. Barney, "Differences Between Entrepreneurs and Managers in Large Organizations: Biases and Heuristics in
Strategic Decision-Making," *Journal of Business Venturing* 12, no. 1 (1997):
9–30, https://doi.org/10.1016/S0883-9026(96)00003-1.

37. Utpal Dholakia, "4 Ways in Which Optimism Helps Entrepreneurs
Succeed," *Psychology Today*, October 2, 2016, https://www.psychologytoday.
com/us/blog/the-science-behind-behavior/201610/4-ways-in-which-optimism-helps-
entrepreneurs-succeed.

38. Ruta Aidis, Tomasz Mickiewicz, and Arnis Sauka, "Why Are
Optimistic Entrepreneurs Successful? An Application of the Regulatory

Focus Theory," The William Davidson Institute at the University of Michigan, February 2008, https://deepblue.lib.umich.edu/bitstream/handle/2027.42/64399/wp914.pdf.

39. O. Arias, "Moral Leadership in Today's World," *Journal of the International Institute* 9, no. 3, accessed March 25, 2023, https://quod.lib.umich.edu/cgi/t/text/idx/j/jii/4750978.0009.303/--moral-leadership-in-todays-world?rgn=main;view=fulltext.

40. Martin Reeves and Mike Deimler, "Adaptability: The New Competitive Advantage," *Harvard Business Review*, August 2011, https://hbr.org/2011/07/adaptability-the-new-competitive-advantage.

41. "10 Proven Ways to Build Resilience as an Entrepreneur," Forbes, May 21, 2021, https://www.forbes.com/sites/theyec/2021/05/21/10-proven-ways-to-build-resilience-as-an-entrepreneur/?sh=b0dc4db5b97b.

42. Michele M. Tugade, Barbara L. Fredrickson, and Lisa Feldman Barrett, "Psychological Resilience and Positive Emotional Granularity: Examining the Benefits of Positive Emotions on Coping and health," *Journal of Personality* 72, no. 6 (2004): 1161–1190, https://doi.org/10.1111/j.1467-6494.2004.00294.x.

43. Carol S. Dweck, *Mindset: How You Can Fulfill Your Potential* (Edinburgh, UK: Constable & Robinson Limited, 2012).

44. "Family-Owned Businesses Are Economic Powerhouses That Drive Local, National, and Global Economies. Here Are Some Statistics," Conway Center for Family Business, accessed December 14, 2022, https://www.familybusinesscenter.com/resources/family-business-facts/.

45. Meredith Somers, "Intrapreneurship, Explained," MIT Sloan School of Management, June 21, 2018, https://mitsloan.mit.edu/ideas-made-to-matter/intrapreneurship-explained.

46. "Intrapreneurs—Why Big Businesses Value the Entrepreneurial Mindset," Hult News, accessed June 23, 2022, https://www.hult.edu/blog/intrapreneurs-big-businesses-value-entrepreneurial-mindset/.

47. Mike Krzyzewski, "Duke Entrepreneur Stories: Coach K & Power-Forward," Duke Innovation and Entrepreneurship on YouTube, video posted January 12, 2017, https://www.youtube.com/watch?v=d6_wHIBDni8.

48. Peter Drucker, *Innovation and Entrepreneurship* (London: Routledge, 2014).

49. Efosa Ojomo, "6 Signs You're Living in an Entrepreneurial Society," *Harvard Business Review*, October 4, 2016, https://hbr.org/2016/10/6-signs-youre-living-in-an-entrepreneurial-society.

50. "Entrepreneurial Optimism Is Warranted, Even During This Pandemic: HBS Professor William Sahlman Makes the Case," Quantum Media, May27,2020,https://www.quantummedia.com/news-item/entrepreneurial-optimism-is-warranted-even-during-this-pandemic-hbs-profess.

51. "The Nature of Government," USHistory.org, accessed November 17, 2022, USHistory.org/gov/1a.asp.

52. "GDP and Labor Force: Derived Using Data from International Labor Organization, ILOSTAT Database," The World Bank, accessed August 16, 2022, https://ilostat.ilo.org/data/.

53. Mark J. Perry, "Putting America's Enormous $21.5T Economy into Perspective by Comparing US State GDPs to Entire Countries," American Enterprise Institute, February 5, 2020, https://www.aei.org/carpe-diem/putting-americas-huge-21-5t-economy-into-perspective-by-comparing-us-state-gdps-to-entire-countries/#:~:text=It's%20pretty%20difficult%20to%20even,the%20entire%20national%20output%20of.

54. Paul C. Light, "The True Size of Government Is Nearing a Record High," Brookings Institution, October 7, 2020, https://www.brookings.edu/blog/fixgov/2020/10/07/the-true-size-of-government-is-nearing-a-record-high/.

55. Pork barrel spending refers to members of Congress funding questionable projects in their home districts for political gain. See Will Kenton, "Pork Barrel Politics: Definition, Purposes, Reform Efforts," Investopedia, July 18, 2021, https://www.investopedia.com/terms/p/pork_ barrel_politics.asp.

56. Jeffrey M. Jones, "Americans Say Federal Gov't Wastes Over Half of Every Dollar," Gallup, September 19, 2011, https://news.gallup.com/poll/149543/americans-say-federal-gov-wastes-half-every-dollar.aspx.

57. "2013 Survey of Americans on the U.S. Role in Global Health," Kaiser Family Foundation, November 7, 2013, https://www.kff.org/global-health-policy/poll-finding/2013-survey-of-americans-on-the-u-s-role-in-global-health/.

58. Derek Bok, "Measuring the Performance of Government," in *Why People Don't Trust Government*, ed. Joseph S. Nye, Phillip D. Zelikow, and David C. King (Cambridge, MA: Harvard University Press, 1997); Rebecca Riffkin, "Americans Say Federal Gov't Wastes 51 Cents on the Dollar," Gallup, September 17, 2014, https://news.gallup.com/poll/176102/americans-say-federal-gov-wastes-cents-dollar.aspx.

59. Vanessa Williamson, "Public Ignorance or Elitist Jargon? Reconsidering Americans' Overestimates of Government Waste and Foreign Aid,"

American Politics Research 47, no. 1 (2019): 152–173, https://doi.org/10.1177/1532673X18759645.

60. Williamson, "Public Ignorance or Elitist Jargon?"

61. Abby Monteil, "50 Inventions You Might Not Know Were Funded by the US Government," Stacker, June 21, 2022, https://stacker.com/stories/5483/50-inventions-you-might-not-know-were-funded-us-government.

62. Audrey Conklin, "What Is the Most Popular Smartphone in the World Right Now?" Fox Business, April 27, 2020, https://www.foxbusiness.com/technology/most-popular-smartphone-world.

63. Rutger Bregman, "Look at the Phone in Your Hand—You Can Thank the State for That," *The Guardian*, July 12, 2017, https://www.theguardian.com/commentisfree/2017/jul/12/phone-state-private-sector-products-investment-innovation.

64. Mariana Mazzucato, *The Entrepreneurial State: Debunking Public vs Private Sector Myths* (London: Anthem Press, 2015).

65. "Operation Warp Speed: Accelerated COVID-19 Vaccine Development Status and Efforts to Address Manufacturing Challenges," U.S. Government Accountability Office, February 11, 2021, https://www.gao.gov/products/gao-21-319.

66. "Space Tech and Geospatial Startups: Ukraine Needs Your SAR Data," Investable Universe, March 1, 2022, https://investableuniverse.com/2022/03/01/eos-data-analytics-eosda-needs-remote-sensing-optical-radar-satellite-imagery-ukraine/.

67. John Maynard Keynes, "Essays in Persuasion: The End of Laissez-Faire," Economics Network, accessed August 17, 2022, https://www.economicsnetwork.ac.uk/archive/keynes_ persuasion/The_ End_of_Laissez-Faire.htm#:~:text=The%20important%20thing%20for%20 Government,occasion%20to%20develop%20practical%20policies.

68. "FACT SHEET: Biden Harris Administration Announces Commitments to Advance Pay Equity and Support Women's Economic Security," The White House Briefing Room, March 15, 2022, https://www.whitehouse.gov/briefing-room/statements-releases/2022/03/15/fact-sheet-biden-harris-administration-announces-commitments-to-advance-pay-equity-and-support-womens-economic-security/.

69. "Gender Pay Differences: The Pay Gap for Federal Workers Has Continued to Narrow, but Better Quality Data on Promotions Are Needed," U.S. Government Accountability Office, December 3, 2020, https://www.gao.gov/products/gao-21-67.

70. Timothy Carter, "The True Failure Rate of Small Businesses," Entrepreneur, January 3, 2021, https://www.entrepreneur.com/starting-a-business/the-true-failure-rate-of-small-businesses/361350.

71. "Program Overview and History," Partnership for Public Service, accessed June 23, 2022. https://servicetoamericamedals.org/about/.

72. "About Humans of Public Service," Humans of Public Service, accessed December 26, 2022, https://humansofpublicservice.org/.

73. Bruno Lanvin, "The World's Most Innovative Countries, 2021," INSEAD, September 20, 2021, https://knowledge.insead.edu/entrepreneurship/worlds-most-innovative-countries-2021.

74. Mike Maddock, "Why Americans Make the Best Entrepreneurs…For Now," Forbes, September 25, 2013, https://www.forbes.com/sites/mikemaddock/2013/09/25/why-americans-make-the-best-entrepreneurs-for-now/?sh=51fe3270bf5f.

CHAPTER 3

1. For more details about this mobilization of public-private partnerships, see Arthur Herman, *Freedom's Forge: How American Business Produced Victory in World War II* (New York: Random House, 2012).

2. Liliana B. Andonova, *Governance Entrepreneurs: International Organizations and the Rise of Global Public-Private Partnerships* (Cambridge, UK: Cambridge University Press, 2017).

3. Tom Donohue, "Business and Government Must Continue to Work Together to Rebuild the Economy," U.S. Chamber of Commerce, January 12, 2021, https://www.uschamber.com/on-demand/leadership/business-and-government-must-continue-to-work-together-to-rebuild-the-economy.

4. "Goldman Sachs Announces 2022 10,000 Small Businesses Summit, the Largest Gathering of Small Business Owners in the U.S.," Businesswire, June 29, 2022, https://www.businesswire .com/news/home/20220629005352/en/Goldman-Sachs-Announces-2022-10000-Small-Businesses-Summit-The-Largest-Gathering-of-Small-Business-Owners-in-the-U.S.

5. Robert Higgs, "World War II and the Military-Industrial-Congressional Complex," Independent Institute, May 1, 1995, https://www.independent.org/publications/article.asp?id=14.

6. Jason M. Rathje, "Essays on Public Funding for Private Innovation," (PhD diss., Stanford University, 2019).

7. Hal G. Rainey and Young Han Chun, "Public and Private Management Compared," in *The Oxford Handbook of Public Management*, ed. Ewan Ferlie, Laurence E. Lynn Jr., and Christopher Pollitt (Oxford, UK: Oxford University Press, 2005).

8. Marcus Ahadzi and Graeme Bowles, "Public-Private Partnerships and Contract Negotiations: An Empirical Study," *Construction Management and Economics* 22, no. 9 (2004): 967–78, https://doi.org/10.1080/0144619042000241471; Hal G. Rainey and Barry Bozeman, "Comparing Public and Private Organizations: Empirical Research and the Power of the A Priori," *Journal of Public Administration Research and Theory* 10, no. 2 (2000): 447–70, https://doi.org/10.1093/oxfordjournals.jpart.a024276.

9. Mark H. Moore, *Creating Public Value: Strategic Management in Government* (Boston: Harvard University Press, 1995).

10. Owen E. Hughes, *Public Management and Administration* (London: Bloomsbury Publishing, 2017).

11. Carlos Rufin and Miguel Rivera-Santos, "Between Commonweal and Competition: Understanding the Governance of Public-Private Partnerships," *Journal of Management* 38, no. 5 (2012): 1634–54, https://doi.org/10.1177/0149206310373948.

12. Barry Bozeman and Gordon Kingsley, "Risk Culture in Public and Private Organizations," *Public Administration Review* 58, no. 2 (1998): 109–18, https://doi.org/10.2307/976358.

13. Rainey and Han Chun, "Public and Private Management Compared."

14. Gerard George, Thomas Fewer, Sergio Lazzarini, Anita McGahan, and Phanish Puranam, "Partnering for Grand Challenges: A Review of Organizational Design Considerations in Public-Private Collaborations," *Journal of Management* (2023).

15. Eduardo Porter, "Wall St. Money Meets Social Policy at Rikers Island," *New York Times*, July 28, 2015, https://www.nytimes.com/2015/07/29/business/economy/wall-st-money-meets-social-policy-at-rikers-island.html.

16. Simone Cesca, Daniel Stich, Francesco Grigoli, Alessandro Vuan, José Ángel López-Comino, Peter Niemz, Estefanía Blanch, Torsten Dahm, and William L. Ellsworth, "Seismicity at the Castor Gas Reservoir Driven by Pore Pressure Diffusion and Asperities Loading," *Nature Communications* 12, no. 4783 (2021): 1–13, https://doi.org/10.1038/s41467-021-24949-1.

17. Heather Whiteside, *Public-Private Partnerships* (Halifax: Fernwood, 2016).

18. "Three Gorges Dam," *Encyclopedia Britannica*, accessed December 14, 2022, https://www.britannica.com/topic/Three-Gorges-Dam.

19. "New Karolinska Solna Project Overview," SKANSKA, accessed November 17, 2022, https://group.skanska.com/projects/57344/New-Karolinska-Solna.

20. Mark Alesia and Kaitlin Lange, "Mike Pence's Infrastructure Mess: What Went Wrong with I-69?" IndyStar, June 18, 2017, https://www.indystar.com/story/news/2017/06/18/mike-pence-donald-trump-public-private-partnerships-mitch-daniels-interstate-69-isolux-bloomington/388756001/.

21. See George et al., "Partnering for Grand Challenges."

22. "A Brief History of Public-Private Partnerships," Lorman, July 19, 2018, https://www.lorman.com/resources/a-brief-history-of-public-private-partnerships-16968#:~:text=The%20first%20public%20private%20partnership,in%20the%202012%20legislative%20sessions.

23. We calculate this percentage using two recent studies. First, The National Center for Science and Engineering Statistics finds that business accounted for 72.2 percent of R&D expenditures in the United States in 2019 ("New Data on U.S. R&D: Summary Statistics from the 2019–20 Edition of National Patterns of R&D Resources," NSF National Center for Science and Engineering Statistics, access December 14, 2022, https://ncses.nsf.gov/pubs/nsf22314#:~:text=Source(s)%3A&text=The%20business%20sector%20accounted%20for,development%20centers)%20(9%25). Second, researchers find that VC-backed companies account for 62 percent of U.S. public companies' R&D spending (Will Gornall and Ilya Strebulaev, "The Economic Impact of Venture Capital: Evidence from Public Companies," Social Science Research Network 2681841, 2021, http://dx.doi.org/10.2139/ssrn.2681841).

24. Quoted in "Independent Science for a Daunting Future," Issues in Science and Technology, accessed December 14, 2022, https://issues.org/tag/salk/.

25. Terrence E. Brown, Per Davidsson, and Johan Wiklund, "An Operationalization of Stevenson's Conceptualization of Entrepreneurship as Opportunity-Based Firm Behavior," *Strategic Management Journal* 22, no. 10 (2001): 953–68, https://doi.org/10.1002/smj.190.

26. Chapter 1, George et al., "Purpose in the For-Profit Firm."

27. Martin Kenney, *Understanding Silicon Valley: The Anatomy of an Entrepreneurial Region* (Stanford, CA: Stanford University Press, 2015).

28. Amy Zegart, "Are We Dumb About Intelligence? Amy Zegart on the Capabilities of American Intel Gathering," Hoover Institution, March 31, 2022, https://www.hoover.org /research/are-we-dumb-about-intelligence-a my-zegart-capabilities-american-intel-gathering-1.

29. Zegart. "Are We Dumb About Intelligence?"

30. Mark Boroush, "New Data on U.S. R&D: Summary Statistics from the 2019–20 Edition of National Patterns of R&D Resources," NSF National Center for Science and Engineering Statistics, accessed December 14, 2022, https://ncses.nsf.gov/pubs/nsf22314.

31. Rebecca Mandt, Kushal Seetharam, and Chung Hon Michael Cheng, "Federal R&D Funding: The Bedrock of National Innovation," *MIT Science Policy Review* 1, (2020): 44–54, https:// sciencepolicyreview.org/2020/08/ federal-rd-funding-the-bedrock-of-national-innovation/.

32. "DoD Open Source Software FAQ," U.S. Department of Defense, October 28, 2021, https://dodcio.defense.gov/open-source-software-faq/.

33. William G. Ouchi and Alan L. Wilkins, "Organizational Culture," *Annual Review of Sociology* 11, (1985): 457–83, https://www.jstor.org/ stable/2083303.

34. "Pay and the General Schedule," Partnership for Public Service, accessed August 17, 2022, https://gogovernment.org/all-about-government-jobs/pay-and-the-general-schedule/.

35. Mike Juang, "A Secret Many Small-Business Owners Share with Mark Zuckerberg," CNBC, July 19, 2017, https://www.cnbc.com/2017/07/19/ survey-shows-majority-of-business-owners-lack-college-degree.html.

36. Dragomir Simovic, "39 Entrepreneur Statistics You Need to Know in 2022," Smallbizgenius, July 28, 2022, https://www.smallbizgenius.net/ by-the-numbers/entrepreneur-statistics/#gref.

37. "Mark Zuckerberg's Commencement Address at Harvard," *The Harvard Gazette*, May 25, 2017, https://news.harvard.edu/gazette/ story/2017/05/ mark-zuckerbergs-speech-as-written-for-harvards-class-of-2017/.

38. Katherine Schaeffer, "10 Facts About Today's College Graduates," Pew Research Center, April 12, 2022, https://www.pewresearch.org/ fact-tank/2022/04/12/10-facts-about-todays-college-graduates/.

39. Patrick Thibodeau, "Federal Workforce Too Reliant on Degrees, Says White House," TechTarget, February 12, 2020, https://www.techtarget.com/

searchhrsoftware/news/252478497/ Federal-workforce-too-reliant-on-degrees-says-White-House.

40. Andrea Laplane and Mariana Mazzucato, "Socializing the Risks and Rewards of Public Investments: Economic, Policy, and Legal Issues," *Research Policy* 49, no. 100008 (December 2020), https://doi.org/10.1016/j.repolx.2020.100008.

41. L. Kiely, D. V. Spracklen, S. R. Arnold, E. Papargyropoulou, L. Conibear, C. Wiedinmyer, C. Knote, and H. A. Adrianto, "Assessing Costs of Indonesian Fires and the Benefits of Restoring Peatland," *Nature Communications* 12, no. 7044 (2021): 1–11, https://doi.org/10.1038/s41467-021-27353-x.

42. Mariana Mazzucato, "We Socialize Bailouts. We Should Socialize Successes, Too," *New York Times*, July 1, 2020, https://www.nytimes.com/2020/07/01/opinion/inequality-goverment-bailout.html.

43. "No Risk, No Innovation: The Double-Bind for the Public Sector," APolitical.co, November 3, 2017, https://apolitical.co/solution-articles/en/no-risk-no-innovation-double-bind-public-sector.

44. Edward D. Hess, "Creating an Innovation Culture: Accepting Failure Is Necessary," Forbes, June 20, 2012, https://www.forbes.com/sites/darden/2012/06/20/creating-an-innovation-culture-accepting-failure-is-necessary/?sh=3063b22b754e.

45. Hsiang-Kai Dennis Dong, "Individual Risk Preference and Sector Choice: Are Risk-Averse Individuals More Likely to Choose Careers in the Public Sector?" *Administration & Society* 49, no. 8 (2017): 1121–42, https://doi.org/10.1177/0095399714556500.

46. Katie Fehrenbacher, "Why the Solyndra Mistake Is Still Important to Remember," Fortune, August 27, 2015, https://fortune.com/2015/08/27/remember-solyndra-mistake/.

47. Jeff Brady, "After Solyndra Loss, U.S. Energy Loan Program Turning a Profit," NPR, November 13, 2013, https://www.npr.org/2014/11/13/363572151/after-solyndra-loss-u-s-energy-loan-program-turning-a-profit.

48. Russ Linden, "Innovation and Government's Fear of Failure," Governing, March 8, 2014, https://www.governing.com/archive/col-innovation-government-overcoming-fear-failure.html.

49. "No Risk, No Innovation."

50. Geoffrey A. Moore, *Crossing the Chasm*, 3rd ed. (New York: HarperCollins, 2014).

51. John T. Reinert, "In-Q-Tel: The Central Intelligence Agency as Venture Capitalist," *Northwestern Journal of International Law & Business* 33,

no. 3 (2013): 677–709, https://heinonline.org/HOL/LandingPage?handle=hein.journals/nwjilb33&div=20&id=&page=.

52. Damian Paletta, "The CIA's Venture-Capital Firm, Like Its Sponsor, Operates in the Shadows," *Wall Street Journal*, August 30, 2016, https://www.wsj.com/articles/the-cias-venture-capital-firm-like-its-sponsor-operates-in-the-shadows-1472587352.

53. For a recent list of IQT investments, see the IQT website at https://www.iqt.org/portfolio/.

54. "The Federal Risk and Authorization Management Program (FedRAMP) is a government-wide program that provides a standardized approach to security assessment, authorization, and continuous monitoring for cloud products and services" ("FedRAMP," U.S. General Services Administration, accessed December 14, 2022, https://www.gsa.gov/technology/government-it-initiatives/fedramp).

55. Laurence Goasduff, "Top Trends on the Gartner Hype Cycle for Artificial Intelligence, 2019," Gartner, September 12, 2019, https://www.gartner.com/smarterwithgartner/top-trends-on-the-gartner-hype-cycle-for-artificial-intelligence-2019.

56. Katrina Manson, "Another Pentagon Official Exits, Saying U.S. Is at Risk of Losing Tech Edge," Bloomberg, April 18, 2022, https://www.bloomberg.com/news/articles/2022-04-18/another-pentagon-official-resigns-and-criticizes-technical-lag.

57. Chris Darby, "2022 Summit Speech," In-Q-Tel, May 6, 2022.

CHAPTER 4

1. "American Dynamism: Investing in Founders and Companies That Support the National Interest," Andreessen Horowitz, accessed July 8, 2022, https://a16z.com/american-dynamism/.

2. Mariana Mazzucato, *The Value of Everything: Making & Taking in the Global Economy* (New York: PublicAffairs, 2018).

3. "Strategy," C5 Capital, accessed March 5, 2023, https://www.c5capital.com/strategy.

4. "We are Razor's Edge," Razor's Edge, accessed March 5, 2023, https://www.razorsvc.com/about.

5. "Blackbaud Acquires EVERFI, a SaaS Leader Powering Corporate ESG and CSR Initiatives That Reach Millions of Learners Each Year," Blackbaud, January 3, 2022, https://www. blackbaud.com/newsroom/article/2022/01/03/blackbaud-acquires-everfi-a-saas-leader-powering-corporate-esg-and-csr-initiatives-that-reach-millions-of-learners-each-year.

6. "About RRE Ventures," Crunchbase, accessed August 17, 2022, https://www.crunchbase.com/ organization/rre-ventures.

7. Josyana Joshua, "Farm Startup with Ties to NYC History Hits $2.3 Billion in Value," Bloomberg, May 25, 2021, https://www.bloomberg.com/news/articles/2021-05-25/farm-startup-with-ties-to-nyc-history-hits-2-3-billion-in-value#xj4y7vzkg.

8. David Ignatius, "How the Algorithm Tipped the Balance in Ukraine," *Washington Post*, December 19, 2022, https://www.washingtonpost.com/opinions/2022/12/19/palantir-algorithm-data-ukraine-war.

9. Tom Davidson, "Taking on the Missing Layer of Education," EVERFI, May 17, 2021, https://everfi.com/missing-layer-of-education/.

10. "Meet Flock Safety," Flock Safety, accessed August 17, 2022, https://www.flocksafety.com/ about/meet-flock-safety.

11. David Ulevitch and David George, "Investing in Flock Safety," Andreessen Horowitz, accessed October 9, 2022, https://a16z.com/2021/07/13/investing-in-flock-safety/.

12. See FlockSafety.com for more details.

13. "5 Cases Where Custom Software Is the Better Choice for Government Agencies," Antares Technology Solutions, accessed July 8, 2022, https://antaresnet.com/government-agencies/.

14. Fraiser Kansteiner, "National Resilience, Months After Launching with $800M, Snags Sanofi Biomanufacturing Plant," Fierce Pharma, March 24, 2021, https://www.fiercepharma.com/manufacturing/manufacturer-national-resilience-helmed-by-former-novavax-chief-snags-sanofi.

15. "Resilience Announces $625 Million Series D Financing to Expand Network, Bring Innovative Technologies to Biomanufacturing," June 6, 2022, Business Wire, https://www.businesswire.com/news/home/20220606005450/en/Resilience-Announces-625-Million-Series-D-Financing-to-Expand-Network-Bring-Innovative-Technologies-to-Biomanufacturing.

16. "Explore Resilience," National Resilience, accessed November 17, 2022, https://resilience. com/explore/capabilities.

17. "About Us," 1901 Group, accessed November 17, 2022, https://www.1901group.com/about/.

18. "About Us," 1901 Group.

19. "Governor Hogan Announces Elimination of Four-Year Degree Requirement for Thousands of State Jobs," Maryland.gov, accessed December 8, 2022, https://governor.maryland.gov/ 2022/03/15/ governor-hogan-announces-elimination-of-four-year-degree-requirement-for-thousands-of-state-jobs/.

20. Austen Hufford, "Employers Rethink Need for College Degrees in Tight Labor Market," *Wall Street Journal*, November 29, 2022, https://www.wsj.com/articles/ employers-rethink-need-for-college-degrees-in-tight-labor-market-11669432133.

21. "Vision," Remora, accessed December 14, 2022, https://remoracarbon.com/vision/.

22. Denise M. Rousseau, Sim B. Sitkin, Ronald S. Burt, and Colin Camerer, "Not So Different After All: A Cross-Discipline View of Trust," *Academy of Management Review* 23, no. 3 (1998): 393–404, https://doi.org/10.5465/amr.1998.926617.

23. Jeffrey L. Bradach and Robert G. Eccles, "Price, Authority, and Trust: From Ideal Types to Plural Forms," *Annual Review of Sociology* 15 (1989): 97–118, https://www.jstor.org/stable/ 2083220.

24. Thomas J. Fewer and Dali Ma, "Working with the 'Enemy': Free Space in Facilitating Cold War Space Collaboration," *Academy of Management Proceedings* 1, no. 10510 (2020), https://doi.org/10.5465/AMBPP.2020.1.

25. "International Space Station Program Oral History Project Edited Oral History Transcript, Jeffrey N. Williams," NASA Johnson Space Center Oral History Project, July 22, 2015, https://historycollection.jsc.nasa.gov/ JSCHistoryPortal/history/oral_histories/ISS/WilliamsJN/WilliamsJN_7-22-15.htm.

26. "How We Work," In-Q-Tel, accessed November 17, 2022, https://www.iqt.org/how-we-work/.

27. "Welcome to the Rebellion," Rebellion Defense, accessed December 12, 2022, https://rebelliondefense.com/company.

28. "Rebellion Defense Inc.," SBIR, accessed November 17, 2022, https://www.sbir.gov/node/ 1627461.

CHAPTER 5

1. "Trust in Government," OECD, accessed December 15, 2022, https://data.oecd.org/gga/trust-in-government.htm.

2. Francis Fukuyama, *Liberalism and Its Discontents* (New York: Farrar, Straus and Giroux, 2022).

3. Robinson Meyer, "A Huge, Uncharted Experiment on the U.S. Economy Is About to Begin," New York Times, February 12, 2023, https://www.nytimes.com/2023/02/12/opinion/economy-ira-infrastructure-clean-energy.html.

4. Mariam Baksh, "CISA Plans to Hire Chief People Officer to Boost Cyber Workforce," NextGov, June 21, 2022, https://www.nextgov.com/cybersecurity/2022/06/cisa-plans-hire-chief-people-officer-boost-cyber-workforce/368421.

5. Grace Dille, "CISA Director Calls for 50 Percent Share of Cyber Field for Women by 2030," MeriTalk, March 21, 2022, https://www.meritalk.com/articles/cisa-director-calls-for-50-percent-share-of-cyber-field-for-women-by-2030.

6. Julie Pattison-Gordon, "Federal Cyber Officials Talk Recruitment, Culture, Collaboration," Government Technology, June 9, 2022, https://www.govtech.com/workforce/federal-cyber-officials-talk-recruitment-culture-collaboration.

7. Catherine Ellwood, "Building Trust Through Transparency," March 25, 2020, The Myers-Briggs Company, March 25, 2020, https://www.themyers-briggs.com/en-US/Connect-with-us/Blog/2020/March/Trust-and-Transparency#:~:text=In%20the%20words%20of%20Jack,your%20opinions%20and%20being%20direct.

8. "Transparency and Open Government: Memorandum for the Heads of Executive Departments and Agencies," The White House Briefing Room, January 21, 2009, https://obamawhitehouse.archives.gov/the-press-office/transparency -and-open-government.

9. "Open Government Initiative," The White House, May 9, 2013, accessed August 16, 2022, https://obamawhitehouse.archives.gov/open.

10. "The Home of the U.S. Government's Open Data," Data.gov, accessed December 12, 2022, https://data.gov/.

11. "Open Government," OECD, accessed August 13, 2022, " https://www.oecd.org/gov/open-government/.

12. "Access and Reuse of Public Information to Improve Open Government," datos.gob.es, March 23, 2018, https://datos.gob.es/en/noticia/access-and-reuse-public-information-improve-open-government.

13. "Trust in Government"; "Open Democracy, The Democratic Innovation Collective," Démocratie Ouverte, accessed August 13, 2022, https://www.democratieouverte.org/.

14. "About Open Government Partnership," Open Government Partnership, accessed August 17, 2022, https://www.opengovpartnership.org/about/.

15. Gordon W. Allport, *The Nature of Prejudice* (Cambridge, UK; Reading, MA: Addison-Wesley, 1954); Thomas J. Fewer and Murat Tarakci, "Aliens on Board: The Effect of Intergroup Contact on Political Ideology at NASA," *Academy of Management Proceedings* 1, no. 10510 (2020), https://doi.org/10.5465/AMBPP.2020.15094abstract.

16. Arnoud De Meyer and Peter J. Williamson, *Ecosystem Edge: Sustaining Competitiveness in the Face of Disruption* (Stanford, CA: Stanford University Press, 2020).

17. "Innovation on a Mission," In-Q-Tel, accessed June 17, 2022, https://www.iqt.org/.

18. Sabrina T. Howell, Jason Rathje, John Van Reenen, and Jun Wong, "Opening up Military Innovation: Causal Effects of Reforms to U.S. Defense Research," *National Bureau of Economic Research*, no. 28700, (2021): 1–102, https://www.nber.org/papers/w28700.

19. "The Future Economy Council: Alliances for Action (AfA)," Ministry of Trade and Industry Singapore, accessed August 13, 2022, https://www.mti.gov.sg/FutureEconomy/AFAs.

20. Laura Reiley, "Cutting-Edge Tech Made This Tiny Country a Major Exporter of Food," *Washington Post*, November 21, 2022, https://www.washingtonpost.com/business/interactive/2022/netherlands-agriculture-technology/.

21. "SG Digital—Digitalising Singapore," IMDA, accessed August 5, 2022, https://www.imda.gov.sg/infocomm-media-landscape/SGDigital.

22. "Harnessing Open Health Data & Methodologies to Serve Value-Based Care Networks," CareJourney, accessed August 13, 2022, https://carejourney.com/harnessing-open-health-data-methodologies-to-serve-value-based-care-networks/.

23. "CareJourney Overview," CareJourney, accessed August 13, 2022, https://carejourney.com/company/.

24. Evie Kim Sing, "GovTech and UK Government Digital Service Sign

MoU agreement," IdentityWeek, August 2, 2022, https://identityweek.net/govtech-and-uk-government-digital-service-sign-mou-agreement/#:~:text=The%20UK%20Government%20Digital%20Service,(MoU)%20agreement%20in%20June.

25. "White House Announces Launch of the International Grand Challenges on Democracy-Affirming Technologies for the Summit for Democracy," The White House Briefing Room, December 8, 2021, https://www.whitehouse.gov/ostp/news-updates/2021/12/08/white-house-announces-launch-of-the-international-grand-challenges-on-democracy-affirming-technologies-for-the-summit-for-democracy/#:~:text=The%20Grand%20Challenges%20will%20bring,stage%20of%20development%20and%20use.

26. "White House Announces Launch of the International Grand Challenges on Democracy-Affirming Technologies for the Summit for Democracy," The White House Office of Science and Technology Policy, December 8, 2021, https://www.whitehouse.gov/ostp/news-updates/2021/12/08/white-house-announces-launch-of-the-international-grand-challenges-on-democracy-affirming-technologies-for-the-summit-for-democracy.

27. Jeff Ubois and Thomas Kalil, "The Promise of Incentive Prizes," *Stanford Social Innovation Review*, Winter 2019, https://ssir.org/articles/entry/the_promise_of_incentive_prizes#.

28. "Market Shaping Accelerator," University of Chicago, accessed March 8, 2023, https://bfi.uchicago.edu/wp-content/uploads/2023/01/Market-Shaping-Accelerator-coming-soon.pdf.

29. Howell, et al., "Opening up Military Innovation."

30. "What Do Universities Do with the Billions They Receive from the Government?" USAFACTS, November 3, 2021, https://usafacts.org/articles/what-do-universities-do-with-the-billions-they-receive-from-the-government/#:~:text=Federal%20grants%20at%20universities%20received,public%20good%2C%20according%20to%20Datalab.

31. Melanie Hanson, "College Enrollment & Student Demographic Statistics," Education Data Initiative, July 26, 2022, https://educationdata.org/college-enrollment-statistics#:~:text=Since%201960%2C%20the%20rate%20of,time%20or%20full%2Dtime%20students.

32. Douglas A. Brook, "Fewer Graduates Are Choosing Government Jobs," The Hill, May 14, 2019, https://thehill.com/opinion/education/443588-fewer-graduates-are-choosing-government-jobs/#:~:text=In%20

2017%2C%2034%20percent%20of,of%20employment%20or%20further%20 schooling.

33. "College Students Are Attracted to Federal Service, but Agencies Need to Capitalize on Their Interest," Partnership for Public Service and The National Association of Colleges and Employees, March 2014, https://www. govexec.com/media/gbc/docs/pdfs_edit/031713e2.pdf.

34. Alexander Stevenson, "3 Skills the Private Sector Can Learn from Government," Government Executive, October 18, 2013, https://www. govexec.com/management/2013/10/3-skills-private-sector-can-learn-government/72257/.

35. Colin Demarest and Molly Weisner, "Pentagon Wants to Spur Cyber Talent Exchange with Tech Industry," C4ISRNet, March 10, 2023, https:// www.c4isrnet.com/cyber/2023/03/10/ pentagon-wants-to-spur-cyber-talent-exchange-with-tech-industry.

36. "White House Tweaks Visa Rules to Attract Scientists, Seeks Broader Reforms," American Institute of Physics, February 2, 2022, https://www.aip. org/fyi/2022/ white-house-tweaks-visa-rules-attract-scientists-seeks-broader-reforms.

37. "Is Gen Z the Most Success-Oriented Generation?" Barna, June 6, 2018, https://www.barna.com/research/ is-gen-z-the-most-success-oriented-generation/.

38. Derek Loosvelt, "Google or NASA: Which Employer Is More Prestigious?," Firsthand, June 13, 2018, https://firsthand.co/blogs/job-search/ google-or-nasa-which-employer-is-more-prestigious.

39. Carly Page, "Big Tech Pledges Billions to Bolster US Cybersecurity Defenses," TechCrunch, August 26, 2021, https://techcrunch.com/2021/08/26/ big-tech-pledges-billions-to-bolster-u-s-cybersecurity-defenses/.

40. "The Opportunity: Begin Your Career at the Intersection of Technology and Public Service," United States Digital Corps, accessed August 13, 2022, https://digitalcorps.gsa.gov/opportunity/.

41. Suman Battacharyya, "Veterans Affairs Taps Former Microsoft Executive to Modernize Tech," Wall Street Journal, March 4, 2022, https:// www.wsj.com/articles/veterans-affairs-taps-former-microsoft-executive-to-modernize-tech-11646391600.

42. Dan Primack, "VA Official Hopes Laid-Off Tech Workers Will Take on a New Mission," Axios, December 9, 2022, https://www.axios. com/2022/12/09/va-official-hopes-laid-off-tech-workers-will-take-on-a-new-mission.

43. Primack, "VA Official."

44. "Overview," Stanford University, accessed August 13, 2022, https://h4d.stanford.edu/details/; "The Gordian Knot Center for National Security Innovation," Stanford University, accessed August 13, 2022, https://gordianknot.stanford.edu.

45. Steve Blank, "Hacking for Defense @ Stanford—Making the World a Safer Place," SteveBlank.Com, January 26, 2016, https://steveblank.com/2016/01/26/hacking-for-defense-stanford.

46. "The Greg and Camille Baroni Center for Government Contracting," George Mason University, accessed December 7, 2022, https://business.gmu.edu/centers/center-government-contracting.

47. "Clearance Ready Program," George Mason University, accessed December 7, 2022, https://careers.gmu.edu/undergraduate-students/clearance-ready-program.

48. Tamara Chuang, "Guild Education's Twist on College Is Working for Cashiers, Sales Clerks and Others Who Abandoned the Idea of a College Degree," *Colorado Sun*, December 3, 2018, https://coloradosun.com/2018/12/03/guild-education-low-income-workers-college/.

49. "Who We Are," Guild Education, accessed December 8, 2022, https://www.guildeducation.com/who-we-are/.

50. "Who We Are," EDB Singapore, accessed August 13, 2022, https://www.edb.gov.sg/en/about-edb/who-we-are.html.

51. "An Economic Powerhouse," EDB Singapore, accessed August 13, 2022, https://www.edb.gov.sg/en/why-singapore/an-economic-powerhouse.html.

52. Michael Aaron Dennis, "Defense Advanced Research Projects Agency," Britannica, accessed August 17, 2022, https://www.britannica.com/topic/Defense-Advanced-Research-Projects-Agency.

53. "About DARPA," Defense Advanced Research Projects Agency, accessed August 13, 2022, https://www.darpa.mil/about-us/about-darpa.

54. "IQT Emerge," In-Q-Tel, accessed August 13, 2022, https://www.iqt.org/emerge.

55. "About EPSRC," UK Research and Innovation, accessed August 13, 2022, https://www.ukri.org/about-us/epsrc/.

56. "Sovereign Wealth Fund (SWF): Definition, Examples, and Types," Investopedia, November 25, 2020, https://www.investopedia.com/terms/s/sovereign_wealth_fund.asp#:~:text=A%20sovereign%20wealth%20fund%20is,country's%20economy%20and%20its%20citizens.

57. Rajiv Sharma, "Sovereign Wealth Funds Investment in Sustainable Development Sectors," Global Projects Center-Stanford University, April 11, 2017, https://www.un.org/esa/ffd/high-level-conference-on-ffd-and-2030-agenda/wp-content/uploads/sites/4/2017/11/Background-Paper_Sovereign-Wealth-Funds.pdf.

58. Yael Selfin, Richard Snook, and Himani Gupta, "The Impact of Sovereign Wealth Funds on Economic Success," PricewaterhouseCoopers, October 2011, https://www.pwc.co.uk/assets/pdf/the-impact-of-sovereign-wealth-funds-on-economic-success.pdf.

59. "Our Portfolio," Temasek, accessed December 15, 2022, https://www.temasek.com.sg/en/our-investments/our-portfolio.

60. "About the Fund," Norges Bank Investment Management, accessed December 15, 2022, https://www.nbim.no/.

61. Richard Milne, "Norway's Oil Fund Makes First Investment in Renewable Energy," April 7, 2021, *Financial Times*, https://www.ft.com/content/ce215b48-03a7-44ae-b614-560f1fa74173.

62. "Who We Are," U.S. International Development Finance Corporation, accessed August 13, 2022, https://www.dfc.gov/who-we-are.

63. "Financing Sierra Leone's First Major Utility-Scale Power Plant," U.S. International Development Finance Corporation, accessed August 13, 2022, https://www.dfc.gov/investment-story/financing-sierra-leones-first-major-utility-scale-power-plant.

64. Kai Wang, "China: Is It Burdening Poor Countries with Unsustainable Debt?" BBC, January 6, 2022, https://www.bbc.com/news/59585507.

65. "Investing in Development," U.S. International Development Finance Corporation, accessed August 13, 2022, https://www.dfc.gov/.

66. Adva Saldinger, "US DFC Looks to Balance Foreign Policy and Development Mandates," Dexex, March 8, 2021, https://www.devex.com/news/us-dfc-looks-to-balance-foreign-policy-and-development-mandates-99326.

67. Daniel F. Runde, Romina Bandura, and Janina Staguhn, "The DFC's New Equity Authority," Center for Strategic & International Studies, April 3, 2020, https://www.csis.org/analysis/dfcs-new-equity-authority.

68. "Public Private Partnerships in India: PPP Supporting Environment," Ministry of Finance-Government of India, accessed August 13, 2022, https://www.pppinindia.gov.in/toolkit/ports/module1-pse-psfafp.php?links=rfpee1d.

69. "The Public's Front Door to Government Services," U.S. Government Services Administration, accessed August 13, 2022, https://labs.usa.gov/.

70. "The Opportunity: Begin Your Career at the Intersection of Technology and Public Service," United States Digital Corps, accessed August 13, 2022, https://digitalcorps.gsa.gov/opportunity/.

71. Chris Kuang, "Introducing the U.S. Digital Corps: A New Path to Public Service for Early-Career Technologists," ChrisKuang.com, September 2021, https://www.chriskuang.com/words.

72. "Leadership," World Wildlife Foundation, accessed December 14, 2022, https://www.worldwildlife.org/about/leadership.

73. Frank Wolfe, "Eric Schmidt to Helm National Artificial Intelligence/ Emerging Technologies Project," Defense Daily, October 5, 2021, https:// www.defensedaily.com/eric-schmidt-to-helm-national-artificial-intelligence-emerging-technologies-project/advanced-transformational-technology/.

74. "In Depth: The Special Studies Project," Rockefeller Brothers Fund, accessed December 14, 2022, https://www.rbf.org/about/our-history/timeline/ special-studies-project/in-depth.

75. "Dr. Eric Schmidt Announces Special Competitive Studies Project," AIthority, October 5, 2021, https://aithority.com/security/ dr-eric-schmidt-announces-special-competitive-studies-project/.

76. "SCSP and RUSI Launch a New Project on Human-Machine Collaboration and Teaming in Military Operations," Special Competitive Studies Project, November 10, 2022, https://www.scsp.ai/2022/11/ scsp-and-rusi-launch-a-new-project-on-human-machine-collaboration-and-teaming-in-military-operations/.

77. "Who We Are," UnBox, accessed December 2, 2022, https://www. unboxproject.org/.

78. "Who We Are," All Tech Is Human, accessed November 29, 2022, https://alltechishuman.org/about#purpose.

79. "Responsible Tech Guide: How to Get Involved & Build a Better Tech Future," All Tech Is Human, September 2022, https://alltechishuman.org/ responsible-tech-guide.

80. "What We Do," Teach for America, accessed August 17, 2022, https:// www.teachforamerica.org/.

81. "From Zero to One," Activate Global, accessed March 8, 2023, https:// www.activate.org/impact.

82. "About MissionLink.Next," MissionLinkNext, accessed March 17, 2023, https://missionlinknext.com.

83. "How We Work," Elemental Excelerator, December 15, 2022, https://elementalexcelerator.com/.

84. "Scaling Climate x Social Equity Solutions, 5 Year Strategy," Elemental Excelerator, April 2021, accessed December 8, 2022, https://elementalexcelerator.com/wp-content/uploads/2021/04/Elemental-5Y-Strategy-Scaling-Climate-x-Social-Equity-Solutions.pdf.

85. "How We Work," Bill & Melinda Gates Foundation, accessed November 29, 2022, https://www.gatesfoundation.org/about/how-we-work.

CHAPTER 6

1. John R. French, Bertram Raven, and Dorwin Cartwright, "The Bases of Social Power," in *Classics of Organization Theory*, ed. Dorwin Cartwright and Alvin Zander (New York: Harper & Row, 1959), 150–67.

2. Suzanne Smalley, "Former Marine, Cyber Exec Nate Fick Selected as State's Inaugural Cyber Ambassador," Cyber Scoop, June 1, 2022, https://www.cyberscoop.com/former-marine-cyber-exec-fick-state-cyber-ambassador/.

3. Herbert C. Kelman, "Compliance, Identification, and Internalization: Three Processes of Attitude Change," *Journal of Conflict Resolution* 2, no. 1 (1958): 51–60, https://doi.org/10.1177/002200275800200106.

4. "Verdant Robotics Raises $46.5 Million to Reduce Ag Chemicals, Improve Farm Profits," News Direct, November 29, 2022, https://finance.yahoo.com/news/verdant-robotics-raises-46-5-143000258.html.

5. Sibile Marcellus, "Millennials or Gen Z: Who Is Doing the Most Job-Hopping?" Yahoo Finance, October 20, 2021, https://finance.yahoo.com/news/millennials-or-get-z-who-is-doing-the-most-job-hopping-112733374.html#:~:text=A%2016%20Gallup%20report%20on,the%20same%2C%20according%20to%20Gallup.

6. Cameron Keng, "Employees Who Stay in Companies Longer Than Two Years Get Paid 50% Less," Forbes, June 22, 2014, https://www.forbes.com/sites/cameronkeng/2014/06/22/employees-that-stay-in-companies-longer-than-2-years-get-paid-50-less/.

7. Alissa Carpenter, "The Importance of Diversity and Inclusion During Uncertain Times," Entrepreneur, March 27, 2020, https://www.entrepreneur.com/article/348209.

8. Nick Lovegrove, *The Mosaic Principle: The Six Dimensions of a Remarkable Life and Career* (New York: Public Affairs, 2016).

9. David J. Epstein, *Range: Why Generalists Triumph in a Specialized World* (New York: Riverhead Books, 2019).

10. Héctor García and Francesc Miralles, *Ikigai: The Japanese Secret to a Long and Happy Life* (London: Penguin, 2017).

11. Reuben Brody, "And the One Fish No One Should Eat Is…The World's Best Sushi Chef Says Sushi Is Doomed. Here's Why," Inside Hook, November 7, 2016, https://www.insidehook.com/ article/food-and-drink/ jiro-ono-says-sushi-is-doomed.

CHAPTER 7

1. "The World Needs Breakthroughs," Breakthrough Energy, accessed August 30, 2022, https://www.breakthroughenergy.org/#:~:text=My%20 basic%20optimism%20about%20climate,invent%20that%20makes%20me%20 hopeful.

2. David Boaz, "Happy New Year: A Time to Celebrate Human Progress," CATO Institute, December 31, 2014, https://www.cato.org/blog/ happy-new-year-time-celebrate-human-progress.

3. "Risk of Dying from Cancer Continues to Drop at an Accelerated Pace," American Cancer Society, January 12, 2022, https://www.cancer.org/ latest-news/facts-and-figures-2022.html#:~:text=The%20risk%20of%20 dying%20from,for%20which%20data%20were%20available.

4. Rick Noack, "For Decades, Global Hunger Was on the Decline. Now It's Getting Worse Again—And Climate Change Is to Blame," *Washington Post*, September 11, 2018, https://www.washingtonpost.com/world/2018/09/11/ decades-global-hunger-was-decline-now-its-getting-worse-again-climate- change-is-blame/.

5. Max Roser, Hannah Ritchie, and Bernadeta Dadonaite, "Child and Infant Mortality," Our World in Data, updated November 2019, https:// ourworldindata.org/child-mortality#child-mortality-around-the-world-si nce-1800.

6. "White House Announces Launch of the International Grand Challenges on Democracy-Affirming Technologies for the Summit for Democ-

racy," The White House Briefing Room, December 8, 2021, https://www.whitehouse.gov/ostp/news-updates/2021/12/08/white-house-announces-launch-of-the-international-grand-challenges-on-democracy-affirming-technologies-for-the-summit-for-democracy/.

7. "Next-Generation Biomanufacturing Market," Emergen Research, February 2021, https://www.emergenresearch.com/industry-report/next-generation-biomanufacturing-market#:~:text=The%20global%20next%2Dgeneration%20biomanufacturing,increasing%20at%20a%20steady%20pace.

8. Raj Daniels, "The Current State of the Climate Tech Market," Nexus PMG, accessed August 30, 2022, https://nexuspmg.com/the-current-state-of-the-climate-tech-market/.

9. "Environmental Technology Market Size to Worth USD 783 Bn by 2030," Globe News Wire, May 17, 2022, https://www.globenewswire.com/en/news-release/2022/05/17/2445241/0/en/Environmental-Technology-Market-Size-to-Worth-USD-783-Bn-by-2030.html#:~:text=According%20to%20Precedence%20Research%2C%20the,4.5%25%20from%202022%20to%202030.

10. "Commonwealth Fusion Systems Raises $1.8 Billion in Funding to Commercialize Fusion Energy," Commonwealth Fusion Systems, December 1, 2021, https://cfs.energy/news-and-media/commonwealth-fusion-systems-closes-1-8-billion-series-b-round.

11. "Commonwealth Fusion Systems Raises $84 Million in A2 Round," Cison PR Newswire, May 26, 2020, https://www.prnewswire.com/news-releases/commonwealth-fusion-systems-raises-84-million-in-a2-round-301064766.html.

12. "Biology by Design," Ginkgo Bioworks, accessed August 30, 2022, https://www.ginkgobioworks.com/.

13. "Ginkgo Bioworks, Transcriptic Awarded $9.5M DARPA Contract," GenomeWeb, April 12, 2018, https://www.genomeweb.com/applied-markets/ginkgo-bioworks-transcriptic-awarded-95m-darpa-contract#.Yv5UnnbMLq4.

14. Riley de León, "Ginkgo Bioworks Begins Trading on the NYSE After Completing SPAC Merger," CNBC, September 17, 2021, https://www.cnbc.com/2021/09/17/ginkgo-begins-trading-on-the-nyse-after-completing-spac-merger.html.

15. Johannes Lenhard, "What Is Public Purpose Technology and Why Does It Matter Right Now?" TechEU, March 17, 2022, https://tech.eu/2022/03/17/what-is-public-purpose-technology-and-why-does-it-matter-right-now/.

16. Jeff Kauflin and Maria Abreu, "How David Vélez Built the World's

Most Valuable Digital Bank and Became a Billionaire," Forbes, April 7, 2021, https://www.forbes.com/sites/jeffkauflin/2021/04/07/fintech-billionaire-david-velez-nubank-brazil-digital-bank/?sh=6c6d-f3b6b279.

17. Gerard George, Ryan K. Merrill, and Simon J. D. Schillebeeckx, "Digital Sustainability and Entrepreneurship: How Digital Innovations Are Helping Tackle Climate Change and Sustainable Development," *Entrepreneurship Theory and Practice* 45, no. 5 (2021): 999–1027, https://doi.org/10.1177/1042258719899425.

18. "Rise of the Rest Seed Fund," Revolution, accessed December 16, 2022, https://revolution.com/entity/rotr/.

19. "We're Restoring Humanity to Health Care," Iora Health, accessed August 30, 2022, https://www.iorahealth.com/.

20. "What Is Primary Care at Iora with One Medical?" Iora Health, accessed August 30, 2022, https://ioraprimarycare.com/what-is-primary-care/.

21. "Iora Health," Crunchbase, August 30, 2022, https://www.crunchbase.com/organization/iora-health.

22. Paige Minemyer, "One Medical to Acquire Iora Health in $2.1B All-Stock Deal," Fierce Healthcare, June 7, 2021, https://www.fiercehealthcare.com/practices/one-medical-to-acquire-iora-health-2-1b-all-stock-deal.

23. Andy Greenberg and Ryan Mac, "How a 'Deviant' Philosopher Built Palantir, a CIA-Funded Data-Mining Juggernaut," Forbes, August 14, 2013, https://web.archive.org/web/20150604110616/http://www.forbes.com/sites/andygreenberg/2013/08/14/agent-of-intelligence-how-a-deviant-philosopher-built-palantir-a-cia-funded-data-mining-juggernaut/.

24. Ryan Mac, "Palantir Aiming to Raise $400 Million in New Round," Forbes, December 11, 2014, https://web.archive.org/web/20150102175054/http://www.forbes.com/sites/ryanmac/2014/12/11/palantir-aiming-to-raise-400-million-in-new-round/; Rob Copeland, "Secretive Data Company Palantir Weighs Giant Public Offering," *Wall Street Journal*, October 18, 2018, https://web.archive.org/web/20181018221959/https://www.wsj.com/articles/secretive-data-company-palantir-weighs-giant-public-offering-1539864003.

25. Chris Metinko, "Report: Palmer Luckey's AI-Powered Defense Tech Startup Anduril Seeks $7B Valuation," Crunchbase News, April 28, 2022, https://news.crunchbase.com/venture/anduril-industries-palantir-military-defense/.

26. "We Are on a Mission to Decode the Immune System and Improve

Health," Immunai, accessed August 30, 2022, https://www.immunai.com/company/.

27. "America's Personal Care," Bravo Sierra, August 30, 2022, https://www.bravosierra.com/.

28. "H.R.3942—Commercial Space Launch Act," Congress.Gov, accessed August 30, 2022, https://www.congress.gov/bill/98th-congress/house-bill/3942#:~:text=Commercial%20Space%20Launch%20Act%20%2D%20Prohibits,case%20of%20a%20license%20holder%2C.

29. "Falcon 9 Launch Vehicle NAFCOM Cost Estimates," NASA, August 2011, https://www.nasa.gov/pdf/586023main_8-3-11_NAFCOM.pdf.

30. Erick Burgueño Salas, "Number of Carrier Rockets Launched by SpaceX from 2006 to 2022, by Type," Statista, March 25, 2022, https://www.statista.com/statistics/1266914/spacex-number-of-launches-by-type/.

31. Carl Berrisford, "Longer Term Investments: Space," UBS, November 30, 2018, https://www.ubs.com/content/dam/WealthManagementAmericas/documents/space-p.pdf.

32. William Harwood, "SpaceX Launches 55 Satellites in Three Launches in Less Than Two Days," CBS News, June 19, 2022, https://www.cbsnews.com/news/spacex-launches-55-satellites-in-three-launches-in-less-than-two-days/.

33. "Investor Updates," C5/Axiom Space, November 11, 2022.

34. "The House Passes the America COMPETES Act," Congresswoman Madeleine Dean, February 4, 2022, https://dean.house.gov/2022/2/the-house-passes-the-america-competes-act; "Foreign Policy Side-by-Side: Division D of the America COMPETES Act Versus Division C of the U.S. Innovation and Competition Act," Akin Gump, February 14, 2022, https://www.akingump.com/a/web/npXZYbf7Pzhm1zHfWEdHuM/akin-gump-competes-act-and-usica-division-d-side-by-side2.pdf.

35. Margaret Mulkerrin, "The America COMPETES Act of 2022 Will Help Ensure Workers and Businesses Can Make It in America," Steny Hoyer Majority Leader, February 11, 2022, https://www.majorityleader.gov/content/america-competes-act-2022-will-help-ensure-workers-and-businesses-can-make-it-america.

36. "President Biden's FY 2023 Budget Advances Equity," The White House Briefing Room, March 30, 2022, https://www.whitehouse.gov/omb/briefing-room/2022/03/30/president-bidens-fy-2023-budget-advances-equity/.

37. "Summary of the Energy Security and Climate Change Investments in the Inflation Reduction Act of 2022," Senate Democrats, accessed August 30,

2022, https://www.democrats.senate.gov/imo/media/doc/summary_of_the_
energy_security_and_climate_change_investments_in_the_inflation_reduc-
tion_act_of_2022.pdf.

38. Anshuman Daga and Himanshi Akhand, "Temasek Pledges $3.6
Billion for Climate-Focused Investment Platform," Reuters, June 6, 2022,
https://www.reuters.com/markets/us/
temasek-pledges-36-bln-climate-focused-investment-platform-2022-06-06/.

39. "NATO Sharpens Technological Edge with Innovation Initiatives,"
North Atlantic Treaty Organization, April 7, 2022, https://www.nato.int/cps/
en/natohq/news_194587.htm.

40. "U.S. Research and Development Funding and Performance: Fact
Sheet," Congressional Research Service, October 4, 2021, https://sgp.fas.org/
crs/misc/R44307.pdf.

41. Daniel Pereira, "Thomas Tull Chairs the $5 Billion US Innovative
Technology Fund; Shield AI Among Early Investments," ODALOOP,
February 20, 2023, https://www.oodaloop.com/archive/2023/02/20/
thomas-tull-chairs-the-5-billion-us-innovative-technology-fund-shield-ai-
among-early-investments.

42. "Our Impact," Ontario Teachers' Pension Plan, accessed November 29,
2022, https://www.otpp.com/en-ca/about-us/our-impact.

43. "TPG Closes Rise Climate Fund at $7.3 Billion," TPG, April 27, 2022,
https://press.tpg.com/news-releases/news-release-details/
tpg-closes-rise-climate-fund-73-billion.

44. Sophie Baker, "Saudi Arabia's Wealth Fund Pledges to Reach Net-
Zero by 2050," Pensions and Investments, November 8, 2022, https://www.
pionline.com/sovereign-wealth-funds/saudi-arabias-sovereign-wealth-fund-pledges-
reach-net-zero-2050.

45. "Climate and Infrastructure Funds," European Investment Fund,
accessed December 15, 2022, https://www.eif.org/InvestEU/climate-and-in-
frastructure-funds/index.htm.

46. "Defying Gravity, 2022 Climate Tech VC Funding Totals $70.1B, up
89% on 2021," HolonIQ, January 3, 2023, https://www.holoniq.com/
notes/2022-climate-tech-vc-funding-totals-70-1b-up-89-from-37-0b-in-2021.

47. "Work," Privos Capital, accessed August 30, 2022, https://www.
privoscapital.com/family-offices.

48. Katarzyna Wilk, "The Role of Family Offices in Accelerating Impact
Investing," InvestESG.eu, February 14, 2022, https://investesg.eu/2022/02/14/
the-role-of-family-offices-in-accelerating-impact-investing/.

49. "Bill and Melinda Gates Foundation: What Is It and What Does It Do?," BBC, May 4, 2021, https://www.bbc.com/news/world-us-canada-56979480.

50. Leslie Hook, "Bill Gates-Backed Fund Aims to Invest $15BN in Clean Tech," *Financial Times*, January 10, 2022, https://www.ft.com/content/f25fd95d-e2d8-43f8-b786-1552a1f0059e.

51. "Systems Change in This Decisive Decade," Bezos Earth Fund, accessed August 30, 2022, https://bezosearthfund.org/.

52. "Emerson Collective," Influence Watch, accessed August 30, 2022, https://www.influencewatch.org/non-profit/emerson-collective/.

53. Alex Knapp, "Why Billionaires Ken Griffin and Eric Schmidt Are Spending $50 Million on a New Kind of Scientific Research," Forbes, March 17, 2023, https://www.forbes.com/sites/alexknapp/2023/03/17/why-billionaires-ken-griffin-and-eric-schmidt-are-spending-50-million-on-a-new-kind-of-scientific-research/?sh=4aee55462847.

54. "Our Story: Working to Achieve Net Zero Emissions," Breakthrough Energy, accessed August 30, 2022, https://www.breakthroughenergy.org/our-story/our-story.

55. Murat Tarakci and Timo van Balen, "Recruiting Talent Through Entrepreneurs' Social Vision Communication," *Organization Science*, forthcoming.

56. "Talent for a New Era: A Vision to Attract and Retain the Next Generation of Federal Public Servants," Partnership for Public Service, 2022.

57. "Strategic Technology Landscape 2023: Risks, Opportunities, and Wild Cards," Denton Global Advisors, February 7, 2023, https://www.dentonsglobaladvisors.com/strategic-technology-landscape-2023-risks-opportunities-and-wild-cards.

58. "The Georgetown Initiative on Tech & Society," Georgetown University Tech & Society, accessed December 17, 2022, https://techandsociety.georgetown.edu/.

59. "Emmett Interdisciplinary Program in Environment and Resources," Stanford Earth, accessed August 30, 2022, https://earth.stanford.edu/eiper#gs.68q05x.

60. "Our Mission," Institute for Applied Computational Science at Harvard University, accessed August 30, 2022, https://iacs.seas.harvard.edu/about.

61. Anthony Fauci and Max Stier, " The Federal Workforce Is Aging. It's Time for a New Generation," *Washington Post*, February 7, 2023, https://www.

washingtonpost.com/opinions/2023/02/07/fauci-government-workforce-aging-hire-young/.

62. "H.R.4818—National Digital Reserve Corps Act," Congress.Gov, accessed August 30, 2022, https://www.congress.gov/bill/117th-congress/house-bill/4818/text.

63. "Our Mission," Institute for Applied Computational Science at Harvard University.

64. Mitchell Weiss, "Public Entrepreneurship," Harvard Business School, revised July 2021, https://www.hbs.edu/faculty/Pages/item.aspx?num=52994.

65. "NobleReach," NobleReach Foundation, accessed December 2, 2022, https://noblereachfoundation.org/.

ABOUT THE AUTHORS

Arun Gupta is a Lecturer at Stanford University for "Valley Meets Mission" and an Adjunct Entrepreneurship Professor at Georgetown University, and has been a venture capitalist for over twenty years. He is currently leading NobleReach Foundation, which is focused on catalyzing and inspiring a renewed spirit of national service through innovation.

Gerard (Gerry) George is Tamsen and Michael Brown Family Professor of Entrepreneurship and Innovation at Georgetown University and Senior Advisor at TPG, a leading global alternative asset manager.

Thomas J. Fewer is a Postdoctoral Fellow in the Georgetown Entrepreneurship Initiative at Georgetown University and VP at NobleReach Foundation, focused on developing innovative talent programs to educate and inspire the next generation of mission-driven change-makers.

ALL OF THE TOOLS TO TACKLE SOCIETY'S BIGGEST PROBLEMS EXIST

The Venture Meets Mission ecosystem's role is to bring together these tools

Find tools and additional resources here:

VentureMeetsMission.com